FORMAL GARDENS
IN
ENGLAND AND SCOTLAND

FORMAL GARDENS

IN

ENGLAND AND SCOTLAND

THEIR PLANNING AND ARRANGEMENT
ARCHITECTURAL AND ORNAMENTAL FEATURES

BY

H. INIGO TRIGGS, A.R.I.B.A.

JOINT AUTHOR OF "SOME ARCHITECTURAL WORKS OF INIGO JONES."

ILLUSTRATED BY
SEVENTY-TWO PLATES FROM DRAWINGS BY THE AUTHOR
AND FIFTY-THREE REPRODUCED FROM PHOTOGRAPHS

BY

CHARLES LATHAM

WITH FORTY-SIX ADDITIONAL COLOUR PLATES SHOWING
THE GARDENS DURING THE 1987 AND 1988 SEASONS

ANTIQUE COLLECTORS' CLUB

First published in 1902 by B.T. Batsford
Second edition published by Antique Collectors' Club 1988

Published for the Antique Collectors' Club
by the Antique Collectors' Club Ltd.

British Library CIP Data
Triggs, H. Inigo
    Formal gardens in England and Scotland
    1. Great Britain. Landscape gardens to 1988
    I. Title
    712'6'0941
    ISBN 1 85149 017 5

Printed in England by Antique Collectors' Club Ltd.
5 Church Street, Woodbridge, Suffolk.

The Antique Collectors' Club

The Antique Collectors' Club was formed in 1966 and now has a five figure membership spread throughout the world. It publishes the only independently run monthly antiques magazine *Antique Collecting* which caters for those collectors who are interested in widening their knowledge of antiques, both by greater awareness of quality and by discussion of the factors which influence the price that is likely to be asked. The Antique Collectors' Club pioneered the provision of information on prices for collectors and the magazine still leads in the provision of detailed articles on a variety of subjects.

It was in response to the enormous demand for information on "what to pay" that the price guide series was introduced in 1968 with the first edition of *The Price Guide to Antique Furniture* (completely revised, 1978), a book which broke new ground by illustrating the more common types of antique furniture, the sort that collectors could buy in shops and at auctions rather than the rare museum pieces which had previously been used (and still to a large extent are used) to make up the limited amount of illustrations in books published by commercial publishers. Many other price guides have followed, all copiously illustrated, and greatly appreciated by collectors for the valuable information they contain, quite apart from prices. The Antique Collectors' Club also publishes other books on antiques, including horology and art reference works, and a full book list is available.

Club membership, which is open to all collectors, costs £15.95 per annum. Members receive free of charge *Antique Collecting,* the Club's magazine (published every month except August), which contains well-illustrated articles dealing with the practical aspects of collecting not normally dealt with by magazines. Prices, features of value, investment potential, fakes and forgeries are all given prominence in the magazine.

Among other facilities available to members are private buying and selling facilities, the longest list of "For Sales" of any antiques magazine, an annual ceramics conference and the opportunity to meet other collectors at their local antique collectors' clubs. There are over eighty in Britain and more than a dozen overseas. Members may also buy the Club's publications at special pre-publication prices.

As its motto implies, the Club is an amateur organisation designed to help collectors get the most out of their hobby: it is informal and friendly and gives enormous enjoyment to all concerned.

For Collectors — By Collectors — About Collecting

The Antique Collectors' Club, 5 Church Street, Woodbridge, Suffolk

LIST OF SUBSCRIBERS.

TO THE FIRST EDITION

The ARCHITECTURAL BOOK CLUB ZINGARI.
ADAM, P., Esq., Kidderminster.
AITKEN, DOTT, & SON, Messrs., Booksellers, Edinburgh.
ALEXANDER, W. C., Esq., F.S.A., Heathfield.
ALLAN, J. A. O., Esq., Aberdeen.
ALLEN & MURRAY, Messrs., Booksellers, London.
AMBLER, LOUIS, Esq., F.R.I.B.A., London.
AMORY, H. M. HEATHCOTE, Esq., Tiverton.
ANDERSON, SIMON, & CRAWFORD, Messrs., Edinburgh.
ANGUS & ROBERTSON, Messrs., Booksellers, Sydney.
ARBUTHNOT, Mrs. M. H., East Grinstead.
ARMY AND NAVY CO-OPERATIVE SOCIETY, Ltd., Booksellers, London.
ARNOT, J. A., Esq., Edinburgh.
ASHER & CO., Messrs., Booksellers, London.
ASTOR, W. W., Esq., Taplow.
ATKINSON, G. W., Esq., Leeds.
ATKINSON, R. FRANK, Esq., London.
AUSTIN, ALFRED, Esq., Ashford.
AUSTIN, HUBERT J., Esq., Lancaster.

The Most Hon. The MARCHIONESS OF BREADALBANE.
The Right Hon. The EARL BEAUCHAMP, K.C.M.G., LL.D.
The Right Hon. The EARL BROWNLOW.
The Right Hon. The EARL OF BUCKINGHAMSHIRE.
The Right Hon. LORD VISCOUNT BOYNE.
The Right Hon. LADY VISCOUNTESS BARING.
The Right Hon. LORD BATTERSEA.
The Right Hon. LORD HENRY BENTINCK, M.P.
The Right Hon. LORD BRASSEY, K.C.B.
The Right Hon. LORD BURTON.
The Right Hon. BARONESS ALEX VON BOESELOGER.
The COUNT BERCHTOLD.
Sir HICKMAN B. BACON, Bart., F.S.A.
Sir HENRY BELLINGHAM, Bart., M.A.
Sir CHARLES HENRY ROUSE-BOUGHTON, Bart.
The Hon. MRS. R. BOYLE.
The BIRKENHEAD CENTRAL LIBRARY.
The BRADFORD PUBLIC LIBRARY.
The BRIGHTON PUBLIC LIBRARY.
The BOARD OF EDUCATION, South Kensington.

BAGOT, JOSCELINE FITZROY, Esq., M.P.
BAIN, Mr., Bookseller, London.
BAIN, JOHN, Esq., F.R.I.B.A., Newport.
BALFOUR, R. S., Esq., A.R.I.B.A., London.
BARDELL, W., Esq., Nottingham.
BARLOW, E. P., Esq., Canterbury.
BATEMAN & SON, Messrs., Birmingham.
BAZLEY, GARDNER S., Esq., Fairford.
BEAN, Miss HELENA, Welling.
BECK, FRED. T., Esq., Wolverhampton.
BECKETT, E. W., Esq., M.P., London.
BELCHER, JOHN, Esq., A.R.A., F.R.I.B.A., London.
BELL, Mr. W., Bookseller, Edinburgh.
BELOE, E. M., Esq., F.S.A., King's Lynn.
BEVAN, ARTHUR T., Esq., Chevening.
BIBBY, FRANK, Esq., Shrewsbury.
BIDLAKE, W. H., Esq., M.A., F.R.I.B.A., Birmingham.
BIRCH, G. H., Esq., F.S.A., F.R.I.B.A., London.
BLANC, HIPPOLYTE J., Esq., R.S.A., F.R.I.B.A., Edinburgh.
BOARDMAN, E. T., Esq., Norwich.
BODLEY, G. F., Esq., R.A., London.
BOLTON, A. T., Esq., A.R.I.B.A., London.
BOSTOCK, SAMUEL, Esq., Winchester.
BOTHAMS, A. C., Esq., Salisbury.
BRADSHAW, C., Esq., Eccles.
BRAIKENRIDGE, GEORGE JOHN, Esq., London.
BRASSEY, H. L. C., Esq., Aylesford.
BRENTANO'S LIBRARY, Booksellers, Paris.
BREWILL & BAILEY, Messrs., Nottingham.
BRIERLEY, WALTER H., Esq., York.
BRIGGS, R. A., Esq., F.R.I.B.A., London.
BRIGHT'S STORES, LIMITED, Booksellers, Bournemouth.
BRINDLEY, W., Esq., London.
BROOKE, F. W., Esq., Littlewood, Cornwall.
BROOKES, Rev. C. C., London.
BROOKS, BOULTBEE, Esq., Bromsgrove.
BROOKS, CECIL, Esq., London.
BROWN, GEORGE T., Esq., Sunderland.
BROWN, W. TALBOT, Esq., F.R.I.B.A., Wellingborough.
BROWN, Mr. W., Bookseller, Edinburgh.
BRYAN, H. DARE, Esq., Bristol.

LIST OF SUBSCRIBERS.

Bryant, Wilberforce, Esq., Stoke Poges.
Budden, H., Esq., Sydney.
Bumpus, Messrs. J. & E. Ltd., Booksellers, London.
Burder, Alfred W. N., Esq., Hereford.
Burgess, Edward, Esq., London.
Burnet, John J., Esq., A.R.S.A., F.R.I.B.A., Glasgow.
Burrell, Miss, Botley.
Butt, Rev. Walter, Cheltenham.

The Right Hon The Earl of Carlisle.
The Right Hon. The Earl of Carysfort, K.P.
The Right Hon. The Earl of Chesterfield.
The Right Hon. The Earl of Craven.
The Right Hon. The Countess Cowper.
The Right Hon. Lord Edward William Pelham Clinton, K.C.B., G.C.V.O.
The Right Hon. Lady Chermside.
The Right Hon. Lady Churchill.
The Right Hon. Lady Crawshaw.
The Hon. Lieut. Gen. Calthorpe.
The Cape of Good Hope Public Works Department.
The Croydon Public Libraries.
The Constitutional Club, London.
Cackett, J. T., Esq., F.R.I.B.A., Newcastle-on-Tyne.
Cameron, R. M., Esq., Edinburgh.
Caröe, W. D., Esq., F.S.A., F.R.I.B.A., London.
Carruthers, F. J. C., Esq., Dumfries.
Carruthers, W. L., Esq., F.R.I.B.A., Inverness.
Carter, T. B., Esq., London.
Cartwright, Fairfax L., Esq., Banbury.
Cassels, Walter F., Esq., London.
Cazenove & Son, Messrs., Booksellers, London.
Chadwyck-Healey, C. E. H., Esq., K.C., F.S.A., London.
Chafy, Rev. W. K. W., M.A., D.D., Evesham.
Chamberlain, Mrs. Highbury.
Chandler, Joseph Everett, Esq., Boston, U.S.A.
Chatwin, J. A., Esq., F.S.A. Scot., F.R.I.B.A., Birmingham.
Chippindale, Harold, Esq., Leeds.
Clapham, F. Dare, Esq., Eltham.
Clare, George E., Esq., Chelmsford.
Clarke, Howard Chatfield, Esq., London.
Clarke, Somers, Esq, F.S.A., London.
Clayton-Browne, R. Tolan, Esq. (Visconte Montague), Ligure, Italy.
Coates, Major Edward F., York.
Cobb, J. W., Esq., London.
Cockrill, J. W., Esq., A.R.I.B.A., Great Yarmouth.
Cole, Mrs. Jane, Newbury.
Collcutt, T. E., Esq. F.R.I.B.A. London.
Conder, Josiah, Esq., F.R.I.B.A., Tokyo, Japan.
Constable, W., Esq., Edinburgh.
Corry, Robert, Esq., Belfast.
Cory, Clifford J., Esq., Monmouthshire.
Cronk, E. Evans, Esq., London.

Courtney, Mrs. E. J., London.
Cross, Alfred W. S., Esq., M.A., F.R.I.B.A., London.
Crosse, Miss, London.
Crouch & Butler, Messrs., Birmingham.
Cullen, Alexander, Esq., F.R.S.E., F.R.I.B.A., Hamilton, N.B.
Cunliffe, Walter, Esq., Epsom.
Currie, L., Esq., London.
Curtis & Davison, Messrs., Booksellers, London.

The Right Hon. Lord Viscount de Vesci.
The Right Hon. Lord Deramore.
The Right Hon. Aretas Akers Douglas, M.P.
Sir Edwyn Sandys Dawes, K.C.M.G.
The Hon. Mrs. Dawson, Ashburton.
Davidson, W. R., Esq., M.A., London.
Davy, R. Clifton, Esq., Maidenhead.
Dawber, E. Guy, Esq., A.R.I.B.A., London.
Dawkins, C. E., Esq., London.
De la Mare, Andrew J., Esq., London.
Denny, Messrs. A. & F., Booksellers, London.
Dick, R. Burns, Esq., Newcastle-on-Tyne.
Disraeli, Coningsby, Esq., M.P., High Wycombe.
Douglas, Greville, Esq., London.
Douglas & Foulis, Messrs., Booksellers, Edinburgh.
Doulton & Co., Ltd., Messrs., London.
Doyle, J. Francis, Esq., Liverpool.
Dunington, Miss Lorrie A., Woldingham.
Dunn & Watson, Messrs., London.

The Hon. Charles Ellis, London.
The Hon. Mrs. C. Egerton.
The Edinburgh Public Library.
Eady, The Hon. Sir Charles Swinfen, LL.D.
Eccles, T. E., Esq., A.R.I.B.A., Liverpool.
Eden, F. C., Esq., London.
Edwards, G. S. F., Esq., Campfer, Engadine, Switzerland.
Edwards, Mr. Francis, Bookseller, London.
Elgood, George S., Esq., Leicester.
Ellice, Capt. Edward C., Invergarry.
Endicott, W. C., Esq.
Every, John H., Esq., Lewes.

The Right Hon. The Earl Fitzwilliam, K.G.
The Right Hon. The Countess of Feversham.
The Right Hon. Lady Viscountess Falmouth.
Fairley, J. McLellan, Esq., A.R.I.B.A., Edinburgh.
Farquharson, Horace, Esq., London.
Feilding, Percy, Esq., London.
Fisher, E., Esq., London.
Fleming, S. H. Le, Esq., Ambleside.
Fletcher, Banister F., Esq., F.R.I.B.A., London.
Fletcher, J. Douglas, Esq., Rosehaugh.
Fletcher, W. H. B., Esq., Bognor.
Ford, John Walker, Esq., Enfield.

LIST OF SUBSCRIBERS.

FRANCIS, T. MUSGRAVE, Esq., Cambridge.
FRANKLIN, W. L., Esq., Deddington.
FREEMAN, P. B., Esq., Southgate.
FRERE, E. C., Esq., A.R.I.B.A., London.
FREWEN, MORETON, Esq., Brede.

The Right Hon. LADY VISCOUNTESS GALWAY.
The COUNT DE GRAMMONT.
Sir JOHN ROBERT GLADSTONE, Bart.
SIR REGINALD HENRY GRAHAM, Bart.
SIR ROBERT GRESLEY, Bart.
The GRAY'S INN BOOK CLUB, London.
GALIGNANI LIBRARY, The, Booksellers, Paris.
GARBUTT, MATT., Esq., A.R.I.B.A., London.
GARDNER, J. STARKIE, Esq., F.S.A., London.
GARNER, THOMAS, Esq., Fritwell.
GARRY, J., Esq., F.R.I.B.A., West Hartlepool.
GEORGE, ERNEST, & YEATES, Messrs., London.
GEROLD & Co., Herren, Vienna.
GIBBS, H. MARTIN, Esq., Flax-Bourton.
GILBERT, Messrs. H. M., & SONS, Booksellers, South-
    ampton.
GILBERT & Field, Messrs., Booksellers, London.
GILSTRAP, Miss.
GLADSTONE, ROBERT, Esq., Woolton Vale.
GODFREY, BERNARD, Esq., Bletchingley.
GOODALL, FRANK, Esq., Cape Town, S. Africa.
GORDON, H. PANMURE, Esq. (The late), London.
GOTCH, J. ALFRED, Esq., F.S.A., F.R.I.B.A., Kettering.
GREAVES, Mrs. EDWARD, Glamorgan.
GREEN, ARTHUR, Esq., F.R.I.B.A., London.
GREEN, HERBERT J., Esq., A.R.I.B.A., Norwich.
GREENWOOD, HUBERT J., Esq., F.S.A., London.
GREGORY, C. M., Esq., Brighton.
GRETTON, JOHN, Esq., M.P., Melton Mowbray.
GREVEL & Co., Messrs. H., Booksellers, London.
GUEST, MERTHYR INWOOD, Esq., Blandford.

The Right Hon. LORD VISCOUNT HALIFAX, F.S.A.
The Right Hon. LORD HAMILTON OF DALZELL.
The Right Hon. LADY HORNBY.
The Hon. ADELE HAMILTON.
SIR ALFRED SEALE HASLAM, M.P.
SIR JAMES DE HOGHTON, Bart.
HARROW SCHOOL (The Art School).
The HULL PUBLIC LIBRARIES.
HALL, W. CARBY, Esq., F.R.I.B.A., Leeds.
HALLAM, J. ALGERNON, Esq., London.
HAMBRO, E. A., Esq., Blandford.
HAMLYN, FREDERICK, Esq., Bideford.
HAMP, S. H., Esq., A.R.I.B.A., Wembley.
HANBURY, E. S., Esq., London.
HARBOTTLE, EDWARD H., Esq., F.R.I.B.A., Exeter.
HARDING, W. AMBROSE, Esq., Histon Manor.
HARDY, C., Junr., Esq., Canterbury.
HARRISON, J. W., Esq., London.

HARRISON, SIDNEY, Esq., Woking.
HARRISON, STOCKDALE, Esq., F.R.I.B.A., Leicester.
HART, Mrs. ERNEST, Totteridge.
HARTLEY, EDGAR, Esq., London.
HARVEY, W. ALEXANDER, Esq., Birmingham.
HASLAM, R. E., Esq., Bournemouth.
HATCHARDS, Messrs., Booksellers, London.
HAYWARD, CHARLES FORSTER, Esq., F.S.A., London.
HEATHCOTE, CHARLES, Esq., Buxton.
HEITON, A., Esq., Perth.
HELLIER, Col. T. B. SHAW, Wolverhampton.
HENDERSON, Mrs. Emma C., Horsham.
HENRY, J. M., Esq., Edinburgh.
HEWETSON, Mrs., London.
HIERSEMANN, Herr, Bookseller, agent for Germany,
    Leipzig.
HODGES, FIGGIS, & Co., Ltd., Messrs., Booksellers,
    Dublin.
HODGKINSON, W. S., Esq., Wells.
HODSON, LAWRENCE W., Esq., Wolverhampton.
HOLDING, M. H., Esq., A.R.I.B.A., Northampton.
HOLDING, W., Esq., Newbury.
HOLLAND, Dr., St. Moritz, Switzerland.
HOLLOND, Mrs., Bampton.
HOLMES, JOHN C., Esq., Shortlands.
HOOPER, FRANCIS G. F., Esq., A.R.I.B.A., London.
HOPE, JAMES, Esq., Hereford.
HORDER, P. MORLEY, Esq., London.
HOUSTON, A. C., Esq., A.R.I.B.A., London.
HUCKVALE, WILLIAM, Esq., Tring.
HUDDART, R. M. F., Esq., London.
HUDSON, Rev. C. H. B., Oxford.
HUDSON, R. W., Esq., Marlow.
HUGHES, E. L., Esq., Hindhead.
HUGHES, H. R., Esq., Abergele.
HULBERT, MAURICE C., Esq., A.R.I.B.A., Ealing.
HUNTER, JAMES KENNEDY, Esq., Ayr.
HURRELL, J. W., Esq., Manchester.
HUTH, A. H., Esq., London.

The Right Hon. LORD IVEAGH, K.P.
I'ANSON, E. B., Esq., M.A., F.R.I.B.A., London.
IZOU, Mrs. ELIZABETH, Evesham.

The Right Hon. Sir FRANCIS JEUNE, P.C., K.C.B.
The JUNIOR CARLTON CLUB.
JACKSON, A. T., Esq., Belfast,
JAMES, ARTHUR J., Esq., Cirencester.
JAMES, WILLIAM, Esq., Chichester.
JARROLD & SONS, Messrs., Booksellers, Norwich.
JENNINGS, W. J., Esq., Canterbury.
JOHNSON, B. VAUGHAN, Esq., M.A., A.R.I.B.A., London.
JONES, RONALD P., Esq., London.
JONES, W. CAMPBELL, Esq., A.R.I.B.A. London.
JONES & EVANS, Messrs., Booksellers, London.

LIST OF SUBSCRIBERS.

The Right Hon. The Countess of Kenmare.
The Right Hon. Lord Kenyon.
Kelway, W., Esq., Langport.
Kempe, C. E. Esq., M.A., Lindfield.
Kenyon, J. W., Esq., Cirencester.
King, Vivian H., Esq., A.R.I.B.A., London.
King, Messrs. Henry S., & Co., Booksellers, London.

The Most Hon. The Marquis of Lansdowne, K.G., P.C.
The Right Hon. The Countess of Lathom.
The Right Hon The Countess of Leven.
The Right Hon. Lady Algernon Gordon Lennox.
Sir James John Trevor Lawrence, Bart.
The Liverpool Public Library.
The Leicester & Leicestershire Society of Architects.
Lacey, A. J., Esq , Norwich.
Lafontaine, A. C. de, Esq., Dorchester.
Lawley & Co., Messrs., Booksellers, London.
Law, Ernest, Esq., London.
Leatham, A. W., Esq., Cirencester.
Lees-Milne, G. C., Esq., Shaw.
Leesmith, B. L., Esq., Haslemere.
Letts, C., Esq., London.
Letts, S. E., Esq., London
Lever, W. H., Esq., Thornton Haugh.
Leveson-Gower, Charles, Esq. Limpsfield.
Levy et Cie., Messrs., Booksellers, Paris.
Lewis, Miss, Cardiff.
Lewis, W. Henry, Esq., Llanisten.
Leycester, Rafe, Esq., Knutsford
Lines, Rowland W., Esq., Tring.
Lishman, Frank, Esq., A.R.I.B.A., London.
Loder, Alfred B., Esq., Harpenden.
Low, Messrs. Sampson, and Co., Ltd., Booksellers, London.
Lucas, Joseph, Esq., Waldron.
Lutwidge, C. R. Fletcher, Esq., Tunbridge Wells.
Lutyens, Edwin L., Esq., London
Lyttelton-Annesley, General A., Weybridge.

His Grace The Duke de Moro.
The Hon. Mrs. S. Meade.
The Hon. Lady Medlycott.
The Hon. A. H. Mills.
Sir James Percy Miller, Bart.
Sir James Montgomery, Bart.
The McGill University, Toronto, Canada.
The Mitchell Library, Glasgow.
McAndrew, John, Esq., Tunbridge Wells.
McIntosh, Mrs., Havering.
McLaren, H. D., Esq., Oxford.
Mackenzie, A. Marshall, Esq., A.R.S.A., F.R.I.B.A., Aberdeen.
Maclean, John, Esq., Kegworth.

Mallows, C. E., Esq., Bedford.
Marchant, Robert, Esq., A.R.I.B.A., London.
Martin, Leonard, Esq., London.
Martin, R. B., Esq., M.P., London.
Marwick, T. P., Esq., F.R.I.B.A., Edinburgh.
Maruya & Co., Messrs., Booksellers, Tokyo, Japan.
Mathews, H. Edmund, Esq., London.
Mathews, C. Elkin, Esq., Chiswick.
Mawson, T. H., Esq., Windermere.
Melvin & Son, Messrs., Alloa.
Meredith-Brown, M., Esq., Chippenham.
Messel, L., Esq., Crawley.
Messer, Arthur A., Esq., Woking.
Methuen, A. M. S., Esq., Haslemere.
Meuleneere, Monsieur De, Bookseller, Brussels.
Meyers, Sydney H., Esq., London.
Miller, James, Esq., Glasgow.
Millet, F. D., Esq., Broadway.
Mills & Shepherd, Messrs., Dundee.
Milner, H. E., Esq., London.
Mitchell, Sydney, Esq., Edinburgh.
Mitton, E. Stanley, Esq., Birmingham.
Moffatt, H. C., Esq., Ross.
Moore, Robert, Esq., Middlesborough.
Moore-Smith, J. R., Esq., A.R.I.B.A., London.
Morgan, J. Pierpont, Junr., Esq., London.
Morison & Co., Messrs., Edinburgh.
Morphew, Reginald, Esq., London.
Morris, James A., Esq., F.R.I.B.A., Ayr, N.B.
Moscrop, W. J., Esq., F.R.I.B.A., Darlington.
Mount, Francis, Esq., London.
Mountford, E. W., Esq., F.R.I.B.A., London.
Mundy, E. M., Esq., Derby.
Munro, James M., Esq., Glasgow.
Muntzer, Fredk., Esq., London.
Murray, John, Esq., Edinburgh.

His Grace The Duke of Norfolk, K.G., P.C.
His Grace The Duke of Northumberland, K.G., P.C.
Lady Naesmyth.
The Newcastle Public Library.
The Nottingham Public Library.
The Nottingham School of Art.
Nesfield, G. S., Esq., Scarborough.
Neve, W. West, Esq., London.
Newbold, Arthur, Esq., Plumpton, Lewes.
Newton, Ernest, Esq., London.
Nicholson, W. G., Esq., M.P., London.
Nield, George Ernest, Esq., A.R.I.B.A., London.
Norman & Burt, Messrs., Burgess Hill.

The Right Hon. Lady Oranmore & Browne.
The Hon. Mrs. Mary Oakeley.
Oakey, Herbert, Esq., London.
Oatley, George H., Esq., F.R.I.B.A., Bristol.
Ogilvy, G., Esq., London.

LIST OF SUBSCRIBERS.

OLIVER, R. D., Esq., London.
OLIVER, VERE L., Esq., Sunninghill.
ORBAN, L., Esq., Brussels.
ORRED, Miss META, Bournemouth.
OWEN, SEGAR, Esq., A.R.I.B.A., Warrington.
OWERS, CHARLES, Esq., Dundee.

The Right Hon. The EARL OF PEMBROKE, P.C., G.C.V.O.
The Right Hon. The EARL OF PORTSMOUTH, F.S.A.
The Right Hon. LORD VISCOUNT PORTMAN.
The Hon. Mrs. PALEY.
PANNETT, A. R., Esq., Haywards Heath.
PARKER, BARRY, Esq., Buxton.
PARKER, JOHN, Esq., Cape Town, S. Africa.
PARRY, Mrs., New Southgate.
PARRY, S. GAMBIER, Esq., A.R.I.B.A., London.
PARSONS, ALFRED, Esq., A.R.A., London.
PARSONS, E. & SONS, Messrs., Booksellers, London.
PARTRIDGE, Capt. W., Newbury.
PATERSON, ALEXANDER N., Esq., M.A., A.R.I.B.A.,
   Glasgow.
PATERSON, GAVIN, Esq., Hamilton.
PAOTN, R. JOHNSTON, Esq., Templetonburn.
PAWLEY, CHARLES H., Esq., London.
PEDDIE, J. M. DICK, Esq., Edinburgh.
PENTON, Mrs. SARAH E., London.
PERRINS, C. W. DYSON, Esq., Malvern.
PETO, H. A., Esq., Bradford-on-Avon.
PHILLIPS, FREDERICK ABBISS, Esq., Leatherhead.
PHILLIPS, GEORGE R., Esq., London.
PHIPPS, J. S., Esq., New York.
PICK, S. PERKINS, Esq., F.R.I.B.A., Leicester.
PICKERING, ROBERT YOUNG, Esq., Dumfries.
PIRIE, J. M., Esq., Aberdeen.
PITCHER, Messrs. W. N., & Co., Booksellers, Manchester.
PITMAN, ERNEST, Esq., Bath.
PITT-RIVERS, A. E., Esq., Salisbury.
POIX, E. DE, Esq., Broome Place.
POTTS, W. E., Esq., Bolton.
PRACTICAL LANDSCAPE GARDENING & ESTATE DE-
   VELOPMENT Co., The, Ltd., London.
PRENTICE, A. N., Esq., A.R.I.B.A., London.
PRESTON, R. BASSNETT, Esq., A.R.I.B.A., Manchester.
PRYNNE, GEORGE H. FELLOWES, Esq., F.R.I.B.A.,
   London.
PULHAM & SONS, Messrs., London.
PULLAR, RUFUS D., Esq., London.
PULTENEY, Rev. A. W., Market Harborough.

QUARITCH, Mr. BERNARD, Bookseller, London.

His Grace The Duke OF RUTLAND, K.G., P.C., G.C.B.
The Right Hon. The EARL OF RADNOR.
The Right Hon. LORD RENDEL.
The Right Hon. LADY REAY.
LADY ROBERTS, Godalming.

The Hon. LADY ROSCOE.
The ROYAL INSTITUTE OF BRITISH ARCHITECTS.
The ROYAL GARDENS, Kew.
RAWLINS, REGINALD S. P., Esq., Bath.
REAVELL, GEO., Junr., Esq., A.R.I.B.A., Alnwick.
REDMAYNE, GEO. T., Esq., F.R.I.B.A., Haslemere.
RHODES, Mrs. HEATON.
RICH, F. W., Esq., F.R.I.B.A., Newcastle-on-Tyne.
RIDLER, Miss, Torquay.
RIMELL, Messrs. J., & SON, Booksellers, London.
ROBERT, ALBERT W., Esq., Paris.
ROBERTS, Miss E. D., Tunbridge Wells.
ROBERTSON, Messrs. G., & Co., Booksellers, London.
ROMAINE-WALKER, W. H., Esq., A.R.I.B.A., London.
ROSS, JAMES W., Esq., Edinburgh.
ROSS, WALTER G., Esq., A.R.I.B.A., London.
ROTHSCHILD, LEOPOLD DE, Esq., Leighton Buzzard.
ROTHSCHILD, Miss ALICE DE, Waddesdon.
ROWNTREE, FRED., Esq., London.
RUNTZ, E. A., Esq., London.

H.R.H. PRINCE CHRISTIAN OF SCHLESWIG-HOLSTEIN,
   K.G.
H.R.H. The DUCHESS OF SPARTA.
Her Grace The DOWAGER DUCHESS OF SUTHERLAND.
The COUNT SEILERN.
SIR CHARLES SEELY.
SANDYS, Col. T. MYLES, M.P., Ulverston.
SAUL, HENRY A., Esq., A.R.I.B.A., London.
SAUMAREZ, F. B. DE, Esq., Cheltenham.
SAXTON, Mr. H. B., Bookseller, Nottingham.
SCHULTZ, R. W., Esq., London.
SCHWARTZ, J. M. W. VAN DER POORTEN, Esq., Holland.
SCOTT, A. GILBERT, Esq., London.
SCOTT, CHAS. TOLLEMACHE, Esq., Nuneaton.
SCOTT, JAMES, Esq., St. Andrews, N.B.
SCOTT, J. OLDRID, Esq., F.S.A., F.R.I.B.A., Oxted.
SCOTT-ELLIOT, W., Esq., Arkleton, N.B.
SCRIBNER'S SONS, Messrs. CHARLES, Agents for United
   States of America.
SEBRIGHT, GUY, Esq., Hever Castle, Kent.
SELBY, E. H., Esq., A.R.I.B.A., London.
SHAND, WILLIAM, Lancaster.
SHAW, STEPHEN, Esq., F.R.I.B.A., Kendal.
SHEEN, WILLIAM, Esq., London.
SHEPHERD, J. J., Esq., Bournemouth.
SHERRATT & HUGHES, Messrs., Booksellers, Manchester.
SHERRIN, GEO., Esq., F.R.I.B.A., Ingatestone.
SIMMS, Mr. S. W., Bookseller, Bath.
SIMON, B., Esq., Ragatz, Switzerland.
SIMPKIN, MARSHALL & Co., Ltd., Messrs., Booksellers,
   London.
SIMPSON, JONATHAN, Esq., Bolton.
SIMPSON, J. W., Esq., A.R.I.B.A., London.
SKELTON, S. GISSING, Esq., London.
SKIPPER, GEO. J., Esq., F.R.I.B.A., Norwich.

LIST OF SUBSCRIBERS.

SLOPER, E. W., Esq., Johannesburg, S. Africa.
SMEE, ARTHUR R., Esq., London.
SMITH, ALBERT W., Esq., F.R.I.B.A., Maidstone.
SNELL, HENRY J., Esc., Plymouth.
SOTHERAN, Messrs. E. & Co., Booksellers, London.
SPEAIGHT, F. W., Esq., London.
SPON, Messrs. E. and F. N., Ltd., Booksellers, London.
SQUIRE, JOHN H., Esq., London.
STANFORD, C. F., Esq., London.
STEBBING, W. P. D., Esq., Epsom.
STEVENS, J. WALLACE, Esq., Mansfield.
STEVENSON, J. J., Esq., F.S.A., F.R.I.B.A., London.
STOCK, ELLIOT, Mr., Bookseller, London.
STOCKS, BEN, Esq., Huddersfield.
STOKES, J. N., Esq., New York, U.S.A.
STONES & STONES, Messrs., Blackburn.
STORY, J. WALDO, Esq., Rome.
STREATFIELD, GRANVILLE E. S., Esq., London.
SUGDEN, Messrs. W. H. & A., Keighley.
SWINFEN-BROUN, M.A., Esq., Lichfield.

The Hon. Mrs. FREEMAN THOMAS.
The Hon. ROBERT MARSHAM TOWNSHEND.
The Hon. Mrs. TREMAYNE.
The TORONTO PUBLIC LIBRARY, Canada.
TAPPER, WALTER J., Esq., A.R.I.B.A., London.
TATHAM, L., Esq., Manchester.
THACKER & Co., Messrs., Booksellers, London.
THOMAS, Mrs. C. E., Wakefield.
THOMSON, HOWARD H., Esq., A.R.I.B.A., Leicester.
TILLOTSON, J. L., Esq., Bebington.
TOWER, WALTER E., Esq., London.
TRAQUAIR, RAMSEY, Esq., A.R.I.B.A., Edinburgh.
TREVELYAN, Mrs., Cacciola, Sicilia.
TRIGGS, A., Esq., London.
TRIGGS, A. B., Esq., J.P., Yass, Australia.
TRUSLOVE, HANSON & COMBA Ltd., Messrs., Book-
    sellers, London.
TURNER, T. WARNER, Esq., Mansfield.

UNDERHILL, C. F., Esq., Burton-on-Trent.

VICTORIA, The LIBRARY, MUSEUMS AND NATIONAL
    GALLERY OF.
VINCENT, SIR EDGAR, K.C.M.G., M.P., Esher.

Her Grace The DUCHESS OF WESTMINSTER.
The Right Hon. The EARL OF WESTMORLAND.
The Right Hon. The EARL OF WILTON.
The Right Hon. The COUNTESS OF WARWICK.

The Right Hon. The Countess WHARNCLIFFE.
The Right Hon. LORD WINDSOR, P.C.
The Right Hon. LADY WANTAGE.
The Right Hon. LADY WENLOCK.
BARON I. WASAKI, Japan.
LADY WOLSELEY.
SIR BOUCHIER SHERRARD WREY, Bart.
The WIGAN FREE PUBLIC LIBRARY.
The WREN BOOK CLUB.
WADDINGTON, W. A., Esq., A.R.I.B.A., Manchester.
WAINWRIGHT, Mrs. W. P., Boston, U.S.A.
WALPOLE, Col. HORACE, Winchfield.
WALTER, MISS NUTTALL.
WARD, W. H., Esq., A.R.I.B.A., London.
WARING, S. J., Junr., Esq., London.
WARREN, E. PRIOLEAU, Esq., F.S.A., London.
WATERHOUSE & SON, Messrs., London.
WATNEY, VERNON, Esq., London.
WATSON, W. CRUM, Esq., Edinburgh.
WATT, GEORGE, Esq., Aberdeen.
WEBB, ASTON, Esq., A.R.A., F.S.A., London.
WEBB, MISS ETHEL MARY, Nottingham.
WELLES, R. DOUGLAS, Esq., London.
WESTON, GEORGE F., Esq., Baltimore, U.S.A.
WEYMOUTH, R. HENRY, Esq., A.R.I.B.A., London.
WHELDON & Co., Messrs., Booksellers, London.
WHITE, JOHN P., Esq., Bedford.
WHITE, Mrs. HENRY, Beaconsfield.
WHITELAW, CHARLES E., Esq., Glasgow.
WHITFIELD & THOMAS, Messrs., London.
WILLETT, W., Esq., London.
WILLIAMS, A., Esq., F.R.I.B.A., London.
WILLIAMS, MORGAN S., Esq., Llantwit Major.
WILLIAMS, W. CLEMENT, Esq., F.R.I.B.A., Halifax.
WILLIAMSON, & INGLIS, Messrs. Kirkcaldy.
WINGFIELD, ANTHONY H., Esq., Ampthill.
WINN, Messrs. THOMAS, & SONS, Leeds.
WISSENDEN, A. C., Esq., A.R.I.B.A., Croydon.
WOLSTENHOLME, HARRY V., Esq., F.R.I.B.A., Black-
    burn.
WOOD, WALTER B., Esq., A.R.I.B.A., Gloucester.
WOODWARD, W., Esq., A.R.I.B.A., London.
WOOLNOUGH, J. W., Esq., Eastbourne.

YOUNG, CLYDE, Esq., London.
YOUNG, KEITH D., Esq., F.R.I.B.A., London.
YOUNG, W. THOMAS, Esq., Woking.
YULE, MISS W. F., Muir of Ord, N.B.

ZAEHNSDORF, Mr., Bookbinder, London.

PREFACE TO 1988 EDITION

The last decade of the nineteenth century saw one of the periodic revivals of interest in the philosophy of gardening which have occurred regularly over the last three centuries. Evelyn, Pope, Repton, Loudon and Jekyll are among the names that can be linked with each heightening of interest. We are in one such period today. Arguably these revivals provide the high tide of intellectual concern as opposed to the ground swell of work done by practical men who continued to make gardens but not always with the same degree of cerebral involvement. The ingredients which accompanied each new episode included a new direction of thinking, often accompanied by peace (in military if not political terms), lively minds and above all, patrons with wealth.

There was certainly great wealth in the Edwardian period; the improvements in the transport system and an interest in the open air meant that it was possible to work in London and live in the country. Commuting had begun and the demand for suitable country homes was created. The self confidence of rich merchants and financiers at the height of the British Empire's prosperity demanded buildings and gardens which would impress. In looking back for architectural examples it is not surprising that the Italian influence should once more make itself felt, as it had done in the early seventeenth century and again in the mid-nineteenth century. The Italian style has an air of order combined with rich decoration which complemented the tenets of the Arts and Crafts movement. What could be more natural for client and architect than to look back at the solid buildings and their gardens created two to three hundred years previously by men with similar ambitions and attitudes?

All this might have passed as yet another revival of interest in the theory of gardening had it not been for the arrival of Hudson and his publishing activities. The books he commissioned on houses and gardens, which became famous under the *Country Life* imprint, were produced by new printing techniques to a standard never seen before. The improvement in print from Caxton to Loudon in the early nineteenth century is less than was achieved in the following eighty years. Apart from technical quality this book was also superbly designed in the tradition of the Arts and Crafts movement. One can sense the enthusiasm of author and publisher in the way in which as much as possible has been put into the book, in the form of photographs, drawings, plans, elevations and sketches. This particular period was marked by its highly scientific approach to recording gardens. For example it may be that Triggs was the first man ever to set about an historic garden with a tape measure. The book itself is a typical product of the Edwardian demand for excellence, something which *Country Life* continued to provide as it chronicled the development of English houses and gardens over the decades — and still provides in its magazine today.

Formal Gardens is not simply a record of gardening at one of its high points, it also carries relevance for today's practical gardener. The early Renaissance gardens are typified by contrasts in the use of space, well proportioned enclosures, long thin walks, tiny well planted shady corners and small intimate gardens like the recent recreation of a small 'Lady's' or herb garden by Rosemary Verey that is included among the colour plates.

ANTIQUE COLLECTORS' CLUB
November, 1988

PREFACE.

THE strong interest in the Art of Gardening which exists in this country is characteristic of its people and their love of out-of-door occupations and amusements. It may also be regarded as constant, for although there have been times when the Art has shown signs of decay, these have been quickly followed by periods of revival; and it may perhaps be safely said that the revival which has taken place during the past decade is not only strong evidence of the continuing interest felt in the Art, but is also of great promise for its future, since it has attracted the attention of various classes, chief amongst which are amateurs of taste and means, together with architects who have made a special study of the Art as it was practised during the best periods of its history, and some of whose work is as good as the old they have studied to such good effect. The Art, too, has in the period above-mentioned acquired quite a new literature of its own, including valuable contributions from the late John D. Sedding, E. V. B. (the Hon. Mrs. Boyle), the Hon. Alicia Amherst, Miss Gertrude Jekyll, Mrs. Earle, Mr. A. Forbes Sieveking and Messrs. Blomfield and Thomas, who have treated it from various points of view—historical, sentimental and pictorial.

The present work has been prepared chiefly with the object of showing, by means of a series of studies of some of the most complete and historical gardens now extant in this country, the principle involved in their planning and arrangement in relation to the house, which is the essential element in what it is the custom to call a Formal Garden. It must be matter for regret that very few of these gardens can be correctly described as old; indeed, there are but few throughout the country to which the term can be applied. Gardens, unlike buildings, are never finished; almost each succeeding season seeing some change in the growth of vegetation, and many so-called old gardens have suffered so greatly from the changes of fashion as to have lost all resemblance to their original schemes.

In order, therefore to supplement the examples of existing gardens the aid of some old prints, contemporary with the subjects they illustrate, has been called in, and a small number of drawings of the most characteristic and interesting of these, made to a larger scale than on the originals, has been included. These will be of practical value, as they show the complete schemes, either as they existed at the time or were designed to be carried out.

The remainder of the plates are devoted to examples of those architectural and decorative accessories, which, when well designed, add so much to the charm of a garden, and include a selection of Columbaries, Garden-houses, Summer-houses, Gate Entrances, Terraces and Steps, Ponds and Fountains, Sundials, Figures, and Vases in Lead and Stone, Lead Cisterns, Mazes, etc. The backgrounds to the initial letters to the descriptions of the Plates are from sketches by the Author, and represent in the majority of cases portions of the gardens described.

The Introduction does not pretend to be more than a brief historical note, based upon the sum of our knowledge of the subject, while in the descriptions of the various plates the endeavour has been made to keep strictly to the intention of the work; treating the matter in as practical a way as possible, and giving only such historical details as appeared essential.

To Mr. Charles Latham much is due, for he has devoted the best of his art to the photographic

PREFACE.

portion of the work. In this he has been somewhat handicapped, as the points of view were necessarily chosen rather to show the general disposition of the gardens than to obtain the most picturesque effect; but in spite of this he has succeeded in producing a collection of pictures doing justice to the beauties of the subjects in a way that no other medium could so well have accomplished.

The cordial thanks of the author are due, first, to all those who so readily granted him access to their gardens; their courtesy and kindness alone rendered his task possible. Next, to Mr. Bradley Batsford, who has materially assisted him in the production of the work, unceasingly giving his best attention to the many important details involved. He is also indebted to Mr. Thomas Ross, of Edinburgh, for some considerable assistance in the selection of the Scottish examples; to Mr. Ernest Law, for his kind help in the description of the gardens at Hampton Court; to Mr. L. Rome Guthrie, for preparing several of the plates of Scottish gardens; and to Mr. J. Tarney, Mr. A. E. Bullock and Mr. J. Davidson for assistance in drawing some others of the plates.

If any apology had been necessary for the publication of this work the author feels it has been rendered needless by the gratifying manner in which it has been taken up by the Subscribers, and the cordial reception accorded to it by the Press, both technical and artistic. He has made every endeavour to fulfil the promise of the Prospectus, and trusts that in its complete form his book will meet with the approval of the Subscribers, and be of some help in the advancement of the Art with which it deals.

H. INIGO TRIGGS.

STAFFORD HOUSE, CHISWICK,
October, 1902.

LIST OF COLOUR PLATES.

LIST OF THE PLATES.

LIST OF THE PLATES.

LIST OF THE PLATES.

LIST OF THE PLATES.

INDEX TO THE PLATES
AND DESCRIPTIVE TEXT.

(Arranged under Names of Subjects or Places.)

INDEX TO THE PLATES AND DESCRIPTIVE TEXT.

INDEX TO THE PLATES AND

DESCRIPTIVE TEXT.

A

INDEX TO THE PLATES AND

DESCRIPTIVE TEXT.

HOLDENBY 1988.

FORMAL GARDENS

IN

ENGLAND AND SCOTLAND

AN HISTORICAL NOTE.

HE History of the Formal Garden in England is one of continuous and gradual growth, from the earliest mediæval period to the close of the seventeenth century, and in this " Note " an endeavour is made to trace, as briefly as may be, the story of its origin and development. Those who desire fuller information should consult "The Praise of Gardens," by A. Forbes Sieveking ; "Garden Craft Old and New," by John D. Sedding ; "The Formal Garden in England," by Reginald Blomfield, M.A., and F. Inigo Thomas ; "A History of Gardening in England," by the Hon. Alicia Amherst ; and some of the early writers on the subject, of which a very complete list will be found in the last mentioned.

Of the garden in the Middle Ages there are no examples extant, but, fortunately, illuminated manuscripts and paintings of the period give us some impression of their arrangement. The garden was in those days regarded chiefly as a place wherein to grow herbs, vegetables and plants for medicinal purposes ; few feudal castles had within their precincts sufficient space for pleasure gardens, and indeed a garden for pleasure was quite a secondary consideration.

There was sometimes a small "ladies" garden, usually consisting of a square enclosure surrounded by high walls or thick hedges, and opening directly off the buildings. This quaint plot was in the first instance designed as a place of rest, away from the troubles and cares of the world without, and was often surrounded by a bank of earth turfed to form a comfortable seat, or used as a flower-bed, the front built up of brick or stone, with here and there a raised mound, which developing later into the "Mount" became an important feature in garden design. Such a garden would also contain its arbour in some sheltered position, carefully screened from curious eyes, with perhaps a fountain and certainly a cistern or wells for watering.

In the early part of the Norman Dynasty gardens were practically what we now call orchards, although few fruit trees were known in England at this period. But near the castles and monasteries a small enclosure surrounded by lofty walls was reserved for the ladies, or for the Abbot, and this was filled with roses or other fragrant plants. An interesting garden of the late fifteenth century, shown in the Flemish manuscript of the "Roman de la Rose," is divided into several enclosures, bounded either by stone embattled walls or by a fence of light trellis-work. In the centre of one of these enclosures is a fountain of elaborate design, from which the water runs into a small canal circulating through the garden.

A garden was an important adjunct to every monastery, and often, as in the case of Canterbury, attained to considerable dimensions. The art of horticulture was indeed principally practised amongst the monastic orders, whose travelled brethren introduced many foreign plants into this country. As vegetables formed the principal daily food of the inmates, the greater portion of the garden was devoted to their cultivation. There would also be some acres of orchard or "Pomerium," a vineyard and a herb garden, wherein were grown the herbs used as medicines.

FORMAL GARDENS IN

Alexander Necham, Abbot of Cirencester and the foster-brother of Richard Cœur de Lion, was the earliest Englishman to write on gardens.[1] He was born at St. Albans in 1157, and died near Worcester in 1217. His account of the herbs, fruit and flowers to be found in a garden of his day is interesting, and gives a good idea of what was considered necessary for the support of a monastic establishment of the time. Another interesting description of a monastic garden is that of the Abbey of Clairvaux, written by a contemporary of St. Bernard (1091-1153), who says: " If thou desire to know the situation of Clairvaux, let those writings be to thee as a mirror. . . . Then the back part of the abbey terminates in a broad plain, no small portion of which a wall occupies, which surrounds the abbey with its extended circuit. Within the enclosure of this wall many and various trees prolific in various fruits constitute an orchard resembling a wood, which, being near the cell of the sick, lightens the infirmities of the brethren with no moderate solace, while it affords a spacious walking place to those who walk and a sweet place for reclining to those who are overheated. . . . Where the orchard terminates, the garden begins, distributed into separate plots, or rather, divided by intersecting rivulets; for though the water appears stagnant, it flows nevertheless with a slow gliding. . . . This water serves the double duty of supporting the fish and watering the vegetables."

In the troublous period which succeeded the Norman Conquest, the quiet pleasures of a garden could not be enjoyed. For the better security of life and property it was necessary to choose positions as inaccessible as possible for castle sites, in direct contrast to the course followed by the monastic orders, who as a rule chose to place their monasteries in some fertile valley, giving shelter for their orchards, gardens and vineyards.

Of the gardens surrounding the Royal Palaces the most prominent was that of Woodstock, where Henry III. carried out many improvements for his Queen. Here was the famous labyrinth which concealed Fair Rosamund's Bower. The labyrinth was an invention of very early times, and, from being merely a winding path cut in the ground, developed into the maze which formed such a feature of the seventeenth-century garden. There were also Royal gardens at Windsor, Westminster, Charing and the Tower, and others of importance belonging to the nobility, and surrounding their houses in the neighbourhood of London.

During the fourteenth and fifteenth centuries more peaceable times permitted an advance in the art of horticulture. A class of smaller landowners was growing up, who, gradually throwing off allegiance to their feudal lords, built for themselves small farms and manor-houses, surrounding them with orchards and gardens, and by the end of the fourteenth century almost every small manor and farm had its garden. During the Wars of the Roses the gentle arts received a check which lasted until the restoration of peace in Tudor times.

We now arrive at a time when a great change came over the Domestic Architecture of this country; a time when the castle with its fortified enclosures, built perhaps in some inaccessible ravine or on the summit of some steep hill, was succeeded by the more comfortable manor-house, surrounded by a moat, and usually situate on a site much more adapted to the development of gardens. In many cases, as, for example, at Broughton Castle, the moat enclosed an area sufficient for the formation of a very fairly sized garden, which would be devoted to the cultivation of flowers and other purposes of pleasure, whilst the orchards or vineyards would be just without the moat. The increasing sense of security diminished the necessity for keeping all property within the protecting lines of a moat, and the space beyond, thus gained for the pleasure grounds, afforded greater scope for play of fancy in garden design.

One of the first innovations was the garden bed, enclosed by a low railing of trellis-work, or raised a little from the ground with a low wall of brick or stone. Another important feature introduced at this period was topiary work, which had been used in Roman gardens. This soon found much favour in this country, and whilst confined to its simpler forms added much to the quaint aspect of a garden. To this period also is ascribed the introduction of the mount in England, though one can readily believe that it is of greater antiquity; it is a feature that came into very common use, and is thus recommended by Bacon in his essay: " I would also

[1] See " The Praise of Gardens," by A. Forbes Sieveking.

in the very middle a fair Mount, with three Ascents and Alleys, enough for four to walk abreast, which I would have to be perfect circles, without any Bulwarks or Imbossments, and the whole Mount to be thirty foot high, and some fine Banquetting House with some chimneys neatly cast and without too much glass."

The mount was, no doubt, originally contrived to enable persons in the garden to look over the enclosing wall, and would serve both as a place from which to enjoy the view and as a point of outlook in case of attack. In early days the mounts were constructed of wood or stone, and were curiously adorned within and without, whilst later on they resumed the old Barrow shape, and were made of earth and utilized for the culture of fruit trees. John Leland, in his "Itinerary" (1540), describing Wressel Castle, Yorkshire, says: "Yn the Orchardes were mounts writhen about with degrees, like the turnings in cokil shelles to come to the top without payne." At Rockingham, in Northamptonshire, there still remains a great terraced mound of earth, covered with turf. It is raised against a part of the high wall which surrounds the garden, and behind which the keep formerly stood. From the top of this the eye ranges across the garden with its quaintly cut yew trees, over a magnificent view of the open country beyond [1] The top of a mount was often surmounted by an arbour or summer-house. The mount at Hampton Court, constructed in 1533 on a brick foundation, was the finest specimen of its day, and the arbour, constructed of wooden pales and trellis-work, was a very elaborate feature. Similar arbours were frequently constructed around three or all sides of the garden, and formed a delightful means of access from one part to another. The arbour or garden-house was often a substantial erection of brick or stone, and frequently built at the corner of a boundary or dividing wall, thus affording a view of more than one part of the gardens.

Another innovation made about the time of Henry VIII. was the "knot" or knotted bed; a bed laid out in a complicated geometrical pattern, the design being formed by borders of brick, tile or box, and sometimes later these knots were filled in with coloured earth; an objectionable practice which was treated with much well-deserved contumely. In the destruction of the many monasteries at the Reformation, great havoc was made of the best of old English gardens, and often nothing now remains beyond an occasional fish-pond or the walls of a vineyard or orchard to show us their former extent and beauty.

The Privy Purse expenses of Henry VIII., of which there are many extracts in Mr. Ernest Law's "History of Hampton Court Palace," give us a good deal of information with regard to his gardening operations there. The land which Wolsey covered with the buildings, gardens and park, amounted to about two thousand acres. The old Manor House stood at the south-west corner of this area, and around it the Cardinal laid out his gardens and orchards. In 1529 occurred the Cardinal's disgrace, and Henry entered into the possession of the Palace. The gardens were soon after enlarged and divided by brick walls, a new orchard was laid out, and a flower-garden provided for the Queen's pleasure. What a truly delightful picture must these gardens have formed with their little walks and parterres, sheltered alleys, arbours and banqueting houses! The largest plot was called the King's New Garden, and occupied the space now known as the Privy Garden. Here there were gay parterres with gravel paths and little raised mounds with sun-dials on them. There was also the Pond Garden, which is still to be seen, and which, though much altered, yet retains something of its Tudor aspect, and another, known as "the little garden," which may perhaps be identified with the enclosed space at the side of the Pond Garden. Studded about in various parts of the gardens and orchards were heraldic beasts on pedestals, holding vanes or shields bearing the King's arms and badges, also many brass sun-dials.

Another famous garden was at Nonsuch, near Ewell in Surrey, which was laid out by Henry VIII. towards the end of his reign. Hentzner, who made a journey into England in 1598, says of Nonsuch: "In the pleasure and artificial gardens are many columns and pyramids of marble, two fountains that spout water one round the other like a pyramid, upon which are perched small birds that stream water out of their bills. In the grove

---

[1] "History of Gardening in England," by the Hon. Alicia Amherst.

of Diana is a very agreeable fountain with Actæon turned into a stag, as he was sprinkled by the goddess and her nymphs, with inscriptions. There is, besides, another pyramid of marble full of concealed pipes, which spirt upon all who come within their reach."

This garden was, perhaps, much in its original state at the time of the Parliamentary Survey in 1650, when it is thus described : " It was cut out and divided into several allies, quarters and rounds, set about with thorn hedges ; on the north side was a kitchen-garden very commodious, and surrounded with a brick wall of fourteen feet high. On the west was a wilderness severed from the little park by a lodge, the whole containing ten acres. In the privy garden were pyramids, fountains, and basons of marble, one of which is set round with six lilack trees, which trees bear no fruite but only a very pleasaunte flower. . . Before the Palace was a neate and handsome bowling green surrounded with a balustrade of freestone."

Theobalds was another famous garden of this period, and the following description is from the same Survey : " In the Greate Garden are nine large compleate squares or knotts lyinge upon a levell in ye middle of ye said Garden, whereof one is sett forth with box borders in ye likeness of ye Kinges armes, one other plott is planted with choice flowers ; the other 7 knotts are all grass knotts handsomely turfed in the intervalls or little walkes . . . a quicksett hedge of white Thorne and Privett cut into a handsome fashion at every angle, a faire cherrie tree and a Ciprus in the middle of the knotts—also a marble fountaine."

The growing popularity of the game of bowls, and a greater appreciation of the delights of a garden induced by the writings of such men as Bacon, did much to further garden designing. Although the game was undoubtedly played in much earlier periods, it was never encouraged, and was often subject to severe legislation. In 1541 it was enacted that no one could at any time "play at any bowle or bowles in open place out of his garden or orchard "; whilst a licence might be granted to anyone worth over £100 per annum to play privately in his own domain. As the game became more popular among the country gentry, bowling lawns, with large expanses of level turf, were formed.

The Elizabethan was a golden era in the history of domestic architecture, and in that also of garden designing. All through her reign her courtiers were vying with each other in the erection of splendid palaces. Hardwicke, Hatfield, Kirby, Longleat, and many others belong to this period, and all had most stately garden surroundings. Nor was the art of garden design confined to the larger houses, for even the smaller manor-houses had their parterres, forecourts and bowling greens. The Elizabethan garden was a combination of much of what was best in the older English garden, combined with the new ideas from Italy, France and Holland, which dominated the architecture of the period, much as they affected our literature. In designing a garden, it was fortunately not so easy as in the case of a building to borrow a complete scheme from one country and reproduce it in another, and it is this which accounts for the many essential differences between the Italian and the English gardens. In the Italian there is always a lack of grass-work, which forms so important a feature in our own, and even if we are bound to admit the foreign influence, it is not too much to claim for our gardens an individuality which certainly belongs to the houses they surrounded, and they obviously played an important part in the general harmony of the design. Thus the primitive mediæval garden gradually developed into the more elaborate and stately garden of the Renaissance.

The plan, subject to much variety in the treatment of detail, was usually drawn up somewhat on similar lines to that of Montacute,[1] having a walled-in forecourt in front of the house, and in the forecourt would be an entrance gate opposite the main entrance to the building, the wings of which gave the leading lines to the design. There was usually in the forecourt a small lawn, a fountain or a pond. Before arriving at this forecourt there was in many cases a sort of ante-court, which seems to have been designed more for the sake of dignity than for its utility. It was not the custom for guests to alight at the front entrance of the house, and

[1] See Plate I. The original forecourt walls here were formerly extended past the Pavilions into the Park beyond, but this was an unusual arrangement.

in these cases they had to traverse at least one court on their arrival. On one side of the forecourt lay the base or bass court, surrounded by the kitchens, stables and other buildings which it was intended to serve, and in it was hidden away all the untidiness associated with its uses, while on the other side were situated the more ornamental pleasure grounds and parterres, with probably one small enclosed garden known as " my lady's " garden, a survival from the Middle Ages.

Overlooking the garden, and generally next to the house, would be the terrace, usually some twenty to thirty feet wide, as at Bramshill and Bradford-on-Avon, and of considerable length, with perhaps an arbour at either end. The terrace would be protected by a balustrade either of detached balusters or of a design pierced in stone and from it flights of steps would lead to the broad sanded walks dividing the parterre into several subdivisions, which were again divided by narrow paths into smaller designs.

The general shape of such a garden would be square, a shape which would commend itself to the taste of the Elizabethan and Jacobean times as being that adopted in classic ages, for the antique garden was designed in a square with enclosures of trellis-work, espaliers and clipped box hedges, regularly ornamented with statuary, fountains and vases. The square shape was common to the Italian and French gardens also. Bacon, in his essay, says : " The garden is best to be square, encompassed on all the four sides, with a Stately Arched Hedge : the Arches to be upon Pillars of Carpenters work some ten foot high, and six foot broad, and the Spaces between of the same Dimension with the breadth of the Arch. Over the Arches let there be an Entire Hedge, of some four foot high, framed also upon Carpenters work, and upon the upper Hedge, over every Arch, a little Turret with a Belly, enough to receive a Cage of Birds, and over every space between the Arches some other little Figure, with broad plates of round Coloured Glass, gilt, for the sun to play upon." [1]

Bacon also recommends the construction of alleys at the sides of the garden, excepting those sides which command a view over the surrounding country. He goes on to say : " For the ordering of the ground within the great hedge, I leave it to Variety of Device. Advising nevertheless, that whatsoever form you cast it into, first it be not too busie or full of Work ; wherein I for my part do not like Images cut out in Juniper or other garden-stuff, they are for Children. Little low Hedges, round like welts, with some pretty Pyramids, I like well ; and in some places Fair Columns upon frames of Carpenters Work. I would also have the Alleys spacious and fair." He approves of fountains, but not of pools ; these, he says, " mar all, and make the Garden unwholesome and full of Flies and Frogs." This essay of Bacon's is an attempt to improve the national taste, and should be studied as such. It must not be taken as an exact picture of the formal gardens of his day, but this does not lessen its value as explaining the general motives of formal gardening at that time.

The mount was not always a raised detached mound, but often took the form of a long bank raised against an outer wall. Fountains and ponds were introduced into the Elizabethan gardens, and made very decorative features. They were frequently used for practical joking, where the water from the fountains being made to play upon unsuspecting visitors caused much merriment. Hentzner, in his description of the gardens at Whitehall, says : " In the garden adjoining to this palace, there is a jet d'eau, with a sun-dial which, while strangers are looking at, a quantity of water forced by a wheel, which the gardiner turns at a distance, through a number of little pipes plentifully sprinkles those who are standing round."

The design of these gardens usually fell within the province of the architect-builder of the house, and this continued to be the custom until about the middle of the eighteenth century, when the landscape gardener established a new profession.

In the Soane Museum are drawings and designs for houses by John Thorpe, one of the most celebrated architects of his day, and the designer of several noble mansions. One of these drawings shows a design for the laying out of the grounds, with a note to the effect that there is to be " nothing out of square." In these

[1] The essay is quoted at length in " The Praise of Gardens."

early garden plans remarkable simplicity is the most notable and pleasing feature, and though the parterres may be intricate, yet the main lines of the designs are invariably quite simple.

The gardens at Wilton, in Wiltshire, which were laid out by Isaac de Caux, are an interesting study in garden design of this period. The designs were published in a folio volume with descriptions, from which we gather that the garden was 1,000 feet long, by 400 feet broad, and was divided into three parallelograms; the first of these from the house being divided into four parts, each having a fountain in the centre, and being subdivided by grass paths into six smaller divisions. The second parallelogram comprised two groves, rather after the French manner, in which were two statues of white marble, and through these groves ran the River Nadar. At the beginning of the third parallelogram were two ponds, with columns in the middle "casting water all their height which causeth the moveing and turning of two crownes at the top of the same." This third parallelogram consisted of a "Compartement of greene with diverse walks planted with cherrie trees and in the midle is the great oval with the gladiator of brass; the most famous statue of all that antiquitie hath left." Unfortunately nothing now remains of these famous gardens, but here and there a small piece of stonework. The River Nadar still runs through the gardens, though its course has been altered, and it is now spanned by the Palladian bridge designed by Morris.

During the reign of Charles I. no great progress was made in the art of gardening, but during the Commonwealth much was done by both Royalist and Puritan towards the improvement of orchards and market gardens. One Hartlib, who received a pension of £100 a year from Oliver Cromwell, did much to help the advancement of agriculture. The Puritan considered the garden from a more practical point of view— what would pay best to cultivate, and how the fertility of his garden could be improved. Consequently, not many pleasure gardens were laid out, and during the Civil Wars many of the finest then existing were destroyed. Nonsuch and Wimbledon were sold, and the fate of Hampton Court itself hung in the balance, but it was eventually left untouched. It was during this period of unrest in England that Le Nôtre, the greatest of all the Formal or Architectural garden designers, was superintending the execution of his gigantic schemes in garden design at Versailles. He was educated as an architect, and is said to have had his first experience in gardening at Reuil. Later on he designed the gardens at Vaux le Villars, which so pleased the King that he was made Comptroller-General of Buildings and Gardens, and was attached to the brilliant court of Louis XIV. when in the height of its magnificence. It has been said that Le Nôtre visited England, but there does not appear to be sufficient evidence in support of this statement; his influence, however, extended to these shores, and with the Restoration a considerable change came over the designs for the larger English gardens. Charles II. during his sojourn abroad imbibed much of the prevalent taste, and one of his first cares after his accession was the renovation and improvement of his gardens, for which purpose he sent for French gardeners. Of the alterations made by Charles at Hampton Court the most important were the laying out of the Home Park in its present form, the planting of the great avenues of limes with the large semicircular avenue enclosing nine and a half acres, and the digging of the great canal, three quarters of a mile in length. These avenues are probably the earliest instances of the introduction of that French taste, which had so much influence upon the laying out of grounds for those country seats of great noblemen which were erected towards the end of the seventeenth century.

John Rose, reputed to be the best English gardener of his time, was sent by his master, the Earl of Essex, to study under Le Nôtre, and on his return was appointed gardener to Charles II. His pupil and successor was George London. John Evelyn (1620-1706), author of the well-known Diary and Correspondence, attained some distinction as a gardener. Besides his great work on "Forest Trees," he intended to write a book on garden design, which unfortunately never got further than a list of the headings to the various chapters. A perusal of these will show to what an advanced state gardening had attained. In Book II. he proposed writing of "knots, parterres, compartments, bordures, and embossments; of walks, terraces, carpets, and allies; bowling greens, mailles, their materials and proportions; of groves, labyrinths, dadales, cabinets, cradles, pavilions, galleries, close walks and other relievos; of fountains, cascades, rivulets; of rocks, grots, crypts, mountains, precipices, porticos, ventiducts; of statues, columns, dyalls, perspectives, pots, vases, and other ornaments."

Evelyn assisted in the laying out of several garden schemes, besides the oval garden at his own house at Sayes Court, near Deptford, which was ruined by Peter the Great, who caused himself to be wheeled about the garden in a barrow over borders and through hedges. Evelyn laid out the gardens at Wotton in Surrey, and Albury near Guildford, where he dug a canal and planted a vineyard.

The many engravings extant showing the houses and gardens of this period give also some idea of the extensive avenues which began to be constructed across the country; thus at Badminton, which was probably the greatest scheme of avenues, Kip's view shows a vast scheme stretching over miles of the country-side. From the entrance lodge to the house was an avenue of two and a half miles in length, and on the opposite side of the house three avenues extended to Marshfield, a distance of six miles to the south. At one point in the park no less than twenty-four avenues met, many of them extending for several miles. Magnificent avenues still exist from Castle Ashby in Northamptonshire, and Belton House, Grantham, and much of the grand scheme which surrounded Wrest in Bedfordshire is still to be seen. Kip's views also show fine avenues at Haughton in Nottinghamshire, at Chatsworth in Derbyshire, Grimsthorp in Lincolnshire, and at Ashdown Park, Berkshire, where long drives cut through the plantations round the house still exist.

The planting of single avenues was customary as early as the reign of Queen Elizabeth, when we may suppose some of the old avenues and walks adjoining noblemen's houses were planted. The arrangement of avenues starting from a central point was introduced from France at the time of the Restoration.

The influence of Le Nôtre and his pupils tended to increase the size of English gardens. Two good examples of the French manner in England are those at Chiswick in Middlesex and Melbourne in Derbyshire, where we have alleys cut through the groves, with here and there a "star," that is to say, a series of five or more alleys meeting in a circular grass plot. In "The Retired Gardner"[1] of Messrs. London and Wise are careful instructions for the laying out of these French gardens, and at the end of the second volume is a plan and description of the garden laid out by them for Marshal Tallard at Nottingham.[2] The use of the French style, however, was limited to large gardens, while those of a lesser size were still laid out much on the old lines, unaffected by foreign influence.

With the accession of William and Mary came further changes in the fashion of gardens, and for a while the Dutch manner was followed. Fountains and waterworks were more largely used, and gave much scope for ingenuity. Extensive alterations to the Royal gardens at Hampton Court were now commenced. Charles II. had laid out the great semicircular avenue of limes there "in pursuance of some great design he had formed in gardening," and in carrying out their magnificent scheme for the improvement of the Royal gardens William and Mary employed George London, who had been a pupil of Rose, head gardener to Charles II. With London was associated Henry Wise, who entered into a limited partnership with him, and worked in conjunction with him in all the improvements that he carried out in the gardens and parks of Hampton Court.

The Diary of Celia Fiennes,[3] a lady who was riding through England for her health in the time of William and Mary, affords a very good idea of the number of gardens existing in the country at this period, and gives a vivid impression of the care and intelligent interest then being taken in garden design, and also enables us to realize, in some measure, how much we have lost by the vandalism of a succeeding age, the age of "Capability" Brown, Humphry Repton, and the like. The chief fault to be found with the Dutch style was

---

[1] A translation from "Le Jardinier Solitaire," a treatise of the Sieur Louis Liger, of Auxerre.
[2] Reproduced in the Appendix to "The Formal Garden in England," by Reginald Blomfield and F. Inigo Thomas.
[3] "Through England on a side-saddle in the time of William and Mary." 1888.

an exaggeration in the old manner of clipping trees. Topiary work in yew and box was carried to an excess which the wits of the succeeding generation treated with well-deserved ridicule. A visit to the gardens at Levens might almost have justified Pope's famous article in the "Guardian," wherein he ridicules the absurdities and excesses of 'verdant sculpture.' In his witty catalogue of 'greens' to be disposed of by an eminent town gardener, amongst other items he notes :

"Adam and Eve in yew ; Adam a little shattered by the tree of knowledge in the great storm ; Eve and the serpent very flourishing.

" Noah's Ark in holly, the ribs a little damaged for want of water.

" The tower of Babel, not yet finished.

" St. George in Box, his arm scarce long enough, but will be in a condition to stick the dragon by next April."

Following London and Wise as garden designers came Stephen Switzer, the author of " Ichnographia Rustica" and other important works on gardening, and later on Bridgeman, who laid out Stowe in Buckinghamshire for Lord Cobham, about 1714. Bridgeman amongst other changes almost discarded topiary work, and, says Horace Walpole, "introduced a little gentle disorder into the plantation of his trees and bushes." What great changes were to result from this " little gentle disorder " ! The reaction had now fairly set in. No doubt the formal style was on the decline ; moreover, the taste for foreign " specimen " trees and shrubs, that had existed for some time previously, being fostered by the nurserymen gardeners, now came to a head, and some difficulty having arisen in accommodating the old fashions in garden design to the new fashion in " specimen " plants, the solution of the problem seems to have involved the abolition of the old formal garden altogether.

The simplicity of the formal garden was now bitterly attacked by those who declared that it was opposed to Nature, which they proposed not to leave untouched but to " improve." " Nor is there anything more ridiculous and forbidding than a garden which is regular," says Batty Langley, and this was the opinion generally held by garden designers throughout the latter half of the eighteenth century.

Foremost among the leaders of the new style in garden design was William Kent, who laid out the gardens at Esher and Claremont, also those at Carlton House for the Prince of Wales, and others at Rousham in Oxfordshire, and who appears to have been inspired with a desire to produce results that should resemble the compositions of classical landscape-painters. Walpole says, describing his work : " Selecting favourite objects, and veiling deformities by screens of plantations, he realized the compositions of the greatest masters in painting. The living landscape was chastened and polished, not transformed." Walpole considers the first step in the landscape style was taken when the sunken fence or " haha " was introduced, and he certainly touched the keynote, for as soon as walls and enclosures, which are the very essence of formal gardening, are destroyed, any piece of adjoining scenery may be included in the garden, and level lawns bounded by forest trees stretch right up to the windows of the house.

In the early part of his career Kent followed somewhat on the lines laid down by Bridgeman, of whom it has been said : " He enlarged his plans, disdained to make every division tally to its opposite, and though he still adhered much to straight walks with high clipped hedges, they were his only great lines ; the rest he diversified by wilderness, and with loose groves of oak, though still within surrounding hedges." As time went on Kent entirely left the formal garden and substituted for it the landscape style. " Nature abhors a straight line," was one of his ruling principles, so he set himself to destroy the grand avenues left by former generations, and to make his paths to wind aimlessly about in all directions, their destination always concealed by an artfully placed clump of bushes. The ornamental sheets of water were either swept away altogether or converted into artificial lakes fed by winding streams, and with miniature waterfalls formed of unnatural rocks. The height of absurdity was attained when he planted dead trees in Kensington Gardens " to give the greater air of truth to the scene."

ENGLAND AND SCOTLAND

The most popular of all the landscape gardeners was Lancelot Brown, better known as "Capability" Brown, from a habit he had of expatiating on the "capabilities" of any place he was asked to improve. Born in 1715, he began his career as a kitchen gardener, first at a place near Woodstock and then at Stowe; his first attempt at designing was in 1750, when he designed and executed a lake at Wakefield Lodge for the Duke of Grafton. He was appointed Royal Gardener at Hampton Court, where he planted the celebrated vine in 1769. He soon had an enormous practice, and the old gardens disappeared with alarming rapidity before the ruthless hand of the "omnipotent magician," as Cowper calls him. The formation of artificial lakes was a strong point in his designs, and one on which he prided himself. "Thames! Thames! thou wilt never forgive me!" he was overheard to exclaim when lost in admiration over one of his pet schemes.

It would be barely possible to enumerate all the villas the environs of which he remodelled, and always according to the system upon which he worked with persevering uniformity. His reputation and consequent wealth gave him almost exclusive pretensions. Clumps and belts were multiplied in wearying degree, and abounded in almost every part of the kingdom; every vestige of the formal or the reformed taste was forcibly removed; whatever approached to a right line was held in abhorrence.

Brown died in 1783 and was succeeded by Humphry Repton; fortunately the wholesale destruction of old places was to be checked, for Repton had not sufficient influence to suggest such sweeping alterations as Brown had made. Repton, who was the first to assume the title of "Landscape Gardener," published in 1795 "Sketches and Hints on Landscape Gardening," wherein he lays down the four following guiding rules for the design of a garden. "First, it must display the natural beauties and hide the natural defects of every situation. Secondly, it should give the appearance of extent and freedom, by carefully disguising or hiding the boundary. Thirdly, it must studiously conceal every interference of art, however expensive, by which the scenery is improved; making the whole appear the production of nature only; and fourthly, all objects of mere convenience or comfort, if incapable of being made ornamental, or of becoming proper parts of the general scenery, must be removed or concealed."

Unfortunately, the taste for landscape gardening was not only confined to England, but after the peace in 1762 the "Jardin à l'Anglaise" became the fashion on the Continent, and many fine old gardens in France and elsewhere were destroyed. Even when the landscape gardener undoubtedly held the field in the larger gardens, England was not completely captured, for there are still remains of many an old garden, formed during this period and adhering to the principles of the formal school, which hand down to our own day the best traditions of the seventeenth century.

During the nineteenth century the introduction of many new plants, with improved methods of cultivation, and the more extended use of hothouse and conservatory, have brought about many changes. In the early part of the century landscape gardening was still fashionable, but towards the middle the Italian style came in with the revival of Italian Architecture, and large schemes were designed by Sir Charles Barry, notable examples of whose work are the gardens at Trentham and Shrublands. Illustrations of a number of gardens of this period will be found in a work entitled "Gardens of England," by A. E. Brooke, published in 1858. The practice of bedding out plants was introduced, and instead of the glorious beds of old-fashioned flowers which had been the pride of our gardens for centuries, we were asked to admire a row of blue lobelias in front of another row of scarlet geraniums, whilst the yellow calceolarias made a gorgeous background.

While it is a matter for regret that the development of the Formal Garden should have been interrupted during the many years that landscape gardening held the field, it must be admitted that this was largely owing to the excesses and abuses which had crept in during the early part of the eighteenth century, when the garden designer ceased to regard the garden as a place for rest and pleasant recreation, in which one loved to be surrounded by familiar flowers and shrubs, and looked upon it rather with a view to showing his own skill in designing elaborate parterres and conventional scrolls, often to be plotted out in coloured sands and box edgings.

Happily during the last few years a revival of the Formal Garden has taken place, and as throughout the Renaissance period architects may be said to have planned the setting out of the gardens surrounding the houses they designed, so it is gratifying to see that those of our own day have awakened to the fact that this work is quite within their province, and that a much more pleasing and harmonious result is likely to be attained when the main lines are laid out by those who have designed and watched the building grow than when left to the practical gardener alone.

In Scotland, gardening like all the other arts was greatly retarded during the fifteenth and sixteenth centuries through the poverty and unrest of the country. Mary and her French courtiers had indeed given an impetus to garden design, but it was not until the seventeenth century that the best gardens were laid out. These could hardly rival the English, on account of the soil and climate of Scotland, but they are often very quaint and picturesque, as, for example, is that at Barncluith in Lanarkshire, laid out in a series of terraces overhanging the River Evan. The scale of these gardens is usually small; gigantic schemes such as were carried out in England having rarely been attempted. Although, of course, there were originally far fewer gardens in Scotland than in the more southern isle, a greater proportion of these seem to have survived, more or less unaltered, to our own times.

HISTORICAL & DESCRIPTIVE ACCOUNTS
OF THE SUBJECTS ILLUSTRATED.

MONTACUTE, SOMERSETSHIRE.

PLATES 1, 2, 3, 4, 5.

ONTACUTE possesses a character and charm, both in the house itself and in the gardens which surround it, hardly to be excelled in England. It lies in one of the most beautiful parts of Somersetshire, some four miles to the west of Yeovil, under the shadow of Ham Hill, whose famous quarries yielded the stone used throughout the building and in the gardens. Built between 1580 and 1601, it remains to-day in a practically unaltered state, and is still the seat of a descendant of the original builder, Sir Edward Phelips, then Speaker of the House of Commons.

The great size of the house gives evidence of the hospitality that prevailed in Queen Elizabeth's days, aptly illustrated in the two inscriptions, one on the front entrance, "*And yours my friends,*" and another over the garden porch, "*Through this wide open gate, none come too early, none return too late.*" The house is built upon a simple plan, in the form of the letter H, a main block with two projecting wings. The entrance court is on the north-west side, and has an approach with an avenue extending nearly half a mile. The original entrance forecourt was on the opposite or south-east side of the house, whence it was approached by a drive through the park. This court, now diverted from its original purpose, is enclosed on all sides; but formerly it had wing walls extending beyond the garden-house into the park. These have now been placed at right angles to the garden-houses. The enclosing balustrade walls are about seven feet high, with piers spaced at short intervals supporting obelisks. Midway between the main building and the garden-houses the continuity of the wall is broken by small circular stone pavilions, each consisting of six stone pillars supporting an ornamental soffite, with open cupola above, formed of three stone ribs joining at the top; this is again surmounted by a finial of intersecting stone circles.

The garden-houses at either angle of the forecourt are charming conceptions; they are shown in elevation on Plate 2 and in the view on Plate 3. They are square on plan, with small circular shaped bay-windows on every side

On the south-west side of the forecourt is the upper garden, an oblong enclosure some 350 feet long by 150 wide. At the further end is a yew tunnel in process of formation, and a stone arched summer-house. On the opposite, or north-east side, the forecourt is bounded by a broad terrace overlooking the lower garden, round which it extends on all four sides. On the side next the house it has a stone balustrade on which vases are placed at intervals.   The other sides have grass slopes.   In the centre is the fountain pond, surrounded by a well proportioned stone balustrade having obelisks at the angles, as shown on Plate 4.   The balusters are widely spaced, an arrangement always to be commended in garden architecture.

Surrounding the gardens on the south, east, and north sides is a well timbered park, abounding in oaks and elms, through which the house is approached by four drives, the one on the south-west being the more generally used ; that on the north-west is bordered by magnificent avenues with a fine broad grass space on either side of the road.

CANONS ASHBY, NORTHAMPTONSHIRE.

PLATES 6, 7.

LONG before the present house was built a priory of Black Canons had been established here, and from this the name is no doubt derived.   In the sixteenth century the property passed into the hands of the Cope family, and from them by marriage into the family of the Drydens, in whose possession it has since remained.   The building is of several dates, but the greater part of the present structure was built between 1551 and 1584, and also between 1708 and 1710.

The garden, originally made in 1550, was altered about the year 1708, but has since defied the changes of fashion, remaining practically the same for nearly two hundred years.   The original entrance forecourt, known as the green court, still remains.   It was approached from the road through the park, and the remains of an avenue about half a mile long still lead to the old entrance gates.   There is a similar pair of piers at another entrance close to the forecourt, and opposite to them is the quaint lead figure of a shepherd playing on his flute, shown on Plate 107.   The green court is now, and probably always was, laid down entirely in grass, and has eight simply cut yews leading to the old front door, now no longer used.   From the garden entrance we have a delightful view through four large cedar trees over the principal part of the gardens, and down a double avenue of stately elms for a distance of half a mile.   The section on Plate 6 shows the gradual fall of the ground, about 21 feet, to the south-west.   The garden is arranged on four different levels, divided from each other by easy grass slopes.   The extreme simplicity of the design is very pleasing, and the parterres being quite simple in character are such as might have been seen in any garden of this date.   Another very pleasing feature is the absence of gravel walks, except immediately round the house.   The value of grass work as an artistic element is well shown here, all the paths and terrace slopes being thus laid out.   The wooden gates shown on Plate 6, which by reason of their dilapidated state are now stored away, are interesting both for the excellence of their form and on account of the rarity of existing specimens of this type, iron having been so much more generally used for gates of this size.   On the upper parterre quite close to the house is a wooden arbour, probably dating from the seventeenth century.   It is quite small, and was designed only as a shelter for a wooden seat.   On Plate 7 are shown the principal gate piers.   Those surmounted by a lion form the entrance to the flower garden from the avenue, and are about 11 feet high to the cap.   The gate and angle piers in the green court are about the same height, and terminate in obelisks supported on groups of scrolls, forming an original and suggestive design ; they are respectively 2 feet 2 inches and 1 foot 6 inches square.

LONGFORD CASTLE, WILTSHIRE.

PLATES 8, 9, 10.

ONGFORD CASTLE, within two miles of Salisbury, stands in the midst of a noble park, on the banks of the River Avon. It was built by Sir Thomas Gorges, from the designs of John Thorpe, and the plan shows much originality, being formed of a triangle with large circular turrets at either angle, a scheme said to have been suggested by the castle at Orienbaum. Much of this original building is still preserved, but additional wings have been built in modern times. The original formal garden is shown in old prints engraved by Nicholas Yeates, dating from the end of the seventeenth century, but this was swept away when extensive alterations and plantings were undertaken between 1790 and 1810, under the advice of "Capability" Brown. The formal garden as it is now was replaced by the third Earl of Radnor between 1830 and 1840, and enlarged by the addition of about one third of its present size on the side nearest the house.

Plates 8 and 9 show the plan of the principal garden, an oblong sunken enclosure, bounded on either side by hedges of yew four feet thick, with openings cut at intervals of a few feet. An overlooking terrace, bordered by a stone balustraded wall, extends round the garden on all four sides. Until within the last few years the end farthest from the house was in the form of a complete semicircle, and is so shown on the photograph, Plate 9; it has since been altered, and the plan on Plate 8, shows the present arrangement, the centre being marked by a stone temple containing a leaden statue of Flora, the work of Sir Henry Cheere, a sculptor who flourished at the end of the eighteenth century (Plate 10).

The main part of the garden is divided into eight square parterres, with small gravel paths, and the centres have large stone vases said to have been brought from Italy by Lord Coleraine about 1680.

ST. CATHERINE'S COURT, SOMERSETSHIRE.

PLATES 11, 12, 13.

T. CATHERINE'S COURT lies in a secluded district amongst the hills, some four miles north of Bath, on the borders of Somersetshire and Gloucestershire. It was originally a grange belonging to the Abbey of Bath, and the fish-ponds constructed by the monks still remain.

At the Dissolution, Henry VIII. gave the property to one John Malte, the King's tailor, and it afterwards passed into the hands of the Harrington and Blanchard families, whose monuments are in the church adjoining. It is said that the terraced gardens were laid out by some member of these families. After passing through the hands of various other owners, St. Catherine's was altered and restored by Colonel Strutt, who purchased the property in 1840. It afterwards passed to the Hon. Mrs. R. Drummond, who made the bowling-green and increased the size of the gardens.

As an example of a hillside garden the plan of St. Catherine's Court presents many interesting features. The position of the house in relation to its garden is not happy, and it would no doubt have been better placed higher up the hill, had it been possible to obtain access from the road below.

As it is, the house lies almost midway on the slope, and is overlooked by the terraces instead of commanding them, which is the more usual and better treatment. It therefore appears to lie low, although this is not really the case, as the ground falls away on at least two sides. The sketch plan shown on Plate 11 is intended to illustrate the gardens only so far as the terraces are concerned, and shows their position in relation to the house. At present the approach is by a drive direct to the front door, but this is a modern arrangement; originally the visitor alighted at the first flight of steps, and had to traverse the two courts before reaching the porch. At a level about eight feet above the forecourt is the parterre, some 80 feet wide by 160 feet long; the beds are cut out in the grass, and there are no gravel paths. This part of the gardens is shown on Plate 12, a view taken from the terrace which skirts one side of the parterre. The beautiful terrace, a view of which is shown on Plate 13 and an elevation on Plate 11, is 160 feet in length and 11 feet broad, and is raised 10 feet above the parterre. The balustrade has piers eight feet apart, slightly projecting beyond the wall face, and carried on corbels surmounted alternately by balls and vases, which in design are very similar to those on the terrace of Kingston House, Bradford-on-Avon, not many miles away, which are shown on Plates 96 and 98. In the centre of the terrace is a flight of steps unbroken by any landing, the effect of which is decidedly good. Skirting the south-east side of the house and ascending the hill is a broad walk of grass, curiously formed into steps, a pleasing and unusual feature. The lower terrace, also shown on Plate 11, is a charming piece of work, with its flight of steps leading down from the forecourt. The detail of the balustrade is similar to that of the upper terrace, and the irregular spacing of the balusters, whether intentional or due to accident, is quaint. The gardens also extend considerably on the south-east side of the house; but these are not so pleasing as the older and more formal parts.

PENSHURST PLACE, KENT.

PLATES 14, 15.

ENSHURST PLACE was granted by King Edward VI. to Sir William Sidney, whose son, Sir Henry Sidney, a Knight of the Garter and Lord President of the Marches of Wales, did much to the house, and, as a tablet over the entrance gateway records, " caused this tower to be builded in 1585." Other parts of the building date from even earlier days, and the baronial hall is one of the finest in the country. The estate, passing through the hands of several families, eventually became the property of the late Lord de l'Isle and Dudley, a nobleman of great culture, under whom the old buildings were carefully restored. From old drawings it would appear that the gardens were never a great feature until they were laid out under his careful guidance, and he was entirely responsible for their design.

The house is approached, on its north side, by a drive through the park, and the plan on Plate 14 shows that the gardens lie principally on its south and west sides. The ground slopes generally to the south and west, and the house stands on a grass platform, raised about nine feet above the garden level. On this platform is the garden or summer-house, a two storey building. Along the south-west side of the flower garden is a broad grass terrace, and near the house a few steps lead up to the yew alley, at the end of which is the quaint old dial known as the Turk's Head.

The principal part of the gardens is the parterre, shown on Plate 15, in which the beds are marked by high box edgings, whose sober green colour serves to effectually set off the gorgeous masses of flowers. A broad grass walk continued past the front of the house leads between high yew hedges to a delightfully cool spot known as Diana's Pool, where the quietude is broken only by the sound of the rippling water as it enters the pool. The walk continues further and is terminated by a fountain pond, from whence a pretty vista is obtained through the whole length of the gardens.

On the west side the parterre is bounded by thick yew hedges, and in the centre a broad walk, bordered with flower-beds, divides the two orchard gardens. A sketch showing this walk from the fountain in the centre of the parterre is given on Plate 14.

The two orchard gardens are arranged as pleasant retreats, laid out with small grass walks; an arrangement well worthy of notice, as making good use of the orchard, a part of the garden not always esteemed at its full value. A similarly effective arrangement of orchard garden is to be seen at Earlshall (Plates 86, 87).

WILTON HOUSE, WILTSHIRE.

PLATES 16, 17, 18, 19.

 NY account of the gardens surrounding Wilton House would be incomplete without at least a passing reference to the famous garden laid out here by Isaac de Caux towards the middle of the seventeenth century. The designs for this garden are fortunately still preserved and were published in a series of twenty-six copperplates about the year 1645. De Caux also published a full description of the gardens, reference to which has already been made in the Historical Note at the commencement of this work.

These Wilton gardens were amongst the most celebrated in England, and more than one contemporary writer has left glowing accounts of their beauties. Evelyn, who visited them in 1654, writes: "The garden heretofore esteemed the noblest in England, is a large handsome plaine, with a grotto and waterworks, which might be made much more pleasant were the river which passes through cleans'd and rais'd, for all is effected by a meere force. It has a flower garden not inelegant . . ."

There are now but few vestiges of this famous scheme left; lawns cover the site of De Caux's gay parterres; the River Nader, shown on old engravings as quite a small stream, is now a river spanned by a fine Palladian bridge, designed by J. Morris. Here and there a column, or a sundial such as that on Plate 116, may still be seen, and opposite the orangery are certain pieces which formed part of the fountains in the old garden. A grotto, probably designed by Inigo Jones, and now used as a schoolhouse, formed one of the attractions in former days; but beyond these few relics nothing remains of the great scheme which in its time ranked with such gardens as Theobalds, Hatfield and Nonsuch.[1]

A plan of the gardens was published by J. Rocque in 1745, at which date the original garden of De Caux had ceased to exist; but one can easily trace the outline of the great parterre. This plan also

[1] A brass statue formerly in the garden is now at Houghton, and is said to have been by John of Bologna. It was a present to Sir Robert Walpole by Robert, Earl of Pembroke (Catalogue of the Houghton pictures, 1752).

shows the original entrance courtyard on the west side of the house, and in front of this the River Wily converted into a long canal.

Lawns now stretch up to the house on the south and east sides; the north is devoted to the entrance court, and on the west side is the Italian or sunken garden, laid out by the then Lady Pembroke between 1808 and 1810. Plate 16 shows a plan of this garden, and Plate 17 a view taken from the house, looking towards the long walk, terminating in what is known as Hans Holbein's summer-house, which was, however, designed by him for the entrance porch to the mansion. On the north and east sides of the Italian garden is a broad terrace entered directly from the house; on the north side is a small sculpture gallery arranged centrally with the garden, and believed to have been used in the old garden. At either end of the terrace is a stone seat.

Around the terrace walls is a series of delightful leaden *amorini*, shown in the view on Plate 17, and to a much larger scale on Plate 19—these figures are about three feet high.

In the centre of the Italian garden is the fountain, shown on Plate 18 and also from a measured drawing on Plate 119; it is of white marble and bronze, surmounted by a charming little figure of a girl wringing the tresses of her hair, through which the water drips. A similar fountain is shown in Solomon de Caux's volume, "Les Raisons des Forces mouvantes," published in Paris in 1624; and it is therefore possible that the fountain may have been designed by him, but it appears to have been partly re-made at a later date.

BOWOOD HOUSE, WILTSHIRE.

PLATES 20, 21.

OWOOD HOUSE lies surrounded by a fine old park some two miles west of Calne and four south-east of Chippenham, in one of the prettiest parts of Wiltshire. Formerly the estate was part of the royal manor of Pewsham, and being abundantly stocked with deer, was much used for royal sport. James I. often hunted here, but under the Commonwealth the estate was disafforested, and being seized by Parliament eventually came into the possession of Sir Orlando Bridgeman. It was afterwards purchased by John, Earl of Shelburne, father of the first Marquess of Lansdowne.

The greater part of Bowood House, including the orangery, is said to have been built from the designs of Robert and James Adam, who took for their model the celebrated palace of the Emperor Diocletian at Spalato. They were commenced by the Earl of Shelburne. The park and pleasure-grounds were laid out by William, Marquess of Lansdowne.[1]

The house is approached from Chippenham, through an arched gateway designed by Sir Charles Barry, by a drive two miles across the park, to the principal front on the south side; the park also extends round the east side of the house, while on the north are extensive kitchen gardens. The Italian Garden, of which a plan and section are given on Plate 20, and a view on Plate 21, adjoins the house on the west. It lies in a well-sheltered position, for the whole of the north side of the garden is occupied by the fine orangery, which at the same time serves as an excellent screen to the stables and offices. A fine hedge and group of trees form a boundary on the west, and on the south side the garden lies open to the park.

The garden is cleverly arranged in three levels. The higher one, on which the orangery stands, is a

---

[1] There is an engraving dated 1768 of a design by R. Adam for a bridge in the park in imitation of an ancient aqueduct.

broad terrace, 285 feet long by 57 feet broad, divided into two parterres, each centred by a white marble fountain. From this level another terrace returns at right angles, and terminates at the end next the park, with a classic pavilion. In the centre of this terrace is a fine mural fountain surmounted by a group of statuary, with on either side a flight of steps leading to the second level, a few feet below. The third level is divided into six plots, each of similar design, intersected by broad gravel walks, while a balustraded wall divides the garden from the park.

The general aspect of the garden, and the clever arrangement of varying levels, can be well judged by the view on Plate 21. The photograph for this was taken in very early spring-time, and does not, therefore, give an idea of the brilliant parterre; it, however, serves better to show the shapes of the beds.

CHASTLETON HOUSE, OXFORDSHIRE.

PLATES 22, 23.

CHASTLETON HOUSE stands on the western borders of Oxfordshire where it adjoins Gloucestershire, and is about four miles from Moreton-in-the-Marsh. It is a stone Jacobean building, of a type not unusual in the western counties. A plan and photographic views, together with an interesting description of the house, are given in Mr. Gotch's folio work, " Architecture of the Renaissance in England."

The house was built by one Walter Jones, who bought the estate in 1602 from the Catesby who was connected with the Gunpowder Plot, and tradition has it that the money he thus acquired was partly expended in the purchase of gunpowder! The building of the house commenced soon after this date and was finished in 1614. The gardens, as they now exist, were re-laid out in 1828, and as at present are no doubt much on the lines of the original scheme. From the road a stone archway gives access to the forecourt. through which a drive leads to the porch. To the left are the stables and the stable court, while on the right a thick laurel hedge separates the forecourt from the old churchyard.

The most curious part of this garden scheme is the old garden on the eastern side of the house, shown on Plate 23. This is almost square, being 190 feet by 170 feet, and, as shown on the plan (Plate 22), is surrounded by a wall. In the centre is a stone sundial, round which the flower-beds are arranged concentrically, and these again are enclosed by a thick hedge. Within this space are twenty-four curiously cut shapes in box, which after the lapse of so many years have lost much of their original form, but here and there they still retain some trace of the shapes into which they were at one time cut by the gardener's shears. They are said to have represented animal forms, including a peacock, horse, bear and swan; also a ship in full sail. When Chastleton was built the custom of cutting box and yew into various shapes had not long been introduced; biblical subjects were frequently represented in this manner, and it is possible that some of the shapes no longer recognizable were of this description.

There are other flower gardens and a bowling-green on the west side of the house, which, though picturesquely situated, are hardly so interesting as the gardens shown on the plan and photograph, and extensive fruit and vegetable gardens to the north, all enclosed within brick walls, and intersected by little paths of turf, bordered by beds of bright flowers.

HATFIELD HOUSE, HERTFORDSHIRE.

PLATES 24, 25, 26.

THE magnificent home of the Cecil family was built by Robert Cecil, the first Earl of Salisbury, who, having exchanged the estate of Theobalds with James I. for that of Hatfield, commenced building his new mansion in 1605, soon after becoming possessed of the property, partly on the site of the palace of the former Bishops of Ely. Thanks to judicious restoration of the fabric as necessity arose, Hatfield House as we see it to-day presents much of its original appearance. It stands surrounded by gardens in the midst of one of the most beautiful parks in England, watered by the River Lea, with fine stretches of open grass-land and many grand old trees, including Queen Elizabeth's oak, around it. Originally there were two parks, one for red and one for fallow deer, and in one of these was the vineyard planted by the first Earl of Salisbury.[1] This experiment of vine-growing, however, met with little success, and after being carried on for a few years was discontinued. Now no trace of the old vineyard exists. Adjoining this vineyard, and on the banks of a stream, was a small garden laid out by one Mountain Jennings, gardener to the first Earl, in connection with which a Frenchman, Simon Sturtivant, planned some elaborate waterworks, which were never executed owing to the Earl's death in 1614.[2]

Solomon de Caux designed a *jet d'eau* for the gardens, with a statue of Neptune, which was made of marble at a cost of £113. John Tradescant, the well-known botanist and traveller, succeeded Jennings as head gardener, and made the gardens famous for the many new plants he introduced from abroad.

The principal approach to the house is by a double avenue leading to a large square gravel courtyard on the north front, but the original approach is on the west side, through the old palace courtyard. Plate 26 shows the gardens as they are seen from the broad terrace on the east side of the mansion, gradually sloping down to the edge of the lake, and from this terrace a double flight of steps leads to the parterre, which is arranged in two patterns with the initial letters S and B (Salisbury and Burleigh), designed on the lines of those in the old Jacobean garden. From this level a few steps lead to the bowling-green, which, together with the maze beyond, is of recent formation. Beyond the maze, and parallel to it, is a pergola overlooking a small sunken garden, enclosed by hedges on three sides.

On the south side of the house wing walls enclose a gravel courtyard, but beyond these the forecourt extends into the park, surrounded by a pierced balustrade, and with pavilions at the four angles. To the south-west is the shrubbery, about five acres in extent, and beyond are the glass-houses, kitchen and fruit gardens, covering about twelve acres.

The gardens on the west side are in some respects the most interesting. The Privy or Queen's garden and the rose garden originally belonged to the old palace; the former is about 250 feet square, having a very fine pleached lime alley on all sides, and in the centre a parterre surrounded by a low hedge. In the middle of the parterre is a fountain pond, as shown on Plate 24, and at either corner still remain the mulberry trees which were placed here by James I., who had planted four acres of these trees at Westminster in his endeavour to promote the cultivation of silk in this country. Westward of the Privy garden, and at a rather lower level, is another garden with two quadrant-shaped lawns, surrounded

---

[1] The vine had been cultivated here at an earlier period by the Bishops of Ely.

[2] "A History of Gardening in England," by the Honourable Alicia Amherst.

by large beds of shrubs and flowers, and in the midst a well proportioned stone sundial. Northward of the Privy garden is a lawn, shaded by large chestnut trees, and a sunken rose garden, overlooked by the older buildings of the Tudor palace, wherein Princess Elizabeth resided.

The gardens have for the last twenty-six years been under the able supervision of Mr. Norman.

DRAYTON HOUSE, NORTHAMPTONSHIRE.

PLATES 27, 28, 29, 30.

RAYTON HOUSE appears to have become in the reign of Elizabeth the property of Baron Mordaunt (1572-1601), who made extensive alterations and additions to both house and garden. His grandson was created Earl of Peterborough by Charles I., and his successor, the second earl, in the leisure intervals of a most adventurous life, found time to make many alterations at Drayton. The general arrangement of the gardens dates no doubt from before his day, but he made many improvements, and added the stone balustrade with the banqueting-houses at either end, also much of the terracing and steps. There is an engraving extant, dated 1729,[1] showing the forecourt, parterre, and garden-houses all as at present, but with the duck pond of greater extent.

From the park a drive leads to the forecourt on the south-east side of the house, past the entrance gates (shown on Plate 29) which were erected by Lord Peterborough's daughter and heiress, after her second marriage to Sir John Germain. The principal piers, which are about twelve feet in height, have small niches, above which are carved escutcheons. These are surmounted by eagles, and on either side connected by wrought-iron grilles with smaller piers, supporting handsome stone vases. On one side of the forecourt are the stable buildings and stable yard, while on the opposite side the courtyard is shut off from the gardens by a high wall, in which is a pedimented stone gateway with handsome wrought-iron gates. From the forecourt an archway leads to the inner court, which is paved with flags and has a Doric colonnade along one end, erected *temp*. William III. by Sir John Germain. This resembles those at Hampton Court and at Knole.

The gardens are entered from the east front of the house, and the view on Plate 28 is from this point, showing the parterre with its leaden figures of Flora and Bacchus. The stone banqueting houses before alluded to, erected by the second Earl of Peterborough, are connected by a balustrade, on which are some very fine leaden urns, as shown on Plates 30 and 120. In the distance, in front of the "ha-ha" separating the garden from the park, is a leaden group of Cain and Abel, a replica of that still standing in the grounds of Chiswick House.

A double row of fine old limes divides the parterre from the kitchen gardens. These are on a higher level, and are approached by a flight of steps at either end of the parterre. As at Penshurst, the gardens are surrounded by high hedges of beech, elm, hornbeam and yew, with grass alleys between. In the enclosure nearest the house are two fine pleached alleys[2] of considerable age; they are of wych elm, with gnarled stems intertwined and form complete tunnels some forty yards long.

---

[1] Engraved by S. and N. Buck.

[2] Similar pleached alleys, formerly not uncommon, are now rarely to be met with, but the famous one at Hampton Court, known as "Queen Mary's Bower," and the Lime Walk at Hatfield, still remain. There is also one at Melbourne Hall in Derbyshire. Hentzner mentions one that existed in his time at Theobalds. The word "pleach" is from the French *plessir*, to weave, and refers to the weaving together or intertwining of the branches.

South-east of the parterre, and at a rather lower level, is the duck pond, reflecting the charming old house in its still waters. It is skirted on one side by a row of old limes, beyond which is another kitchen garden. A small flight of steps, circular on plan, leads from the parterre to the bowling-green, a long narrow alley terminating in a *clair voyée* or open railing, through which a vista is obtained down an avenue across the park. Four examples of the leaden vases for which Drayton is so justly famous are shown on Plate 30.

It is interesting to note that some vases here are from the same moulds as the Penshurst example on Plate 110, whilst others have the mythological subjects in bas-relief which are cast round the body of the vase, from the same moulds as those at Chiswick House, Middlesex, though the vases differ entirely in their general design: thus probably indicating a common origin. There are many fine examples of ironwork, all attributable to Lady Mary Mordaunt, who married, first, Henry, seventh Duke of Norfolk; secondly, Sir John Germain; the date 1699 is on one of these gates.

ROSE GARDENS AT ROCKINGHAM CASTLE AND BROUGHTON CASTLE.

PLATE 31.

THE two examples of the treatment of enclosed rose gardens given on this plate will suffice to show how charming a feature such a garden can be made.

The Rockingham garden is well arranged within its circular trimmed yew hedge, in which are six arched openings, marked with little pyramids. It lies not far from the south side of the house, and is surrounded by fine old trees. The circular space it occupies is about forty-five yards in diameter, and is divided by six paths meeting in an inner ring. The flower-beds between have neat grass borders and are mostly filled with roses, an outer flower border and path following the circular form of the garden.

The walled-in garden from Broughton Castle was laid out under the tasteful guidance of Lady Algernon Gordon Lennox within quite recent years, and one who knew the old castle but a few years ago —when pasture land extended right up to the house—could hardly fail to be struck· by the immense improvement that has been wrought. The rose garden may have originally occupied the position of an old walled-in garden, and retains the enclosing walls that have stood in their place for generations, but until recently the space was used as a drying-ground. Although the view shown on the plate fails to give an idea of the glories of the garden in all its summer beauty, it answers its purpose in showing the forms of the beds and the general disposition of the garden. A rich herbaceous border runs under the wall, and the middle space is cut out in beds of *fleur-de-lis* shape; in the centre is a sundial of somewhat unusual form, raised on two grass steps, stone-edged, with an inscription :

" I tell men hourlie how the shadowes fly,
For men are shadowes and a shadowe I."

Other examples of the planning of rose gardens shown in this volume are to be found at Hatfield (Plate 25), Chastleton Manor-house (Plate 22), and Saighton Grange (Plate 60), and the series of designs for small parterres given on Plates 104 and 105 are also very suitable for this kind of garden, where it is essential that the beds should be rather small and narrow.

HADDON HALL 1988.

HAMPTON COURT PALACE.

PLATES 32, 33, 34, 35, 36, 37.

OF all the old garden schemes left to us, Hampton Court stands unrivalled in the grandeur of its conception. The history of the palace has been so fully and admirably dealt with in the comprehensive work by Mr. Ernest Law, that it would hardly be possible to add anything to it, and in briefly sketching the history of the gardens which partake of its glory, the author must acknowledge his indebtedness to Mr. Law for most of the historical data.

In early days the Knights Hospitallers had a garden here, together with a dovecote and some two thousand acres of arable land, which they farmed for the benefit of the ruling body. When Cardinal Wolsey became possessed of the property, he converted this land into two parks, partly fencing them in with palings, and partly with a brick wall, portions of which are still remaining. At the same time he surrounded both house and gardens with a moat that remained for many years, and may still be traced on the north side of the old melon yard.

Wolsey devoted much attention to the surroundings of his palace, and the gardens, although of comparatively small extent, were among the finest of the period. Here the Cardinal used to retire for rest and meditation, and, Cavendish tells us, might often be found in the evenings, walking with his chaplain or saying the office in a secluded arbour. In 1529 came his downfall, and Hampton Court passed into the hands of his royal master.

Henry VIII. made many alterations to the gardens, and in 1533 constructed the King's New Garden (now the Privy Garden), appointing one Edward Gryffyn to superintend the work. In the Bodleian Library is preserved a drawing by Antonius Wynegaarde [1] showing the gardens in the reign of Queen Mary, which gives a good idea of their appearance at this date, with their innumerable sundials, vases, and pedestals bearing heraldic beasts, studded about in all parts.

At the southern end of the garden stood the Great Mount with its fine arbour. Nothing now remains of these Tudor gardens except perhaps the small pond garden, shown on Plate 35. To the north of the palace and occupying the site of the present Wilderness, were the orchards, and close by, the kitchen gardens, on ground still used for this purpose.

Queen Elizabeth took great delight in the garden, wherein, we are told, she was accustomed to walk every morning, and here took place the famous interview with Melville, the envoy of Hans Casimir, eldest son of the Elector Palatine, who had come to Hampton Court hoping to be able to effect a marriage between the Queen and his royal master.

Oliver Cromwell devoted some attention to the gardens, repairing the fountains and ponds, but it was left to Charles II., fresh from having seen the glories of Versailles, to inaugurate the great scheme that we see to-day. He constructed the Long Canal, and planted the large semicircle and the grand avenues in front of the palace, but did not live to see the completion of his great schemes.

When William and Mary made the extensive alterations to the palace from Sir Christopher Wren's design, they carried to completion the works commenced by Charles, acting under the advice of George London, whom they appointed to the post of Royal Gardener. London, together with his partner Henry Wise, was responsible for all the alterations which took place at this date, although no doubt acting in concert with the master-mind of the great architect. They shifted the avenue of lime trees further

---

[1] Reproduced on a small scale in Mr. Law's work.

eastward into the park, and laid out the great parterre in front of the palace. The plan of the Privy Garden on Plate 33 is taken from an original survey in the Soane Museum, probably made under the supervision of Sir Christopher Wren a little after this date. It does not show the fountain which existed here until 1712.

There are several engravings of the gardens at this period, including one by Sutton Nicholls, published about 1695, which shows the great Fountain Garden with grass lawns and scroll patterns in box, together with a central fountain in a similar position to that which it still occupies, as well as other smaller fountains and ponds. Another engraving of the Privy Garden shows what was probably the arrangement just prior to the plan shown on Plate 33, that is to say, with the raised grass terrace extending on all three sides, and the so-called "Diana" (really Arethusa), fountain in its original position at the river end of the garden.[1] Kip's view, published in the "Nouveau Théâtre de la Grande Bretagne," 1710, shows the gardens almost as they are indicated on the Soane plan (Plate 33), save that on the south-east corner of this plan is a waste piece of ground, whilst Kip shows here a triangular pond. The two drawings do not agree in a few other minor details. Kip also shows the design of the great Fountain Garden with one principal and twelve minor fountains, the three grand avenues across the park, and the pavilion terrace, overlooking the river, with the bowling-green and four pavilions.[2]

The new greenhouse shown on the Soane Museum plan and on Kip's view was built to house the collection of rare plants formed by Queen Mary; it was divided into several rooms, each furnished with a stove. The pond garden appears to have been used at this time as an orange garden, and the smaller garden adjoining was called the auricular quarter.

When Sir Christopher Wren remodelled the palace, he made plans for a new entrance front on the north side, and it was proposed to build a grand courtyard, between the palace and the Wilderness, with a fine approach from the north. The only part of this magnificent scheme actually carried out was the grand chestnut avenue across Bushey Park. One of the most interesting relics of the days of William and Mary is the old wych-elm pleached alley, raised on a grass terrace overlooking the Privy Garden.

When Queen Anne came into possession of the palace the gardens were again remodelled, alterations were made to the Fountain Garden, and all the box scrollwork of William and Mary was rooted up, plain lawns being substituted. The gardens were again altered under William Kent, about 1736, in the early days of the landscape-gardening movement. A plan engraved by J. Rocque shows the alterations then carried out, with the great Fountain Garden in much the same state as at present. In 1750 Lancelot Brown was appointed to the post of Royal Gardener, who fortunately, "out of respect to himself and his profession," refused to make any alterations to the gardens, and they thus escaped the wholesale destruction which overtook nearly all the old gardens in England at this period. Brown retained his post under George III. and resided at Hampton Court for many years.

Plate 32 shows a plan of the gardens as they now exist. The carriage drive and principal entrance are on the western side of the palace, and from this entrance we pass through the base court, fountain court, and clock court, on to the centre of the east front, from which the three great avenues diverge. Each avenue consists of four rows of lime trees and stretches across the Home Park, giving some long and beautiful vistas. The Central Avenue encloses the Long Canal and extends about three-quarters of a mile. It may be noted that one of the side avenues was so planned as to give a view of Kingston Church tower.

On the eastern front of the palace, the Broad Walk extends a distance of nearly half a mile, from

[1] The fountain was removed in 1712 to the position it now occupies in the centre of the round pond in Bushey Park.
[2] Only one of these pavilions remains at the present day.

the River Thames to the entrance on the Kingston Road, known as the "Flower-pot" gate, where stands the beautiful stone gateway designed by Sir Christopher Wren about 1699. A view of this is shown on Plate 36, and in the measured drawing on Plate 37. It is of Portland stone, handsomely carved with circular alcoves on either side of the piers, and shields containing the Royal Arms above. The piers are surmounted by leaden groups of boys supporting baskets of fruit and flowers, modelled by Van Noste.

Along the entire length of the Broad Walk, and continued at right angles past the "Flower-pot" gate, is the brick wall shown in elevation on Plate 37. This has brick and stone piers at intervals of a few feet, and the tone of the old brickwork forms a delightful background to the brilliant masses of colour in the flower border. This wall terminates the lime avenue and the canal, which in its turn forms the boundary of the gardens on the eastern side of the palace. It is interesting to note that the soil excavated in constructing the canal was used in the formation of the terraces on which the avenues were planted by Charles II. The gardens thus enclosed include the great semicircular Fountain Garden and the two long wings on either side, laid out with flower-beds, whose gorgeous colours are well set off by the sombre green of the old yews, which, trimmed into various shapes, once formed points in the design of the great parterre.

Along the river front is the grand terrace, nearly half a mile in length, leading past some fine iron gates to the bowling-green and pavilion.

On the south front of the palace is the present Privy Garden, a very good idea of which may be obtained from the view on Plate 34, taken from the upper storey of the palace. The garden is now principally laid out with evergreen trees and flowering shrubs, with intervening grass walks and many delightfully cool retreats for hot summer days. In the centre is a large fountain pond, and on either side are terraces, raised with the soil excavated from the garden, for there was no fall in the land to give the change in level, as desired. The east terrace overlooks the Broad Walk, and on the west is Queen Mary's Bower.

The boundary wall of the Privy Garden on this side forms the division between the public gardens and those still retained by the Crown. The latter consist principally of three enclosed oblong spaces: the first, next Queen Mary's Bower, being all orchard garden; the next, the interesting old pond garden, shown on Plate 35, enclosed by low brick walls. The gateways in the wall on either side, shown in Kip's view, still remain, but are no longer in use. Plate 35 also shows the Banqueting House, standing in a small garden of its own, overlooking the river. It was built by King William III., and here he was wont to come and spend many leisure hours. Not far away is the vinery, with its celebrated vine planted in 1769, and adjoining is the greenhouse with a long garden plot in front.

On the northern side of the palace buildings is the old melon ground, now used chiefly for glass-houses, and between this and the Kingston Road is the Wilderness, occupying the site of the orchards of Tudor days. It is still arranged on very similar lines to its original plan, except that there were formerly two semicircular labyrinths quite close to the Maze, known as "Troy Town." The Maze occupies a triangular space in the north-west angle; it has hedges of hornbeam, and is one of the finest examples in existence, the walks amounting altogether to nearly half a mile in length. Close to the Maze are the Lion Gates, so called from the lions surmounting their handsome piers. They were erected in 1714, but the gates, which appear dwarfed by the large proportion of the piers, were added at a later date.

On the whole the disposition of the gardens surrounding Hampton Court must be regarded as a most masterly conception, which can hardly be equalled by any in the kingdom, and it is to be hoped that in future generations those in authority will endeavour to keep up their old characteristics rather than alter their appearance as fashion in gardening may change.

BRIDGE END GARDENS, SAFFRON WALDEN.

PLATE 37*.

THE little Dutch garden, illustrated on this Plate, was laid out about sixty years ago, and is an interesting example of the formal style, since it shows that the older tradition was never entirely obliterated in country places during the days when the landscape garden had become so popular as to have spread well-nigh all over England. As shown on the Plate, it has little walks bordered with box-edging, and a fountain and pond in the centre, while close by is a summer-house with a rather elaborate doorway and scroll pediment. These gardens are now the property of the Right Hon. Lewis Fry, who has generously thrown them open to the public as a pleasure ground.

An old garden, not however one of any great pretension, formerly occupied part of the ground, and at one time was attached to a neighbouring house, though not actually adjoining it. The gardens occupy an irregular piece of ground, partly surrounded by meadow land. On the north east is a small circular maze set in a shrubbery with a pleached alley adjoining, on one side of which is an oblong kitchen garden. There is also a circular rose garden and lawn, with here and there a stone vase or sundial or statue dotted about which are all of good detail. A well-proportioned open balustrade separates the garden from the meadows.

ARLEY HALL, CHESHIRE.

PLATES 38, 39.

FOR upwards of four centuries Arley Hall has been the residence of the Warburton family. A quadrangular house of wood and plaster, built by Piers Warburton, formerly occupied the site of the present hall, and in 1746 this house was cased in brick and otherwise altered. Omerod, in his "History of Cheshire" (1819), describes the house as forming a quadrangle enclosing a courtyard laid out with parterres of flowers. In 1834 this building was demolished and the present house commenced; the works were carried on at intervals until 1849. Old maps show that there was a garden attached to the old hall, but the present garden was laid out when the house was rebuilt in the Jacobean style. On the north side is a chapel built in 1845, from the design of Anthony Salvin, and enlarged in 1856-1857 by G. E. Street. To the west of the house, by the stables, is an old barn supposed to date from the time of Henry VII.

The general appearance of the surrounding country is flat, though Arley lies on high ground; the land slopes away on the south-eastern side of the Hall towards a large piece of water and extensive plantations. A drive through the park leads to the forecourt on the south front of the hall, in which is a leaden figure of the kneeling slave. From the forecourt a gate leads to the flower garden, an oblong space about 300 feet by 200, enclosed within an open balustraded wall, and with a fountain pond in the centre. Beyond the flower garden, on the north, is the archery ground.

A broad walk, 200 yards long, skirted on one side by a "ha-ha," leads from the forecourt to the gardens on the south-west side of the house, and about midway is an oblong enclosure some 300 feet by 40, known as the Alcove walk. Here, on either side of a gravel walk, are flower-beds, divided into little plots by substantial yew buttresses, as shown in Plate 39. At the end of this walk is a stone summer-house, and on the south side of the enclosure is another smaller garden, with curiously shaped yews (Plate 39, lower half), and at one end a small rose garden overlooked by a picturesque summer-house. Close adjoining is the bowling-green, 180 feet by 54, sunk about two feet, and circular at one end; and behind this is a wilderness with a hexagonal-shaped maze, shown to a large scale on Plate 122. The south-west corner of the garden is laid out as a rock-garden.

BELTON HOUSE, GRANTHAM, LINCS.

PLATES 40, 41, 42, 43.

BELTON HOUSE lies about three miles north of Grantham in Lincolnshire, in the midst of a large park, and is approached by a drive down an avenue of magnificent elms. The grounds of the present building partly occupy the site of the former Manor-house, of which the gate piers to the entrance forecourts are all that now remain. These are in the north wall of the rose garden, and the present conservatory probably occupies the site of the original house, which, together with the surrounding estate, was purchased from the trustees of the Packenham family by Richard Brownlow, Esq., Prothonotary of the Common Pleas during the reigns of Elizabeth and James I. Succeeding owners added to the property, and it eventually came into the hands of Sir John Brownlow, the fourth baronet, who built the present house, which is said to have been designed by Sir Christopher Wren, between the years 1685 and 1689. In 1690 a license was obtained to enclose the park, round which a wall was built some five miles in length. The garden was laid out about the year 1700, and this design is shown in a view by Badeslade, unfortunately without a date. The plan reproduced on Plate 41 is taken from Campbell's "Vitruvius Britannicus," and is probably a few years later than Badeslade's view.[1]

It is an interesting study in garden arrangement of the period, and shows the house approached on its south side through two courtyards. A carriage drive traverses the first court, and the second has paved pathways leading to the flight of steps in the centre of the house, which give access to the Salon. On the right hand of the entrance courts is the bowling-green, and on the opposite side the pheasant-yard, wood-yard, and the various household offices. On the west side of the house a flight of steps leads into the flower garden, a small enclosure rather more than 100 feet square; beyond this, arranged centrally with the house, was the great pond, about 250 yards long, with, on either side, two large groves or bosquets in the French manner of Le Notre, which at this date had not long been introduced into England. Many of the trees now existing in this part of the garden were no doubt originally part of these groves. John James, in his "Theory and Practice of Gardening" (1712), gives many designs for groves very similar to these at Belton, but examples are now rarely to be met with.

The parterre occupied an oblong space about 400 feet wide by 650 feet long, and was divided by

[1] It differs from Badeslade's plan in several respects, principally in the arrangement of the forecourt, which Badeslade shows as one large courtyard with an oval grass plot. The grand canal shown in Campbell's plan does not exist in that of Badeslade, and its position is occupied by a broad gravel walk in the centre of which is an obelisk. The groves on either side, however, agree in both the plans. The parterre shown on Campbell's plan is indicated by Badeslade as a plain grass plot.

broad gravel paths. In the centre was a fountain, and at the end a little summer-house overlooking the churchyard. To the west were kitchen gardens, plantations, poultry yard, stables and brew-house. The house was approached on its west side through a court past the offices to the outer court.

In 1754 Belton passed into the hands of Sir John Cust, Speaker of the House of Commons, and he was succeeded by Sir Brownlow Cust, who was created Lord Brownlow shortly after his father's death. He employed James Wyatt to alter and improve the house, and alterations were made in the gardens. In the year 1777 they were entirely demolished and re-laid in the prevailing taste, and a " natural " treatment of the land replaced the trim yew hedges, straight alleys, and bosquets. The present Earl Brownlow partly restored them to their original shape in 1880, and Plate 40 shows the plan of the gardens as existing at the present time, from which it will be seen that the entrance courtyard now occupies the site of the former outer court, the original entrance being rarely used. The parterre on the north side of the house has been restored to something like its original form, though much curtailed in extent. Plate 42 is a view over this part of the garden, showing in the distance the figure of Father Time supporting a sundial (which is given on Plate 116), and Plate 43 is a view of the garden in front of the conservatory. The circular part of this garden is sunk about two feet and a half, and has a central pond with a fountain, charmingly arranged within a rose walk. In the lime avenue, east of the house, are marble statues representing the four seasons, the work of the sculptor C. G. Cibber, and there are some fine examples of wrought-iron work in the railings and screens to the courtyard, also at the end of the lime avenue on the west. side of the house, which leads to the Gothic ruins, cascade, and wilderness, through which the River Witham pursues its course.

TRENTHAM HALL, STAFFORDSHIRE.

PLATE 44.

THE present classic pile of buildings, which Sir Charles Barry designed for the second Duke of Sutherland, occupies the site of an old hall built by Sir Richard Leveson in 1633. This building, surrounded by its formal courtyards, flower gardens and trim yew hedges, must have been a charming old place. Two engravings, published in 1636,[1] show the house and garden as they existed then, with a forecourt surrounded by a balustrade of open letters, similar to that at Castle Ashby in Northamptonshire.

The front of the old house faced west, as does the present building, and the principal gardens looked down the valley of the Trent towards the south, partly occupying the site of the Italian garden shown on the plate; but the great lake which is seen in the distance had not then been formed. The house remained until the end of the eighteenth century, when it was pulled down and replaced by a plain Georgian structure, which was surrounded by gardens in accordance with the taste of that day. In 1833 Sir Charles Barry laid out the gardens as we see them to-day. The situation is one of great beauty, overlooking a large lake, and the River Trent, which formerly flowed through the lake, has been diverted in recent years, and now runs through the grounds on the east side. Trentham Hall is purely classic in design, and the garden surroundings, both in size and style, are well in keeping with the building.

Plot's " Natural History of Staffordshire," 1636.

Plate 44 is a view of the Italian garden, and it will be seen that the ground falls slightly towards the lake, and the garden has therefore been designed on two levels; the first level is about 200 feet square, and is divided from the second by a stone balustrade. In the centre is a circular plot with fountain and pond. A flight of circular steps leads to the second level, an oblong enclosure 700 feet long by 510 feet in breadth, divided by a broad gravel walk, bordered with trees in tubs, and on each side are ponds. At the further end, overlooking the lake, is a handsome stone terrace, 460 feet long, with a statue of Perseus, and a circular stone landing place.

LEVENS HALL, WESTMORLAND.

PLATES 45, 46, 47.

THE old Dutch garden at Levens Hall is probably the most perfect example, remaining in England, of a garden designed under the Dutch influence prevalent soon after the accession of William and Mary, although curiously enough the designer happened to be a Frenchman; but there is certainly nothing French about the aspect of Levens, which was evidently copied almost directly from a Dutch model, and in all their main features the gardens have been handed down to the present day exactly as they were originally designed.

Levens Hall dates back to very remote days, and was probably built as a border "pele" tower, of which there are many examples still to be met with in these parts. In 1489 the property was acquired by one Alan Bellingham, and it remained in his family until 1689, when it was sold to Colonel James Grahame, Keeper of the Privy Purse to James II. and one of his most trusted servants, who, after the revolution in 1689, for political reasons found it safer to live in the north. Soon after becoming possessed of the estate, Colonel Grahame began to make alterations to the hall, and, to create the gardens he called in the assistance of M. Beaumont, a pupil of the famous French gardener Le Notre. In the house there is an old portrait of Beaumont, whereon is the inscription " Monsieur Beaumont, Gardener to King James 2nd and to Coll: Js Grahme. He laid out the gardens at Hampton Court, and at Levens." It is probable that at Hampton Court he worked in the capacity of a foreman.

The gardens were commenced about the year 1700, and a letter written in 1701, describing a great storm that took place in the autumn of that year, tells of the terrible havoc wrought amongst the newly planted trees. We are able to form a very correct idea of the appearance of the gardens at this date, for there is fortunately preserved in the house a plan of them dated 1720, which shows that, with the exception of a few alterations on that part of the garden south of the bowling-green, every path and hedge remains as originally planned; this is probably a unique instance in England. Even the topiary work, though of course considerably grown, still retains its character and many of the trees are believed to have been planted when large enough to have been partly shaped into the forms they were intended afterwards to present.

Plate 45 is a plan of the gardens as they now exist, from which it will be seen that the forecourt is on the north, the parterre and flower garden on the east, and the kitchen garden and bowling-green on the south side of the house; the view on Plate 46 gives a good idea of the quaint and fantastic appearance of the topiary work.[1] Plate 47 is a view over the kitchen garden, taken from a tower at the

[1] Unfortunately the photograph for this plate had to be taken in winter, and it therefore fails to convey an idea of the brilliant aspect of the flower-beds.

angle of the house, and shows the great hornbeam alley, with hedges eight feet thick traversing the garden ; this plate also shows the bowling-green beyond.

Whatever may be one's feelings with regard to the use of topiary work—and many will think it is used to excess at Levens—the old world aspect and great variety of these different forms, if not beautiful, is intensely quaint and interesting. At one corner stands the King with his crown upon his head, and opposite, the Queen with her arms akimbo; here a crowned lion with a fine tail, there an archway or a gigantic helmet, an umbrella like construction shading a seat, Queen Elizabeth with her maids of honour, and many another creation in yew standing out with its wealth of deep green foliage amidst the flowers, with walks of soft green turf between the beds. (The outlines of several of these yews are shown on Plate 106.) Near by are two quite small enclosures with substantial hedges surrounding them and overlooked by the old gardener's house, still known as "Beaumont Hall." A broad walk separates the flower garden from the kitchen gardens, and at one end is an old yew arbour known as "The Judge's Wig."

The garden on the south side of this walk is divided into four parts by grass alleys opening into a circular plot in the centre with high hornbeam hedges, as shown on Plate 47. Three of these plots are used for fruit and vegetable gardens, whilst the fourth is the bowling-green whereon many generations have delighted to play. The ground between this and the boundary road is now covered with fine old beeches ; but on the plan of 1720 this part is shown divided into two parterres, all signs of which are now gone.

HESLINGTON HALL, YORKSHIRE.

PLATE 48.

HESLINGTON HALL lies within two miles of York, and was built about 1565 by Thomas Eymes, a member of the famous Council of the North. After his death the hall was occupied by the Hesketh family, and later by the Yarborough family. It was restored in 1854, but still retains many of its original features, including the square angle turrets, which recall such houses as Hatfield and Charlton, in Kent, although much smaller in extent than these. The gardens would appear to have been laid out at a rather later period than the house, and probably date from the end of the seventeenth century. The Topiary garden, which is the only part of the old garden remaining, recalls that at Levens Hall, and, indeed, has been attributed to Beaumont ; but instead of the huge umbrellas, lions, and other fantastic creations, the topiary work here assumes much simpler forms, and is cut into huge cylinders, globes, and beehive shapes. At present these are set on a grass lawn, but probably they were formerly grouped amongst gay flower-beds. The remaining parts of the grounds have unfortunately been modernized, which is the more to be regretted when we consider the rarity of examples of this period. Until within the last half century the garden was allowed to fall into decay, but in recent years it has been well cared for. Overlooking the topiary work is a Georgian summer-house, in the lower storey of which is an arbour looking on to a picturesque bowling-green.

THE SKATING POND, ASHRIDGE PARK, HERTS.

PLATE 49.

THE pond illustrated on this plate is situated in the beautiful grounds surrounding this seat of Earl Brownlow, which lies in the hilly and well-wooded country on the north slopes of the Chilterns. The park, which is of considerable extent, lies on the borders of Hertfordshire and Buckinghamshire, and is in fact partly in both counties. It is an example of a somewhat unusual treatment of water in a garden, and besides being a good ornamental feature serves a useful purpose as a pond for skating, when the weather is favourable for the indulgence of that pastime. It is rectangular in shape, partly enclosed on three sides by banks formed by the earth excavated. These banks form a good shelter, and help to keep the water still whilst freezing. The pond is surrounded on all sides, close to the water, by a low yew hedge, and has several descents by flights of stone steps to the water's edge.

BRICKWALL, SUSSEX.

PLATES 50, 51.

AMONG the many delightful old gardens surrounding the smaller country houses in England, there are certainly few to be found as quaintly picturesque as Brickwall. Both house and garden seem entirely to belong to one another, and the old world character of the latter has fortunately never been disturbed, so that to-day the gardens present much the same appearance as they have done during the last two centuries. The house, which is situated close to the village of Northiam, was built towards the close of the sixteenth century, on the site of an earlier building, and on a west gable is the date 1617. Additions were made during the reign of James II. by Sir Edward Frewen, whose family are still the possessors of the property, and under their hands the house has been well restored during recent years. Plate 50 is a plan of the garden, and Plate 51 is a general view of it from the house.

The entrance from the main road is on the north side of the house, through gates with well designed piers supporting lions, and with small gates on either side. From here a short drive leads to the entrance; to the left are the stables, and on the right a wing wall, behind which, on the west side of the house, is a small garden. On the south side of the house are the flower garden and kitchen gardens, and on the east is a large paddock with orchard and enclosures. These are on a rather higher level than the house itself, and instead of a terrace on the garden front, a paved brick path with flights of steps at either end communicates with a raised walk, 9 feet wide, which extends round the remaining three sides of the flower garden. This walk is screened by yew hedges on two sides, in which are openings at intervals marked by sentinel-like yews.

On one side of the flower garden is a rectangular fish-pond 75 feet long by 25 wide, with grass sloping sides. The central walk has twelve yews in the shape of triangular cones, set in the midst of old-fashioned flower-beds. On the west side, next the road, is a brick boundary wall with a palisade of hornbeam, whose branches are intertwined and trimmed square to form a continuous hedge with the trunks left bare as high as the top of the wall. From the flower garden three openings give access to the kitchen garden, an oblong enclosure about 80 yards by 45, intersected by narrow grass paths. In the centre is a sundial, of which a sketch is given on Plate 60, and at the farther end of the kitchen garden, and separating it from the park is a grass bowling-alley, 9 feet wide by 130 feet long, raised a few feet, and with seats at either end.

MELBOURNE HALL, DERBYSHIRE.

PLATE 52.

THE early years of the eighteenth century saw the creation of many garden schemes, principally under the direction of the royal gardeners, London and Wise, but of these few are now remaining, especially of the smaller class designed by them. Of this kind Melbourne may be considered a very good example. Early in the reign of Charles I. the estate of Melbourne was leased by the Bishop of Carlisle to Sir John Coke, Secretary of State, who on his retirement settled there, and occupied his time in the pursuits of a country gentleman. On the outbreak of the Civil War he returned to London, and at his death the property passed to his son. The present house dates from the commencement of the eighteenth century, and occupies the site of the older Manor-house. Between the years 1704 and 1711, the grounds were entirely remodelled for Thomas Coke, afterwards Vice Chamberlain to George I., from the designs of Henry Wise, and with the exception of some alterations made about sixty years since, the plan remains practically as it was then designed. Henry Wise appears to have left untouched the older parts near the house, and to have extended the gardens towards the east and south, making the great water-piece, planting the groves, and forming the grass alleys with their yew hedges and high palisades of lime trees.

Plate 52 gives a plan of the gardens as they are now existing, from which it will be seen that they occupy an irregular space, and are to the east of the house, whilst on the south-west side is a large lake. The forecourt is on the south side of the house, the offices, stables, and dovecote being on the north. The land slopes away from the house on the east side, and the garden is arranged on two levels with a central and two side walks, bordered with thick yew hedges.

The upper level has been remodelled in recent years; the lower consists of an oblong grass plot in four divisions, with a good lead figure of Mercury in the centre. Beyond is the fish-pond, an oblong pool 80 feet by 200, with a half quatrefoil extension on the further side, surrounded by grass verges on either side of a gravel path, and yew hedges with recesses for statuary and seats, while in the centre is a curious wrought iron garden house known as the Birdcage. Along the east side of the house is a terrace walk bounded at one end by an arbour and "clair-voyée," overlooking the lake. From this point a path leads to the yew-alley, a tunnel extending 100 yards, where the yew has become impenetrable to light overhead, and is thick enough to be proof against an ordinary shower of rain. It is terminated by a circular pool with a little leaden fountain, from whence walks extend right and left across the garden.

From the Birdcage grass alleys extend in two directions, one leading to a small circular enclosure, the other, known as the "crow walk," to the "crow's-foot," a very favourite feature in gardens of this period. The walk has broad yew hedges on either side, and its soft green turf and overhanging trees make it a truly delightful retreat for hot summer days. From the "crow's-foot" alleys and paths radiate in different directions, and the two principal alleys have lime palisades, 35 feet high, cut in the manner of the old French gardens. In the centre of the "crow's-foot" is the famous leaden vase, probably the most elaborate work of its kind in existence. The Fountain Walk crosses the "crow-walk" at right angles, and has three fountain ponds. At one end is a wooden summer-house, from whence a delightful vista down the walk is presented when the fountains are playing, and here and there a bright gleam of sunshine falls across the grass walk, and lights up the sombre greens of the old yew hedges.

Like Drayton Hall, Melbourne is famous for its magnificent collection of leadwork, for most of which one John Noste[1] was responsible. The vase referred to above was cast in 1706. It is supported by four kneeling monkeys, and is ornamented all over in a manner rather rococo, finishing above with four busts of the seasons and a bouquet of fruit and flowers. It is said to have cost only £100.

On either side of the fish-pond are lead statues of Perseus and Andromeda, the former being a particularly good example. There is also a flying Mercury, after Giovanni Bologna, and two fine examples of the kneeling slave, painted black with white drapery, and supporting a vase instead of the usual sundial, also several cupids, both single figures and in groups of two. One peeps out of a hedge, ready to let go his shaft, another is busily engaged in sharpening his bow, another is falling off a tree, another flying upward. A series of groups show the little figures engaged in quarrelling for the possession of a garland of flowers; words soon come to blows, a battle royal ensues, and the fourth group shows the youthful amorini making friends again. All these statues were supplied by John Noste, and old accounts are still preserved at Melbourne in which it appears that the Perseus cost £25, the Mercury and Syca £50, and a "young Triton with brass pipe in middle" £6 9s.; this is no doubt the fountain still at the end of the yew alley.

WESTBURY COURT, GLOUCESTERSHIRE.

PLATES 53, 54, 55.

 WESTBURY COURT is situated amid pleasant surroundings overlooking the River Severn, on the old main road from Monmouth to Gloucester, and within a few miles of the latter city. Plate 53 gives a plan of the garden partly as it existed in the early years of the eighteenth century, according to a view given in Atkyns' "Gloucestershire,"[2] and partly measured from the garden as it exists to-day, the boundary line dividing these two portions being a brick wall, as noted on the plan. The old house, which probably stood here in Elizabethan days, was burnt down and a new building in the Georgian style erected by Maynard Colchester, Esq., in 1755-1757, when, fortunately, the old gardens were left intact. For some reason unknown this second house was destroyed in the year 1809, and the place remained unoccupied until a few years ago, when the house was rebuilt, though on a different site, adjoining the old garden-house, which has been incorporated in the new building. At the present time that part of the ground on which stood the Elizabethan building with its parterre, kitchen garden, and bowling-green, has been devoted to other purposes, and a straight carriage drive now leads direct to the house through this part of the garden.

[1] See description of Plates 107-112, "Leadwork."
[2] Sir Robert Atkyns, "The Ancient and Present State of Gloucestershire." London, 1712.

The old building stood close to the road, and was approached by a forecourt with gateways leading to the house and stable courts. On the south side of the house was the bowling-green and parterre, beyond which a pleached alley divided the kitchen garden, which was surrounded by a formal arrangement of fruit trees, all now gone. Beyond, and occupying the greater part of the ground, is the Dutch garden, bounded on the east and south by a brook. A very good idea of this part of the gardens is conveyed by the views on Plates 54 and 55. These show the two large water-pieces, one in the form of the letter T; the other a straight piece, 450 feet long by about 22 feet broad, at the end of which is the quaint two storey garden-house supported on columns, now incorporated in the new building. At the other end of the two water-pieces, "clair-voyées," flanked by stone piers with handsome leaden vases, are placed in the wall, and in the angle north-east of the garden is the "gazeebo," or corner garden-house, overlooking the road on one side, and a small walled-in garden on the other.

GROOMBRIDGE PLACE, KENT.

PLATES 56, 57.

THE old moated Manor-house at Groombridge is situated on the banks of a stream separating the counties of Kent and Sussex, about three miles to the west of Tunbridge Wells, in the midst of a beautiful park, and sheltered from the north by well-wooded hills.

In the reign of Edward I., Groombridge was in the possession of a younger branch of the ancient Kentish family of Cobham; it afterwards passed to Sir John de Clinton, and during the last years of Henry IV.'s reign became the property of John Waller, whose son Richard, fighting at the battle of Agincourt, took prisoner Charles, Duke of Orleans, who for many years was confined within the old moated castle of Groombridge. The estate was again sold, to Thomas Sackville, Earl of Dorset, during the reign of James I., but the Sackvilles never resided here, and the castle, deserted for many years, was eventually sold to John Packer, clerk of the Privy Seal to Charles I., whose son, Philip Packer, the friend of John Evelyn, decided to pull down the old castle, which had fallen into a sad state of disrepair. No doubt in carrying out his ideas he was much influenced by the taste of Evelyn, who, but recently returned from Italy, induced him to build his new home in the prevailing style; and it is possible that Sir Christopher Wren himself may have given his advice and direction concerning the new building.

But Packer did not follow the advice of his friend in choosing the site, and preferred rather to build within the old moat than to act on Evelyn's advice and build on the edge of the wood, on rising ground commanding a magnificent view of the surrounding country, which would have been in many respects a more desirable site. The house was therefore built within the moat, in the form of the letter H, the principal approach being on the western side over a beautiful old stone bridge, with a gateway marked by large stone piers having semicircular niches. On the south side of the house the various outbuildings are grouped around the stable yard, adjoining which is a small kitchen garden. The quaint dovecote shown on Plate 56 is perched over the entrance gate to this small enclosure.

The gardens still bear their ancient character; they are enclosed on all sides with brick and buttressed stone walls, now mellowed by time and the soft gray lichen into a variety of beautiful tints. The stately walks, the broad grass terraces and hedges of yew, carry the mind back to the days when

Evelyn must have wandered there with his friend, when, by his advice, no doubt, the gardens were first planned and laid out. Two old fir trees, rising to a great height, formerly stood on either side of the entrance to the house, and are said to have been planted by Evelyn; only one of these venerable trees now remains.

The gardens are to the north of the house on a slight rise, and are approached by a bridge across the broad moat. From this point a walk leads through their entire length, and a vista is thus obtained, through an old gateway into the park beyond. The gradual slope of the ground has caused the garden to be arranged on three levels, each varying but a few feet. Through the lower level a shallow stream runs, kept within bounds by low walls, as shown on Plate 57. Beyond the stream a grass slope leads to the first terrace, bounded on one side by a thick yew hedge of some antiquity; the next level is principally devoted to lawns, with here and there a straggling apple tree, a small stone figure of a boy, and the peacock-house; for the peacocks are one of the chief glories of Groombridge Place. The upper level is divided into two small gardens, in one of which is a sundial and in the other a fountain. These gardens occupy the site of a former kitchen garden.

HOLLAND HOUSE, KENSINGTON.

PLATES 58 AND 58*.

STANDING to-day well within the boundary lines of Greater London, Holland House is one of the very few survivors of the great seats of the nobility which formerly surrounded the metropolis. Whilst all around streets and houses have long swallowed up all available ground, this house still stands surrounded by a beautiful park and gardens, and as one rests amongst its shady groves it is hard to realize the proximity of the great city.

About the end of the sixteenth century, Sir Walter Cope acquired the manor of West Town, and in the year 1607 commenced the erection of Holland House, which was then known as " Cope's Castle." The original plan, by John Thorpe, is in the Soane Museum. Sir Walter Cope died in 1614, and the property passed to Sir Henry Rich, who had married his daughter, and who was created Earl of Holland in 1624. He fought during the Civil War, and being taken prisoner by the Parliamentarians, was beheaded in 1649. From the Restoration until the middle of the eighteenth century, Holland House was occasionally let, and William III. is said to have inspected it with a view to its conversion into a royal residence, but preferred Nottingham House.

Many notable people subsequently resided here, and in 1716 Addison, who had married the widow of Edward Rich, Earl of Warwick and Holland, came here to live, and Holland House soon became a famous literary centre. From the family of Rich the mansion passed by sale to Henry Fox, first Lord Holland of a new creation, and it was for him the gardens were laid out in 1769 by Charles Hamilton, of Pains Hill. Of these old gardens the principal part now remaining is the Dutch garden on the west side of the house, shown on Plate 58, with flower-beds surrounded by high box-edging, and divided by broad paths.[1] This was not formerly so extensive as at present, and in the early years of the eighteenth century part of the land was occupied by a cherry orchard.

Towards the end of the garden is an ivy-covered arcade, part of the original stable buildings which

[1] A plan of the Dutch garden was published in " The Book of the Garden," by C. Mackintosh, 2 vols., London, 1853-5.

were removed by Lord Holland about 1820, while close by is a large bronze bust of Napoleon. The garden is interesting to all horticulturalists, for it was here that the dahlia was first successfully cultivated by the third Lady Holland, who brought the seeds from Spain.

The original entrance forecourt was on the south front, but this was altered in 1873, when the entrance was moved to its present position on the east side of the house. At right angles to the east front of the house, and as if forming one side of an entrance courtyard, is the perforated wall and the stone gateway, shown on Plate 58*, which were erected in 1629 by Nicholas Stone, from the design of Inigo Jones, and for which, according to Walpole, Stone was paid the sum of £100.[1] The gates are reached from the forecourt by a double flight of steps on either side of a fountain in the wall. These steps lead to the pleasure grounds on the north side of the house.

HADDON HALL, DERBYSHIRE.

PLATE 59.

 THE very name of Haddon Hall is so surrounded with romance that it is difficult to consider it in any but a romantic spirit, and to analyze its beauties by means of plan and section would seem to approach the old place without a due spirit of reverence; still it forms so interesting a study in garden planning, and so well demonstrates the importance of considering the house and garden as one design, that the latter has been measured for illustration in this work.

Situated on a rather steep hillside, overlooking the valley of the Wye, here only a narrow stream, one of Haddon's greatest charms is the way in which house and gardens seem to fall into harmony with the surrounding landscape. The Hall consists of buildings round two courtyards, on levels varying about two feet, and the principal rooms, including the Long Gallery, are on the south-east side.

The Great Hall or Banqueting-House was built about 1452, and formed the principal feature of the original building. The famous Long Gallery is later, being Elizabethan in character. It has three fine bay windows overlooking the garden. In the panelling of the gallery the arms of the Manners and Vernon families are found, and there is no doubt that the work of this period was done by John Manners, who married Dorothy Vernon. He became Sir John in 1603, and it was his grandson, on the failure of the elder branch, who became Earl of Rutland in 1641. Haddon still belongs to the Rutland family.

The gardens, as now existing, date from between the middle of the sixteenth century and the end of the seventeenth. A flight of steps leads from the ante-room, between the Long Gallery and the state bedroom, on to the terrace, now overshadowed by the grand old yews that no doubt formerly marked the angles of a parterre, and have been allowed to remain uncut since the commencement of the eighteenth century, when the Hall ceased to be occupied. At the north-east end of this terrace a rectangular flight of steps leads up to the fine old sycamore avenue known as Dorothy Vernon's Walk (although it was probably made after her romantic marriage), which even when first planted must always have been a shady and secluded retreat. This walk forms the north-east boundary of the gardens. At

---

[1] Walpole's " Anecdotes of Painting."

the south-east end of the large terrace existed a rustic arbour, occupying the site of a former summer-house, the base of which exists.

From the terrace a broad flight of steps leads down to the upper garden, now a square plot of ground divided into two lawns by a gravel walk, but which in all probability was originally a parterre. At present its picturesque aspect is much enhanced by a fine old apple tree—the last of several—whose straggling branches and gnarled trunk are just sufficient to break the too formal appearance that would otherwise be presented. The lower garden was in all probability used for household purposes, either as a vegetable and herb garden or as an orchard, most likely the former. At the end of this garden a long flight of steps leads to a small postern gate and Dorothy's Bridge.

The sketch section through the gardens will give a good idea of the manner in which the earth excavated from one part was made to form the terrace of some adjacent portion; the whole being entirely the outcome of the necessities of the site. The gardens probably never extended beyond their present boundary, but above, on the hillside overlooking the Hall, are the remains of the old bowling-green with its house, since converted into a farmhouse, but still retaining part of its original outside staircase, by which spectators ascended to the flat roof to witness the game or admire the scenery. The green is now cut up and made into a garden for the farmhouse.

Below and to the north-east of the Hall is the old archery ground, surrounded with sycamore trees, and a small avenue of the same, leading down to the original entrance to the Hall, the present entrance being that to the park.

SAIGHTON GRANGE, CHESHIRE.

PLATE 60.

AIGHTON GRANGE was originally one of the three castellated residences of the Abbot of St. Werburgh. After the Dissolution it came into the possession of Charles Walley, whose great grandson dying without issue, it was purchased in 1755 by Foster Cunliffe, whose descendant, Sir Foster Cunliffe, sold the estate to the Marquis of Westminster, and the house is now the residence of Lady Grosvenor. In Ormerod's " History of Cheshire " is a view of the Grange as it appeared in 1817, showing the original entrance gateway, built by Simon Ripley in 1489, in a very dilapidated condition. The house has been restored, and the gardens are the creation of recent years. Plate 60 gives a plan of them. The entrance is on the west side of the house, a short drive leading to the forecourt and continuing to the stables, which are on the east side. The whole of the gardens have a slight fall from north to south.

The principal flower gardens are on the south side of the house, arranged centrally with the entrance, within two enclosures surrounded by yew hedges; on the east side of these enclosures is the quaint little " saints' garden," encompassed with hedges, while the beds are filled with flowers supposed to blossom on various saints' days. Adjoining the house on the west side is another flower garden, with little square beds divided by flagged paths, and beyond is the lime walk, a charming arrangement of small limes planted a few feet apart, reminding one of little gardens in Normandy. The kitchen garden is to the north of the house, and is well arranged in four plots with grass walks lined with fruit trees.

CHISWICK HOUSE, MIDDLESEX.

PLATE 61.

CHISWICK HOUSE, as it stands at the present time, partly occupies the site of a country seat purchased by the Earl of Burlington from the Earl of Somerset in the latter part of the seventeenth century, and the property still belongs to his descendant, the Duke of Devonshire. A view by Kip, published in the "Britannia Illustrata," gives an excellent idea of the estate in those days, when fields stretched away to the northward, which have long since been entirely built over. Soon after becoming possessed of Chiswick House, Lord Burlington began to make alterations in the gardens, the character of which he almost entirely changed, and extensive groves were planted in place of the square parterres and low hedges of the Jacobean garden. Lord Burlington, himself a keen amateur in gardening, was assisted by Bridgeman, and in later years by William Kent, who returned from Italy in 1730.

The plan on Plate 61 is taken from a survey by J. Rocque, and represents the gardens as they were previous to the year 1736, that is, in the period immediately preceding the landscape style. Some parts, indeed, away from the house, already show a tendency to the "little gentle disorder," the delight of the landscape gardener who was so soon to follow. It is hardly probable that Kent had much to do with the garden shown on Rocque's survey, as the years immediately following his return from Italy he devoted to architecture.

All through the eighteenth century, and until the commencement of the nineteenth, Chiswick House was in the heyday of its popularity, and a favourite resort of fashionable London. The gardens were kept with considerable care, but of late years they have lost much of their former magnificence, many vases and pieces of statuary having been removed by the Duke of Devonshire to his other gardens at Chatsworth.

The House stands not far from the banks of the Thames, and formerly a broad gravel forecourt led from the road to the south front, with its handsome stone portico of Corinthian columns. The forecourt was bordered on either side by four cedar trees with antique busts between them, while on the west side of it was the flower garden, laid out as a formal parterre.

On the north side of the house the "Grande Allée," about 350 yards long, led to a pavilion at the further side of the garden, while about midway other walks branched to right and left, the one to a summer-house in the north-east corner of the grounds, the other to a pavilion with a small court overlooking the lake. The intervening triangular spaces were laid out as wildernesses with tortuous paths. A broad grass walk, bordered on either side by groves of trees, regularly disposed, led from the north front of the Palladian villa to the "Poets' Corner," a semicircular alcove ornamented with antique statues of Caesar, Pompey, and Cicero. There were also marble seats, brought by the Earl of Burlington from Adrian's Villa, near Rome.

On the east side were the kitchen gardens, and an orangery overlooking a grass plot.[1] This building no longer exists, but the floor may still be seen cleverly laid out with a mosaic of pebbles and the vertebrae of sheep. A long walk extends on the north front of the house, to the gateway brought here in 1737 from the gardens of Beaufort House, Chelsea. This gateway was designed by Inigo Jones, and

---

[1] In the summer time the orange trees with their tubs were disposed in tiers round the circular pond, overlooked by a little classic temple.

was given by Sir Hans Soane to the Earl of Burlington. Early in the nineteenth century the gardens were greatly extended on this side, and a large conservatory, 300 feet long, was constructed, with a semicircular Italian garden in front, and groves with grass walks, all still existing.

The gardens were divided by a large lake and an artificial river which were fed by a small stream flowing eventually into the Thames. This stream, which is shown on Kip's view, was originally quite small, and when it was enlarged and the lake formed, a long terrace was made with the ground excavated. The river was crossed by a bridge, from whence avenues diverged in three directions, and the grounds on this side were laid out with woods and groves, intersected by grass walks, and here and there an open space.

Since the time of Rocque's plan many alterations have been made to both house and grounds. In 1788 James Wyatt added two wings to the Palladian villa, which had been previously described by the wits of the day as a place " too small to inhabit and too large to hang on one's watch chain." There are still some fine garden ornaments in stone and lead, including the large lead group of " Cain and Abel " by Sheemaker, a replica of that at Drayton ; also a pair of leaden sphinxes beautifully modelled, and many vases, two of which are given on Plate 109. The orange-tree garden too, still exists, with its semicircular terraces and circular pool.

HAMPTON COURT, HEREFORDSHIRE.

PLATE 62.

THIS plan is taken from " Vitruvius Britannicus," and is an interesting type of an early eighteenth century garden. There is also an engraving of the garden made at a rather earlier date, by Kip, in the "Britannia Illustrata," which shows it in a very similar condition. At the time this was made the house was in the possession of the Earl of Coningsby, the first and last to hold that title. He took a great interest in the estate, on which he spent much of his fortune.

An interesting account of the gardens as they appeared at this date has been left by Dr. Stukely, the author of " Iter Curiosum," who says : " The gardens are very pleasant (the finest greens I ever saw), terminated by vast woods covering all the side of the hill. . . . Here is a great command of water on all sides of the house for fountains, basons, canals. . . . There are lawns, groves, canals, hills, and plains ; There is a pool three-quarters of a mile long, very broad, included between the two great woods. The dam that forms it across a valley cost £800, and was made in a fortnight by 200 hands. There is a new river cut quite through the park, the channel of which for a long way together is hewn out of a rock. . . . Here are new gardens and canals laid out and new plantations, and timber in proper places to complete its pastures." From the plan it will be seen that an avenue 200 yards long, bordered on either side by grass verges, led direct to the forecourt, an arrangement differing from the earlier type, when it was customary to traverse at least one court on foot before arriving at the front door. The buildings, which were anterior to the garden, surrounded an inner courtyard. The parterre, bowling-green and flower gardens were on the opposite side of the house, and beyond these the great water-piece, extending the total width of the garden (rather more than 400 feet), was fed by a brook, which flowed into the River Lugg.

Bounding the garden on one side was a long, straight canal about 30 feet wide, terminating in a square fish-pond, overlooked by a small lodge. A bridge crossed the canal opposite the house, and from this point avenues diverged in three directions. There was another flower garden on one side of the great courtyard, laid out with oblong beds and grass paths between. A central walk through the garden traversed a kitchen garden, with little square ponds at intervals between the beds, and beyond was a square fountain garden. On the opposite side of the avenue were the stables, kitchen offices, and orchard, with two circular dovecotes. The garden did not exist for many years, as it was unfortunately one of those which fell under the destroying hand of the landscape gardener in the middle of the eighteenth century.

LITTLE COMPTON, GLOUCESTERSHIRE.

PLATE 63.

LITTLE COMPTON was situated near the village of Compton Abdale in Gloucestershire. The manor was purchased in 1608 by Sir Richard Grubham, who bequeathed it to his nephew Sir John Howe, who in his turn was succeeded by his son Sir Richard Howe, and it was whilst in his possession that the engraving was made from which this view is taken. According to Atkyns (1768) it was a large newly-built house having delightful gardens and a pleasant river running through them, with an agreeable prospect over large woods, and a park of great extent. Hardly any traces of the mansion now remain, and its site is occupied by a farmhouse. The house, a classic building with a central block and side wings, was approached through the forecourt by a circular drive. The visitor alighted some little distance from the front door and crossed a flagged court. On the left of the forecourt were the stable buildings, and on the right a long narrow canal, running through the garden. On one side of the house was a stone flagged terrace bordering a canal over which a little bridge led into the principal part of the garden. This was laid out in grass, with a circular fountain pond at one end, from which a little cupid gaily spouted water. On either side were oblong plots raised some few feet above the general level, the soil excavated from the canal being used for the purpose. One of these plots was used as a bowling-green, and the other laid out as a parterre, while all were enclosed within a high boundary wall. The kitchen gardens, which were of considerable extent, occupied the ground on the opposite side of the house; they were divided into plots by hedges, with grass alleys between, and innumerable little formal trees dotted about.

KING'S WESTON, GLOUCESTERSHIRE.

PLATE 64.

OF this quaint old garden there are now hardly any remains, for the old Tudor Manor house, which is shown on the plate, was pulled down in the early years of the eighteenth century to make way for the present building, a stately classic pile, erected in 1711 from the designs of Vanbrugh. The view on Plate 64, taken from Atkyn's " Gloucestershire," shows the house when it was the seat of Edward Southwell, Esq., one of the clerks of the Privy Council, and principal Secretary of State for Ireland. Atkyns says, " He hath a pleasant seat with delightful gardens, and a full prospect over King-road the harbour of the city of Bristol and over the

Severn Sea into Wales." The house was encompassed by a park of nearly 500 acres, with extensive avenues on one side. The entrance was through a stable court to the grass forecourt, whence a flagged path led to the front door, across another court enclosed by the two wings of the house. At the further end of the forecourt was a long narrow bowling-alley with pavilions at either end, and beyond was the kitchen garden. The flower gardens lay to the south of the house, and consisted of two principal parts, with a small walled garden and orangery adjoining the stable court. The garden next the house consisted of a double parterre, mostly laid out in grass, and the remaining part was laid out with large beds of flowers, surrounded with high box borders; this garden was terminated by a raised terrace, and a gazeebo overlooking the park.

SANDYWELL, GLOUCESTERSHIRE.

PLATE 65.

 ANDYWELL HOUSE was situated about five miles from Cheltenham, and its site is still occupied by a residence, but nothing more than the outlines of the kitchen garden can now be discerned. The view of the gardens here given is also taken from Atkyns' "Gloucestershire," and shows the house when it was the seat of Henry Bret, Esq., who bought the property in 1680, and commenced building the mansion. The gardens, with the oblong water-piece, are of about this period, but they cannot have enjoyed a very long existence, for they had entirely disappeared by 1779, when an engraving of the house was published in Samuel Rudder's history of the county. From this view it appears that the old formal gardens, sharing the fate of so many, had been destroyed and grassy lawns extended to the front of the house, where formerly stood the neat little forecourt.

The house was approached on its east side by an avenue, which led to the little forecourt laid out with grass parterres, and adorned with vases and statues. The stable court, kitchen yards and paddock were on the opposite side of the house. A flight of steps led to the principal gardens from the south side of the house, and an oblong fish-pond, bordered by trees, occupied the central part of the garden, with fruit trees planted on either side. To the east of this was the kitchen garden, divided by paths and fruit trees at regular intervals, while in the centre was a leaden figure of the kneeling slave supporting a sundial. A walled-in orchard was close adjoining. The house was surrounded by a park nearly a hundred acres in extent.

MOUNT MORRIS, KENT.

PLATE 66.

 HIS view of Mount Morris is taken from Badeslade's "Views of Noblemen's Seats in Kent," a folio volume published in 1720, containing a series of interesting views of houses and gardens. The house, like nearly all those of this period, was approached through two courtyards, the second being traversed on foot. The arrangement of the first court is interesting, with its open wooden railing and quaint gates, the posts surmounted by wooden pinnacles. In the centre was an oval grass plot with a leaden figure, and to the right was a paddock with a square brick dovecote—a rather unusual form. The forecourt was laid out with grass parterres, and small yew

trees, while in front of the house, raised about two feet from the general level, was a broad paved terrace. On the left-hand side was the kitchen garden and duck-pond, and the right the stable court. The parterre and flower garden were situated on the other side of the house, partly in the park across which the main lines of the garden were extended by avenues.

DAWLEY, MIDDLESEX.

PLATE 67.

 RACTICALLY nothing now remains of this once celebrated garden, which was situated near Hillingdon, not far from the borders of Middlesex and Bucking-hamshire. The house was an extensive classic building, and was approached through a large grass forecourt on the north side. On the south side were very extensive flower gardens and parterres, those near the house being grass. The middle parts consisted of six parterres, and beyond was a flower garden with central grass walks and four little treillage arbours. East of this was another enclosed garden, laid out with ten small parterres, and having an extensive orangery at one end, in front of which a space was reserved for the orange trees, placed out of doors during the summer months. On the opposite side of the garden was the bowling-green and a small orchard. An elevated terrace ran the entire width of the garden from east to west, and was terminated at either end by a square gazeebo. A house still exists on the site, known as Dawley Court, but the gardens, shown on this old view by Kip, have long ceased to exist.

FAIRFORD, GLOUCESTERSHIRE.

PLATE 68.

 HE original Manor-house at Fairford was purchased in 1498 by John Tame, a wealthy London merchant, who had introduced the manufacture of woollen cloth into the town. The property was successively held by his son and grandson, but at the Restoration belonged to one Andrew Barker. The view on Plate 68 is from an engraving in Atkyns' "Gloucestershire," and the house shown here was built by Samuel Barker, who was high sheriff of the county in 1691. The gardens were afterwards demolished, as we may gather from an account published a century later, which states that "the Park was about 200 acres in extent, well planted, with an avenue a mile in length, and the grounds were long and deservedly admired, when in that style of embellishment which distinguished the close of the last century. From the modern art of gardening they have gained additional beauty! the river widened for a great distance with its extremities artificially concealed." Nothing now remains of this fine old garden.

A double avenue gave access to the house from the town of Fairford, and both house and gardens occupied an oblong space enclosed within walls. At the end of the avenue was a single forecourt leading directly to the house, on the left-hand side of which were the stable and laundry yards, with outbuildings.

On the right-hand side were two small gardens with grass plots enclosed within walls, one of which led into the principal garden. Down the centre of this garden was a large oblong parterre, with a fountain in the centre, and each of the plots adorned with statuary. At the further end was a semicircular raised terrace, with a handsome pair of gates leading into the park. On either side of the parterre were kitchen gardens enclosed within hedges, and with broad grass walks between, terminated by little summer-houses, from whence vistas might be obtained through the entire length of the gardens. In one corner was an oblong bowling-green.

OLD BUCKINGHAM HOUSE, MIDDLESEX.

PLATE 69.

THIS plan of the gardens which originally surrounded Buckingham House, now Buckingham Palace, is taken from an original coloured survey preserved in the Soane Museum, and is particularly interesting both on account of the present world-wide celebrity of the palace erected on its site, and as a contemporary plan of a garden dating from the early years of the eighteenth century.

The House was built by John Sheffield, Duke of Buckingham, in a magnificent manner in the year 1703, on the site of the once famous Mulberry Gardens.[1] The duke, who had purchased the property from the Earl of Arlington, did not live long to enjoy the pleasures of his beautiful house, in which he took a keen delight, for he died in 1720.

The duke, who retired here after a busy life, has left an interesting account of the house and gardens in a letter to a noble friend, wherein he says : " The avenues to this house are along St. James's Park, through rows of goodly elms on one hand, and gay flourishing limes on the other ; that for coaches, this for walking, and the mall lying betwixt them ; this reaches to an iron palisade that encompassed a square court, which has in its midst a great basin with statues and waterworks : and from its entrance rises all the way imperceptibly till we mount to a terrace in the front of a large hall. . . . To the gardens we go down from the house by seven steps into a gravel walk that reaches across the gardens with a covered arbour at each end. Another, of thirty feet broad, leads from the front of the house, and lies between two groves of tall lime trees planted upon a carpet of grass : the outsides of these groves are bordered with tubs of bays and orange trees. At the end of this broad walk you go up to a terrace four hundred paces long, with a large semicircle in the middle, from whence are beheld the Queen's two parks and a great part of Surry ; then going down a few steps, you walk on the bank of a canal, six hundred yards long and seventeen broad with two rows of limes on each side. On one side of this terrace, a wall covered with jessamines, is made low, to admit the view of a meadow full of cattle just beneath, and at each end is a descent, into parterres with fountains and waterworks.[2] From the biggest of these parterres we pass into a little square garden that has a fountain in the middle, and two greenhouses on the sides, with a convenient bathing appartment, and near a flower garden. Below all this a kitchen garden, filled with the best sorts of fruits, has several walks in it fit for the coldest weather. . ."

On the death of the duke in 1720 the property passed to his duchess, and she was succeeded by the duke's natural son, who died a minor.

[1] Knight's "London," 6 vols., 1841-4.

[2] To supply the fountains a reservoir over the kitchen wing contained fifty tons of water ; this was forced up by an engine from the Thames.

An engraving by Le Rouge, published in Paris in 1787, shows the gardens entirely dismantled, but the long canal still remained; also the house, courtyard, and outbuildings. In 1793 Buckingham House was purchased by George III. as a residence for Queen Charlotte, and a view taken a few years later, given in Pyne's History,[1] shows the red-brick house with Corinthian pilasters, and two side wings connected by quadrant arcades. Pyne says: "The front was modernized and the grounds, which were according to the old style over-ornamented with parterres, fountains, statues, etc., were changed to the succeeding style, which excluded ornament altogether. . . . The situation when occupied by its founder must have been delightful, no buildings extended beyond St. James's to the left, the north was open to Hampstead, and a view of the Thames almost uninterrupted from the south-west corner of the Park."

The "goodly elms" and "gay flourishing limes" went to decay; a plain iron rail took the place of the handsome palisade, and the fountain of Neptune entirely disappeared; many of the statues were deposited in the famous lead statue yard in Piccadilly, and may still exist scattered over the country.

In 1825 the present palace was commenced from the designs of Nash, and the garden surroundings, the scene of so many important gatherings, were laid out anew in the prevailing taste.

LOWTHER HALL, WESTMORLAND.

PLATE 70.

LOWTHER HALL is situated on the right bank of the Lowther river, and this present castle is the third or fourth residence that has been erected on the site. The plan on this plate is taken from Campbell's "Vitruvius Britannicus," but whether the gardens actually existed in the form here depicted it is difficult now to say; the plan, however, is certainly of sufficient interest to warrant reproduction here. In Kip's "Britannia Illustrata" there is a view showing the house with different and more extensive garden surroundings, and the probability is that Campbell's view was a design for the remodelling of only those parts near the house.

The arrangement of forecourts is interesting and somewhat unusual. On either side of the entrance gates, leading into the forecourt, were small lodges, and the ground rose slightly towards the house from this point. A drive encircled the forecourt, and visitors alighted at a terrace in front of the principal entrance, whilst on either side were blocks of stables and other domestic buildings.

From the house a flight of steps led to the grand parterre, arranged in four plots with statuary in each, and beyond, a broad walk led past the bowling-green to the greenhouse, with bosquets on either side. A long canal bounded the garden on one side, and along its entire length was a raised grass terrace with seats at intervals. On one side of the parterre a wood was laid out, with rectangular walks leading to a small enclosure in the centre. Adjoining this wood and overlooked by the house was a small nursery garden. The Hall was burnt down about 1720, and possibly it was in connection with a scheme for rebuilding that these gardens were designed. After the fire the hall remained in a ruinous condition, until 1802, when the existing Gothic castle was commenced from the designs of Sir Robert Smirke.

[1] "A History of the Royal Residences," by W. H. Pyne, 1819.

FORDEL HOUSE, FIFESHIRE.

PLATE 71.

ORDEL is situated on high ground a few miles east of Dumfermline, on the edge of a rocky ravine, at the junction of two streams, with a deep ditch on the third side. The whole area of the plateau on which the castle stands is now a garden, but formerly only the east side was used for this purpose. The garden is of considerable extent, and in the midst stands the old castle, which is still in a good state, and, having from time to time undergone some alteration, is now used as a kind of summer-house. On a panel is the date 1567, and, on a carved bracket above the door, is a painted frame bearing the arms of the Henderson family, who for many generations have been the owners of Fordel. It is now, however, the property of the Countess of Buckinghamshire.

The garden illustrated on Plate 71 occupies an irregular piece of ground, and extends principally east and west of the castle. On the north side is a very elaborate parterre, which is hardly in keeping with its simple surroundings ; to the east of this is a long bowling-lawn, with raised grass terraces on two sides, while close by is a triangular shaped piece of land bordered on one side by a gravel path, and with beds in circles and heart shapes cut out in the grass. On the south side of the bowling-lawn is an oblong plot, with clipped yew trees and flower-beds, whilst round the castle are some massive old trees. South of this plot, is an oblong parterre with circular beds ; the design being formed in box edging nine inches wide, and the points marked with little balls. All the south part of the garden is laid out with curiously shaped beds of circular, oval, square and pear-shaped forms, arranged without much regard for symmetry, though they are none the less picturesque.

From the castle a massive yew hedge, 25 feet high and 11 feet thick, runs north and south, dividing the garden into two parts. The eastern part has been already described ; the western has an oblong parterre, about 170 feet by 50, with circular beds of flowers divided by box edging ; the remaining part of this enclosure, a triangular space, is arranged as a rose garden, with a circular arbour in the centre. Beyond the hew hedge is a small chapel.

STOBHALL, PERTHSHIRE.

PLATE 72.

TOBHALL is a singular group of four separate buildings clustered round a knoll overlooking the left bank of the River Tay, some eight miles from Perth. The principal building forming this group is known as the Dowry House, and the garden illustrated in the view on Plate 72, is situated on the west side of this house, which appears in the background of the drawing. At the rear of the Dowry House other buildings are arranged around two irregularly shaped courtyards. The garden is bounded on the north side by the approach to the house, and on the south is enclosed by a low wall, which on its outer side is of considerable height owing to the fall of the ground. The River Tay curves and winds round the old house, presenting throughout its course for a mile or two on either side of Stobhall, as charming a piece of lowland scenery as may be found in its whole length. In a way it dominates the place both to the eye and ear, as it runs with considerable speed over a rocky and stone strewn channel, and its murmur is never absent from the air.

As an example of picturesque and simple treatment of a small garden space, it would be difficult to find a more pleasing subject than Stobhall. There is but little originality in its plan; a piece of ground oblong in shape, thirty or forty yards wide by about double that in length, divided by narrow grass paths into four plots, containing beds of hardy flowers. Nothing could be more simple, and yet there is a quaint charm about the garden, with its bright flowers and sentinel like trees at regular intervals, that has appealed to no less an artist than Fred Walker, who painted Stobhall as the setting to his lovely water-colour of " The Lady in the Garden." Almost in the centre of the garden, and raised on a mound of grass, is the sundial, consisting of a circular shaft supporting a square block with hollowed sides. In the middle of the shaft is another block with the Drummond Arms and the initials of Earl John Perth, who succeeded to the estate about the year 1612, and is said to have been the builder of the Dowry House. Another sundial here is shown on Plate 117.

BALCASKIE, FIFESHIRE.

PLATES 73, 74, 75.

 ITUATE in the south-eastern parts of the county of Fife, about a mile and a half from the Firth of Forth, Balcaskie lies in the centre of a good, well watered stretch of arable land. It has changed hands more than once since the days of "Thomas de Balcaskie," who lived in the early part of the thirteenth century, and was held between 1665 and 1684 by Sir William Bruce, the royal architect, who completed Holyrood Palace and other well known buildings. It was acquired by the ancestor of the present owner in 1698.

The house is of various periods, but the principal portion, together with the terraced garden, dates from the end of the seventeenth century. Sir Robert Sibbald, in his " History of Fife " (published in 1710), mentions it as " a very pretty new house with all modish conveniences of Terraces, Gardens, Park and Plainting." The gardens have been skilfully adapted to the fall of the ground, as a reference to the plan on Plate 73 and the bird's-eye view on Plate 74 will show.

An avenue of limes and elms leads to the square grass forecourt, which is partly enclosed by the two projecting wings of the house, and partly by a thick yew hedge. The garden is arranged on the south side of the house, in three different levels almost too broad to be called terraces. The upper level is divided into three parts, two of which are sheltered on three sides by yew hedges, which were formerly very large, but in recent years have been cut down to their present size, and are now kept at a height of 5 or 6 feet. One of these three enclosures is laid down in grass; the other two have beds, the shape of which being hardly satisfactory are to be brought more in keeping with the character of the garden. The rose garden on the west side of the house was laid out in the seventies.

The present arrangement of the lower terraces was designed by the late Sir Ralph Anstruther, who found this part of the garden planted as an orchard. It was he who introduced the balustrade in the middle of the upper terrace wall, and built the stone staircases at either end of the terraces. The effect of this is harmonious and thoroughly in keeping with the style of the place, according well with the massive buttresses above referred to with their quaint busts of Roman Emperors. This arrangement of buttresses is not infrequently met with in Scotland and is a good one, as besides supporting the retaining wall, they afford shelter for a series of delightful little flower-beds (see Plate 75). The second level is also divided into three parts, the central one being a bowling-green, slightly sunk from the general level, the other two having parterres of simple design.

There were at one time summer-houses in the east and west corners, similar to those still existing at Hatton House, Midlothian. The third and lower level, marked "orchard" on the plan, is principally devoted to the kitchen garden, and, as is the Scotch fashion, has flowers and shrubs intermingled with the fruit and vegetables; the centre walk leading from the old stone staircase agreeably completes the view from the terrace above.

BALCARRES, FIFESHIRE.

PLATES 76 AND 77.

SPLENDIDLY situated on high ground some three miles from the Firth of Forth, the old garden surrounding the house of Balcarres deservedly ranks amongst the finest in Scotland. The house commands a magnificent view over the Firth, and out to sea as far as the Bass Rock, whilst the city of Edinburgh and the Lammermoor hills complete the view in another direction. For many years Balcarres has been in the possession of the Crawford family, and the original house was built in 1595 by John, Lord Menmuir, who, like his brother, Sir David Lindsay of Edzell, took a keen interest in his gardens. The house has of late years been remodelled, but the garden retains many of its ancient characteristics, and has always been an object of attraction and pride to its owners.

The entrance is on the north-west side of the house where the forecourt is enclosed by an iron railing with stone piers. From the plan given on Plate 77 it will be seen that the gardens are arranged chiefly on three levels, to the south of the house. The garden entrance leads into the east court, which is laid out with a single parterre and several grass plots, and in the centre of the parterre is a delightful little fountain, while around the sides are trees in tubs. The garden is well sheltered by a thick yew hedge on one side, and on the opposite side is a pergola overlooking the tennis lawn.

From the east court a few steps lead to the west court, with its quaint old pedestal sundial cut into many facets, and raised on three octagonal steps, after the manner of most old Scotch dials, but unusual in that it consists of two heads instead of one, each with about twenty little gnomons, whilst the pedestal itself has curious sinkings.

A handsome balustraded terrace overlooks the lower garden, part of which is shown on Plate 76, in a view taken from the flight of steps leading from the east court. The terrace wall is supported by buttresses, between each of which small partitions of box project, forming a series of charming little flower-beds. The lower garden is about fifteen feet below the east court and is laid out with three parterres of box some eighteen inches high. In the central one of these is a circular fountain pond enclosed within thick hedges, and with four conical shaped yews at the two entrances and a broad gravel walk runs parallel to the terrace. On the western side of the terrace is another parterre, having in the centre a beech tree raised on a square grass mound. On the south side of the garden is another broad walk bounded by an old hedge curiously cut into compartments, or bays, and at the east end of this walk is a garden-house. Not far from the house is the beautiful old kitchen garden, with grass walks bordered by a profusion of old-fashioned flowers and some grand old hedges.

BARNCLUITH, LANARKSHIRE.

PLATES 78 AND 79.

IT would be difficult to find a more romantic or picturesque site for a garden than this. The position is one that does not often present itself to the garden designer, and those responsible for the arrangement of the terraces have certainly made the most of their opportunities, for although quite small in extent the garden is of considerable interest. From the plan and section shown on Plate 78 it will be seen that the ground falls precipitously to the river Avon, a distance of nearly one hundred feet, at an angle of about fifty degrees. The garden is arranged to the westward of the house in a series of five terraces, each about one hundred feet long. The lowest, which is of grass, about fifty feet above the river, is nineteen feet broad, and is protected by an open balustrade and a stone wall. At the west end of this terrace is a circular pool with a fountain consisting of a short fluted column bearing a bowl, which is illustrated on the same plate. Near by is a stone-arched seat, and at the opposite end of the terrace, under the shade of a beautiful acacia tree, is the quaint two storey summer-house, with a twisted double stairway leading to the upper storey, from whence a door admits to another terrace on the east side, ornamented with shrubs and a row of clipped yews. This is shown on Plate 79, a view taken from the third terrace.

The second terrace, some fourteen feet above the first, consists of a narrow gravel walk, with a retaining bank of solid masonry behind, reaching nearly to the level of the third terrace, and covered with wall-flowers, ferns and shrubs. It is unprotected by any balustrade, and is approached from the west end of the first terrace by a narrow flight of steps, adjoining which is a second summer-house. At the opposite end of the terrace is an archway, beyond which on the same level, is the house, some two hundred feet away, overlooking the river. Still mounting the steep, by a narrow flight of steps, we reach the third terrace, nine feet broad, consisting of a grass walk, with a border of flowers. At the east end is a wall, and at the west end further steps leading to the fourth terrace, with its retaining wall clustered with flowers, forming a contrast to the neighbouring row of dark clipped yews. This terrace opens on to the flower garden at the east end. Above is the fifth and topmost terrace, from which a narrow pathway leads to the house.

NEWBATTLE ABBEY, EDINBURGH.

PLATE 80.

NEWBATTLE ABBEY is situated within a few miles of Edinburgh, and is surrounded by a magnificent park. The entrance gate, shown on the Plate, forms a monumental approach to an avenue leading to the house. It is of a type met with in several parts of the country, and consists of two square buildings joined by a stone screen, very similar to one at the entrance to Sion Park, Middlesex, the seat of the Duke of Northumberland. The two lodges are about fifty feet apart, and the screen, which is curved on plan, has small rusticated Doric columns, supporting an entablature with lions. In the centre are two massive stone piers, about twenty feet high, bearing handsome vases, ornamented with swags of flowers and fruit. An open balustrade surmounts the two lodges, with obelisks at the angles and vases on the intermediate piers. In the gardens surrounding the house are a pair of monumental sundials, one of which is shown on Plate 118.

KINROSS HOUSE, KINROSS-SHIRE.

PLATES 81 AND 82.

INROSS HOUSE stands close to the shores of Loch Leven, within sight of the island castle for ever associated with the name of Mary, Queen of Scots. The house is encompassed by lawns and thickly wooded parks, so that it lies hidden amidst the surrounding landscape. The whole place, which has not been inhabited since the year 1819, has now a very desolate and ruinous aspect, which is the more to be regretted as the house is of a good Renaissance type, well worthy of preservation. Unfortunately the site is low and very liable to damp; it was originally a marsh and has been under water on several occasions.

In 1675 Sir William Bruce, the well known architect of Holyrood, purchased the estate from the Earl of Montrose, and ten years later began the erection of the house from his own designs. It was roofed in 1690, and in December of that year, he says, "the building is not far from finishing." It is believed to have been built for James, Duke of York, afterwards King James II.

Sir William Bruce was a son of Robert Bruce of Blairhall, and took an active interest in the restoration of Charles II., in consequence of which promotion followed rapidly, and he was knighted in 1668, and in 1681 made King's Surveyor. He occupied Kinross House until the year 1700, when he gave it up to his son.

On the walls of the office courts are two sundials, cut in 1686 by John Hamilton, mason. One James Anderson, a local mason, was responsible for some of the garden architecture, and "hewed the basses for the diall," erected the gate pillars, and the summer-houses in the garden. Tobias Buchop, an architect and builder of Alloa, erected a "great gate of curious architecture" at the principal entrance from the town, from a timber model delivered to him by Sir William Bruce in 1684. Of this gate only two pillars remain, and these are somewhat fragmentary.

The house and grounds occupy an oblong plot of land, being exactly a double square, 650 feet broad by 1,300 feet long. This space is almost divided in two parts by the house and wing walls separating the garden from the entrance forecourt. The principal entrance is on the west side, up the remains of an old avenue, shown in the plan on Plate 81. On either side of the entrance, or western front of the house, are small enclosed gardens with high walls, surmounted by a balustrade, and close to the house are the quaint little pavilions, with their ogee roofs, as shown on Plate 82. They have entrances from the forecourt, and overlook the small enclosed gardens at the back. The angles of the wall are marked by massive stone piers supporting vases, and the globe sundials before alluded to. The pleasure garden was on the east side of the house, overlooked by the two summer-houses built by Anderson, which, though roofless, are still standing. At the points marked c c on the plan are fine stone piers, about sixty feet apart, surmounted by handsome vases, and in the eastern boundary wall are the curious gates, shown on Plate 82, known as the "Fish Gates," with rusticated piers, fifteen feet high and spaced twenty feet apart, surmounted by boys riding on dolphins.

DRUMLANRIG CASTLE, DUMFRIESSHIRE.

PLATES 83 AND 84.

MAGNIFICENTLY situated, on a considerable elevation, Drumlanrig Castle commands a fine view down the valley of the Nith, and forms a conspicuous object in the landscape for miles round. The present castle, now one of the seats of the Duke of Buccleuch, dates from between the years 1675 and 1689, and occupies the site of an ancient castellated mansion, the home of the Douglas family as early as the fourteenth century. It was built by William, first Duke of Queensberry, who was, however, so impoverished by the cost that he was never able to enjoy the fruits of his enormous outlay. He also laid out the park and grounds. An interesting account, written by the Rev. Peter Rae,[1] describes the gardens as they appeared in the early part of eighteenth century; he says: "The gardens of Drumlanrig are very beautiful and the rather because of their variety. . . . The regular gardens, with one designed to be made on the back of the plumery, the outer court before the house, and the house itself, make nine square plots of land, whereof the kitchen garden, the court before the house, and the garden designed make three; My lady Duchess' garden, the house, and the last parterre and the flower garden make other three, that is nine in all, and the castle is in the centre. Only as to the last three, the westernmost is always more than a storey above the rest. As to those called irregular gardens, because the course of the Parkburn would not allow them to be square, they are very pretty and well suited to one another. They call one part thereof Virginia, the other Barbadoes; then goes a large gravel walk, down betwixt them from the south parterre to the cascade." This cascade is no longer in existence, but not so very many years ago the remains of it, with a leaden figure of a man who was known as "Jock and the Horn," could still be seen. The gardens were still in their original form in 1772, when Pennant described them in his "Journey through Scotland." From the plan on Plate 83, which shows the present arrangement of the gardens, it will be seen that in general shape they still adhere to the nine plots described by Rae, but that one on the north-east corner has been thrown into the park.

The principal approach is up a long, straight avenue, consisting of a double row of lofty limes, to the entrance courtyard on the north front of the Castle, with its handsome double stairway. The court-yard is enclosed by low buildings on either side, and the stables are arranged to the right on entering. Two stone stairways lead from the south front of the Castle to open terraces extending round three sides, and commanding a glorious outlook over the whole of the gardens. From these terraces grass banks slope away on either side to square plots laid out as parterres, and, in front, to the long terrace which extends right across the garden, a distance of nearly two hundred and fifty yards. On the same level, east and west of the Castle, are large square parterres; that on the east side having beds arranged concentrically, while that on the west has rectangular beds planned within a circle. Beyond this parterre, and adjoining the stables, is the rose garden, sheltered by high hedges. At the east end of the long terrace, a broad flight of steps descends to the lower part of the garden, which is on three different levels. Of these, the upper or western one is used as a plantation of trees, the central one is a square parterre, of which a good idea may be gathered from the view shown on Plate 84, and the lower level is another parterre of grass and flower-beds. The garden is divided from the woodland and park on the south by a large semicircle of grass plots and flower-beds, with trees placed at intervals.

[1] Printed in "The History of Drumlanrig Castle," by C. T. Ramage.

COWANE'S HOSPITAL, STIRLING.

PLATE 85.

THE old hospital of the guild brethren at Stirling was founded by one John Cowane in 1633. It is splendidly situated on the top of the rock of Stirling, under the shadow of the old Greyfriars Church, and commanding magnificent views of the winding Forth and the hills of the Trossachs. It is a good example of a simple stone building of the period, with crow-stepped gables, preserving many of the characteristics of Scottish architecture with some infusion of Renaissance detail. The design consists of a main block with wings projecting on either side, and enclosing a small forecourt. The statue of the founder stands in a niche on the building, and over the entrance door is a tablet with the following quaint inscription: "This hospital was erected and largely provyded by John Cowane, Deane of Gild, for the Intertainement of Decayed Gild Breither. John Cowane 1639. I was hungrie and ye gave me meate: I was thirstie and ye gave me drinke: I was a stranger and ye tooke me in: I was sicke and ye visited me."

Instead of the twelve decayed brethren who, according to the wish of the pious founder, were to be maintained in the Hospital, yearly allowances are now made to a much larger number, and the building has been converted into a Guildhall for the meetings of the guildry.

Plate 85 is a plan of the building and its garden surroundings, reproduced by the kind permission of Mr. J. J. Joass, from which it will be seen that the building occupies the northern part of the triangular site, and that the forecourt is on the north side. Along the east or garden front of the building is a stone terrace overlooking the bowling-green, which occupies the greater part of the garden. There is a balustrade with balusters spaced widely apart, and a double flight of steps leading to the green. The awkward corner at the south-east of the site was formed into a garden after the Dutch manner, with flower-beds bordered by box, and intersected by narrow paths curving about in an aimless fashion. In the centre of the south side of the bowling-green is a sundial of rather unusual design, with a pedestal resting on two octagonal stone steps. A drawing of this is shown on the plate.

EARLSHALL, FIFESHIRE.

FOR seventy years previous to 1891 Earlshall existed only as a picturesque ruin, set within its garden wall, in the midst of the remains of an ancient forest, nearly a mile south-east of the village of Leuchars. The woods of Earlshall, though of comparatively recent date, probably occupy the places of their ancient predecessors, and the course of the old avenue, leading to the house, may yet be traced by following the lines of ancient beech trees that preserve its symmetrical form.

The earliest mention of Earlshall is to be found in a charter of James IV., dated 1497, bestowing anew on Sir Alexander Bruce the lands of Earlshall, but the present building owes its origin to Sir William Bruce, and was finished in the beginning of the seventeenth century. All through the troublous times that followed, Earlshall was the scene of many exciting incidents, and continued in the possession of the Bruce family until 1825, when it was sold by Sir Robert Bruce Henderson to Lieut.-Col. Samuel Long, a grandson of the seventh Earl of Lauderdale. He, however, never resided in it, and the property passed to his daughter. In 1891 it was rapidly going to absolute decay, when it was purchased by the present owner, Mr. R. W. Mackenzie.

Fortunately, much of interest still remained, and the fact of its having been so long abandoned saved it from the fate of many other fine old Scottish houses that suffered from injudicious restoration. Assisted by Mr. R. W. Lorimer, the owner took up the work of restoring the old house, in the true sense of the word, preserving as much as possible of the original and so handing down to us a fair specimen of sixteenth century Scottish architecture, with its main features practically intact and as originally planned.

Of the old garden only the wall remained, enclosing an oblong plot about three acres in extent, with, unfortunately, not a tree or shrub remaining. The fruit trees of the little orchard had first been removed, as in the untenanted condition of the place they had proved too great an attraction to the youth of the neighbourhood. Later the hedges and alleys were ruthlessly uprooted in order that the land might be more readily cultivated with the plough. But partly by the help of an old plan the gardens were restored to their original condition, and to-day have all the old-world appearance of a seventeenth century Scottish garden, forming a delightfully quaint setting to the old house.

A short drive leads from the gatehouse to a grass ride along the western boundary wall of the house. The gardens are divided into several small enclosures by hedges. To the north is a fruit and vegetable garden with grass walks in the centre ; opposite the house is a lawn with clipped yew trees dotted about in groups of five, while in the centre of the boundary-wall is the garden gate shown on Plate 121, with the appropriate inscription, " Here shall ye see no enemy but winter and rough weather."

Adjoining the lawn on the south side, is an alley with a grass walk and little paved paths. On either side are ten alcoves divided by hedges, and in the centre are four topiary arches. A bowling-green occupies the south-east corner of the garden, and on the opposite side is the orchard, intersected by grass paths and with a little mound in the centre, and a pedestal from which a cupid is making ready to let fly his arrow.

DRUMMOND CASTLE, PERTHSHIRE.

PLATES 88 AND 89.

RUMMOND CASTLE is built upon a rocky eminence, about three miles from Crieff, in an extensive and beautiful park commanding a fine view over Strathearn. The property was purchased by Sir John Drummond in 1487, and the original castle was built on the highest point of the rock a few years later. On the removal of the family from Stobhall, his descendants, as Earls of Perth, possessed it for some two hundred and fifty years, after which it passed to the Earl of Ancaster, the present owner. The wing adjoining the old keep was erected in the early part of the seventeenth century, and some few years later the castle is said to have suffered greatly at the hands of Cromwell. In 1715 it was greatly strengthened, and garrisoned by royal troops, and in 1745 the Dowager Duchess of Perth caused the walls to be levelled to the ground. Buildings more adapted to modern requirements have since been erected to the east of the old castle.

A drive of more than a mile in length leads through the park to the Castle, the approach being on the north side, through an archway leading to the outer court, and thence through another archway under the older buildings to the inner court, one side of which is occupied by the newer buildings. On the eastern side of the house is a small garden having an octagonal fountain basin in the centre. Along the south side the garden is bounded by a series of large yews, cut into the form of huge pyramids.

From the upper terrace, adjoining the house, a double flight of steps leads to the next terrace, a few feet below, at the eastern end of which a few steps lead to the small garden already referred to. Descending another stairway, one arrives at the middle terrace walk, which, descending to right and left, encompasses the entire garden, a distance of nearly half a mile. In the centre of this terrace is the grand stairway leading to the lower garden, from the foot of which a broad grass walk extends for three hundred yards, having a slight ascent towards either end. The lower garden occupies an oblong space 1,000 feet long by 300 wide, which is crossed by diagonal grass walks. Here the parterres have small beeches and shrubs instead of flowers. A broad gravel walk leads from the foot of the grand stairway, across the garden to a fountain.

In the centre of the garden is the quaint sundial, consisting of an obelisk supported on a square shaft. It was erected in 1630 by the second Earl of Perth and was made by one John Mylne. The dial contains five stanzas of rhyme, in which the hours, as sisters, descant on the flight of time.

GARDEN-HOUSES.

PLATES 90, 91 AND 92.

THE Garden-house was the most important of all the accessories of a formal garden, from the early Tudor days to the middle of the eighteenth century, when it became the fashion to adorn gardens with Greek temples or Chinese pagodas, and the substantial and comfortable garden-house gave place to rustic wooden arbours overgrown with vegetation, which were far from being comfortable places from which to survey the beauty of the surroundings.

A very favourite position for a garden-house was at the end of a long walk enclosing a vista, or overlooking a bowling-green, and many such examples might be noted. At Wilton House, terminating a long walk through the Italian garden, is a stone summer-house of two stories, dating from the seventeenth century. At Haddon Hall are the remains of a garden-house which overlooked the bowling-green. This had an outside staircase by which spectators ascended to the flat roof to watch the progress of the game or admire the scenery. Such buildings were generally fitted up with panelled woodwork round the walls, window seats, and often with a fireplace. At Heslington is a two-storey building with an external stone staircase leading to the first floor, whilst below is an open arbour overlooking the bowling-green.

In some cases garden-houses were used as retreats, but instances are not often to be found. The one at Severn End, illustrated on Plate 91, was erected in 1661 by Judge Lechmere, and here he was wont to retire, perhaps for several days together, for quiet contemplation amongst the fragrant flowers. The example from Charlton House, on the same plate, is placed on a grass mound overlooking the road, and has a basement opening on to a lower level. For many years it was used as a guard-house and is now converted into a museum; it has a curved roof and is surmounted by a wooden cresting.

Another favourite position for garden-houses was at the two angles of a court, like those at Montacute, shown on Plates 2 and 3, which are of two storeys, and are perhaps the finest of their kind existing. Similar ones, but in a ruinous condition, are to be seen at Hatton House, a few miles from Edinburgh. In this case there is a fall in the ground and the garden-house was raised, and the lower part used as a tool house, the structure being conveniently near the kitchen garden. Those at Kinross House, illustrated on Plate 82, are also placed in a somewhat similar position, and with their quaint roofs lend a picturesque air to the forecourt.

On Plate 90 are two good examples from the neighbourhood of Bath, which in all probability were designed by the same architect. The one from Belcombe Brook is placed on a slight mound, surrounded by water and shelters a lead figure of Perseus which is shown on this plate. The octagonal summer-house from Iford Manor has a series of well proportioned Ionic pilasters with carved caps. At present it is roofed with thatch, while the interior is panelled, and has a fireplace on one side.

The gazeebo was another variety of summer-house. The origin of the term is obscure, but it was applied to those garden-houses which were built in a corner position overlooking the garden on one side and the road on the other. A good example from Westbury Court is shown on Plate 55, and another from Beckington on Plate 92. The latter is a small square brick building with stone quoins and a handsome pedimented doorway. At the apex of the stone slate roof is a small finial. The other example, on the same plate, is from the little Dutch garden at Nun Moncton near York. It is placed at the end of a walk lined with lead figures (some of which are shown on Plate 108), and clipped yews, and its double-domed roof is richly covered with lichen. The window on one side overlooks the trim bowling-green, and from that on the other a picturesque corner of the River Ouse.

Although hardly coming under the designation of summer-houses, the fishing lodge and banqueting house may here be mentioned. These were to be met with in many gardens ; one at Beckett Park near Shrivenham, which was designed by Inigo Jones, is charmingly situated overlooking a lake, with broad eaves overshadowing a small balcony. At Dovedale in Derbyshire is a similar building, though some-what later in date, known as Isaac Walton's fishing-house.

Besides the garden-houses, arbours were frequently formed of clipped yew. Such a one still exists at Canons Ashby, probably dating from the end of the seventeenth century. The example at Levens Hall known as " The Judge's Wig " is a little later.

DOVECOTES AND PIGEON-HOUSES.

PLATES 93, 93*.

DOVECOTE or pigeon-house, also designated a columbary, was formerly considered to be one of the most necessary of the numerous small buildings surrounding a country house, and although, strictly speaking, it was considered as outside the range of garden buildings, and more appertaining to the farmyard, yet occasionally it was to be found within the garden walls, and was then frequently made a most picturesque and appropriate addition, as is well shown on Plate 93, where an example at Shipton Court, with its picturesque little lantern and wrought-iron weather vane, is illustrated. At Basing House an octagonal dovecote still exists in an angle of the old garden wall that so long withstood the siege of Cromwell's troops.

There was in those days hardly a manor-house without its columbary or pigeon-house, and pigeons formed a very important source of food supply. The right to keep them was strictly confined to the lords of manors, and any who infringed these rights were severely dealt with.

Of the many very good examples still to be met with, the majority are circular on plan, with a revolving ladder attached to a central post in the interior, as, for example, those at Rousham, Oxfordshire ; Hurley ; Severn End; and the two examples shown on Plate 93* from Old Sufton and Richard's Castle, the latter having three ventilating louvres and gables.   They were also frequently octagonal, like the example at Much March on the same plate, and sometimes square, like those shown on Plate 93.   The variations in shape depended on the material used, and the internal construction. Those shown on Plate 93 from Dormstone and Oddingley are square, a form better suited to half-timber construction ; that from Chastleton Manor, on the same plate, is in a park adjoining the house, and is a well proportioned stone building with a graceful little leaden cupola.   The dovecote occupies the first floor, and access is gained by a ladder and trap-door ; the lower part is a shelter for cattle.   The example from Buttas has some very good carving ; the barge-boards and sill being ornamented with a running pattern in which figures alternate with foliage.   It would be quite an acquisition to any garden. Erected in 1632, it is said to have been originally used as a falconry.

As a rule dovecotes were windowless, and no ivy or other creeping plants were allowed to grow upon them.   An old example at Severn End still retains its massive revolving central post, and a ladder suspended from an arm attached to the post enables any one of the myriad nesting-places to be easily reached.

TERRACES.

PLATES 94, 95, 96, 97, 98, 99, 100 AND 101.

N Tudor gardens terraces were usually placed in a position next to the enclosing walls of a garden, overlooking the surrounding country and forming a convenient point of vantage from which to view the arrangement of the garden plots.   One such may be seen in the Privy garden at Hampton Court, where the terrace rises to within a few feet of the top of the wall.   At Severn End there is a similar terrace overlooking the bowling-green, and an old engraving of Drayton Hall shows a grass terrace down one side of the garden, raised against a wall and overlooking the park beyond. Sometimes, as at Montacute, terraces completely surrounded the garden plot, but the position in which they are most generally placed is immediately in front of the house, and overlooking the flower garden.

The terrace at Claverton Manor House, shown on Plate 94, was placed at the entrance front of the house, which was erected in 1628 by the Basset family.   The house was surrounded by gardens which remained until the beginning of last century, and were only destroyed when the house was pulled down in 1820 ; but fortunately the terrace which formed one side of the forecourt was allowed to remain.   The Manor house was placed on the side of a hill, and entered from the road through the forecourt, which was enclosed on two sides by lofty walls, the side next the road having a pierced stone balustrade of similar design to that of the terrace, also a pair of handsome gatepiers which are shown on the same plate. Owing to the fall of the land, the terrace was arranged on two levels.   A broad flight of steps led from the forecourt to the the first level, which was 164 feet long and 44 feet broad, and was laid out as a garden.   From here another flight led to the terrace on a level with the house.

On Plates 96, 97 and 98, are shown plans and details of the terraces at Kingston House, Bradford-on-Avon, and at Bramshill, Hampshire.   The former is skilfully arranged on the garden front of the house.   It has four bays and is ornamented with stone vases over each of the piers.   In the centre a flight of fourteen steps leads to a grass platform, and a gravel path runs to right and left, descending on either side to the lower garden by flights of steps. The balustrade is formed of stone panels 3½ inches thick, pierced with open work of alternate lozenges and ovals, with engaged balusters to the piers. The house is a few years later in date than Claverton, but a similarity is noticeable between the masonry detail of the two places, which are only a few miles apart.

The terrace at Bramshill is on the east side of the house, overlooking the park. It is 135 feet long by 25 feet broad. Down the centre is a narrow strip of turf with stone flags on either side, used as a bowling-lawn. At either end of the terrace is an arbour, as shown on Plate 97. The elevation on Plate 98 shows the terrace as it was originally arranged, with the balustrade along the entire front, but now only fragments remain. At either end steps lead to the level of what was formerly the garden.

Plate 95 is a view of the terrace at Brympton Manor House in Somersetshire. It is about 30 feet broad, and 5 feet above the level of the garden in front of the house, and is said to have been built early in the last century, but the house itself is considerably older. There is a broad central flight of steps, and at either end two smaller flights are arranged at right angles to the terrace. The piers support urns of different designs, with the exception of one which carries a sun-dial with gnomons on the sides of a square die.

The arrangement of the steps at Clifton Hall, Nottingham, is rather an unusual one. On plan it takes the form of a hexagon, which is intersected by the balustrade. The piers are ornamented with statuary, those in the centre supporting cupids. A similar arrangement of stairway is to be seen at Drayton Hall, Northamptonshire, though here the steps are circular, and altogether on a smaller scale. Plate 100 shows an arrangement of steps in three flights leading from a terrace; at Ven House, Somersetshire. The piers to the balustrade are surmounted with handsome stone vases, and the stairway, with its old mossy stonework, forms quite a beautiful picture, overshadowed by the spreading branches of a grand old walnut tree.

On Plate 101 is a view of a terrace at Hadsoe, with a fountain at the foot, and stairways at either side; the whole forming a pleasing architectural composition, surrounded as it is with very beautiful foliage and dark yew hedges.

GATEPIERS.

PLATES 101, 102 AND 103.

IN nearly all old garden schemes, much attention was lavished on the gateways giving admittance to the various enclosures, and often, when every other vestige of the garden has disappeared, these remain, solitary survivors of the many details of all they enclosed and which surrounded them. Of the many different types of gatepier the most familiar is the square pier of brick or stone surmounted by a stone ball, either with or without a necking. Such a one is shown on Plate 101, from Bulwick Hall, Northamptonshire, and on Plate 102 from Penshurst. This latter is of brick, 12 feet high to the top of the cornice, with piers on either side. It is placed in an old wall, and forms the entrance from the park to the stables. The gateway from Iford Manor illustrated on Plate 102 has stone piers, 10 feet 9 inches apart, supporting heraldic lions, the crest of the Hungerford family, who formerly owned the house. The piers are 2 feet square, and 9 feet 9 inches to the top of the cornice. The piers from the Botanic Garden at Oxford are in the walls surrounding the

old garden, which was founded in 1632 for the advancement of the study of botany. They are nearly eighteen feet high to the top of the cornice, and each supports a massive stone vase with a bouquet of fruit and flowers. The well-known gateway from St. John's College, Cambridge, is an excellent example situate at one end of the picturesque old bridge which gives entrance to the college. The piers are of stone, delightfully toned by age, and they support heraldic beasts, with further armorial bearings carved below. The iron gates themselves are very fine. The remaining example on Plate 102 is from Belton House in Lincolnshire, and is situate at the end of the avenue on the west side of the house. It is 13 feet 6 inches in height. Between the cornice and necking, and immediately below, are small flutings in the stone.

Plate 103 shows a gateway in the gardens of Stoneleigh Abbey, Warwickshire, with a magnificent pair of wrought-iron gates ; the piers support leaden vases which, owing to the action of the sun, have almost lost their original shape. The other example on this plate is from Sydenham in Devonshire, and leads to the porch on the south side of the house ; a charming vista is obtained through the old gate across the forecourt.

Other examples of gateways and piers may be found on Plate 7, where the interesting series from Canons Ashby are illustrated, and on Plates 36 and 37 which give a view and scale drawings of the "Flower Pot" and other gates from Hampton Court, also on Plate 94, which shows one of the piers at the entrance to the forecourt of old Claverton Manor, and Plate 120, where the small piers in the balustrade at Brympton are illustrated.

KNOTS AND PARTERRES.

PLATES 104, 105.

IN the laying out of a garden much may depend upon the shape and disposition of beds in a parterre, or the arrangements of paths in a grass-plot, and the series of designs shown on Plates 104 and 105, which are taken from a quaint old book preserved amongst the Harleian Manuscripts, at the British Museum, will no doubt prove of service to those in search of suggestion for such forms. The book from which they are drawn evidently formed part of the stock in trade of some eighteenth-century garden designer, and the many excellent designs it contains— there are more than a hundred—were obviously intended to be used mostly for grass-plots, although they are equally applicable to flower-beds.[1] The designs are of quite a simple form, and are all drawn to fit into a square shape, but they can be easily altered to fill oblong, octagonal, or circular spaces. As suggestions for rose gardens, or for laying out any small enclosed space, with perhaps a sundial or fountain in the centre, they are particularly suitable.

Knots were the chief adornment of the Tudor gardens, such as those which existed at Hampton Court, and among the quaint pictures in David Loggan's views of Oxford and Cambridge[2] many a charming design may be found. These early forms are invariably the best, but their simple character had later on, when the French influence of Le Notre and other gardeners became predominant, to give

[1] It is interesting to note that nearly all the designs correspond with a Dutch work on gardening published in Amsterdam in 1710, entitled " Twee hundert modellen van Bloem-perken."

[2] David Loggan, " Oxonia Illustrata," Oxford, 1675, folio ; " Cantabrigia Illustrata," Cambridge, 1688, folio.

place to more elaborate parterres of intricate design, having paths of various coloured sands, and more resembling patterns in lace than a flower garden. This meretricious excess in the treatment of the parterre had much to do with the revulsion of taste which culminated in the introduction of the landscape garden.

TOPIARY WORK.

PLATE 106.

THE use of topiary work was first introduced into this country in the early years of the Tudor period, and soon growing into favour it became a conspicuous feature in gardens during the next two centuries. Although the system of cutting trees and shrubs eventually became very much abused, it serves to restrain the undue spreading and the amount of shadow caused by thick and heavy foliage, and there is no doubt that, rightly used, it invests a garden with attractive quaintness. Of the various trees most useful for topiary work, the yew is perhaps the best, and its rich green tones and soft velvety texture cannot be surpassed. Most of the examples left to us are of yew, partly owing to the fact that it is a slow grower, and, once having attained maturity survives for many years. Privet, box, and rosemary were also used, but examples of topiary work in these are not frequently to be met with. The peacock was the form into which the trees were most commonly cut, and has always been a favourite device. At Bedfont in Middlesex two gigantic peacocks overshadow the church porch, and in a small garden at Haddon a similar peacock sits sedately among the flowers. Sometimes biblical subjects were represented, such as the well-known example at Packwood, where the Sermon on the Mount is represented in yew, also the small circular garden at Chastleton shown on Plate 23.

On Plate 106 is given a variety of shapes, several of which are taken from Levens Hall, where certainly the most varied collection is to be found. The view on Plate 46 gives a good idea of the quaint aspect of this garden. Other examples are from Montacute and Canons Ashby, where the green court contains eight yews cut into the form of pyramids resting upon half globes. Two are given from the garden at Heslington (illustrated on Plate 48). Another shows the old hedge at Cleeve Prior near Evesham, known as the Twelve Apostles, which forms the entrance to the Manor-house from the road. Other examples are taken from the more modern gardens of Elvaston in Derbyshire, and Earlshall in Fifeshire, the former containing a large variety of pyramids, columns and other creations in yew.

GARDEN LEADWORK.

PLATES 107 TO 112.

AMONGST the many delightful accessories that go to make up the charm of a garden, few are more satisfactory than the figures, vases, and other objects formed of lead. The adaptability of this material and the delicacy of its colouring make it eminently suitable for such objects, and one can readily recall many instances of the fine effect produced by the soft silvery gray colour of a leaden figure against the rich green background of an old yew hedge.

Throughout the eighteenth century leadwork was very much used, both in the large gardens of the nobility and in those of the small manor-houses, and there is no lack of good examples still to be found in excellent preservation, showing both how extensive its use in gardens has been and its lasting value in this climate. Whereas a terra-cotta or stone vase is liable to be much damaged by frost, and marble is for obvious reasons unsuitable for the garden, a leaden vase or statue may easily last for a couple of centuries, retaining its original form and taking a more charming colour as it increases in age.

The making of leaden statues was undertaken largely in England during the latter part of the seventeenth and all through the eighteenth centuries, under such workers as Cheere, (whose brother, Sir Henry Cheere, was responsible for the figure of Flora at Longford Castle) and the Dutch modeller Van Nost, who towards the middle of the eighteenth century established himself in St. Martin's Lane, and seems to have had a flourishing business. His stock principally consisted of classic subjects; Flora and Bacchus, Venus, Juno, Neptune, Minerva, were all represented, as well as little leaden cupids, such as those at Wilton, known as " Lady Pembroke's boys," some of which are shown on Plate 19, and the very perfect series of groups at Melbourne Hall, known to have been supplied by Van Nost. Portrait statues in lead also are frequently to be met with, as, for example, those at Wilton and at Wrest, and the William III. in the courtyard at Houghton Tower, Lancashire. Of statuary groups in lead, perhaps the finest example is the Cain and Abel at Chiswick House, by Sheemaker, of which a replica exists at Drayton, Northamptonshire. The leaden slave, usually supporting a sundial or vase, seems to have been a very favourite subject, and is frequently to be met with. Copies exist at Enfield Old Park, Middlesex (see Plate 115); Melbourne, Derbyshire; Arley, Cheshire; Guy's Cliff, Warwickshire; and Hampton Court, Herefordshire. These statues are sometimes picked out in colours or painted to imitate stone, and where this is the case, in order to carry the imitation even further, sand was frequently thrown on the wet paint, an attempt at deception quite unworthy of the artists who had executed the statues. Lead fountains, such as the Flying Mercury at Sion House, and the little Triton at Melbourne Hall, are sometimes met with.

Plates 107 and 108 show various examples of lead figures, including a pair from the very fine collection of garden leadwork at Enfield Old Park, which date from the middle of the eighteenth century and remind us of the little figures in porcelain of the same period. They are four feet in height, and are probably the work of an English artist. A similar pair from a garden at Shrewsbury are now in the Victoria and Albert Museum. In the Enfield collection there is a small Harlequin, a replica of which exists at Inwood, Dorsetshire.

The cupid riding on a swan, and the figure of Bacchus, both shown on Plate 107, are from the garden laid out by William Kent at Rousham in Oxfordshire. The rustic figure of a shepherd playing on his flute, with one of his sheep lying at his feet, was placed in the garden at Canons Ashby by Sir Edward Dryden between 1708 and 1717. It is of a similar type to the charming series of rustic figures, shown on Plate 108, from Nun Moncton, an old Dutch house at the junction of the Rivers Ouse and Nidd, not many miles from York. On Plate 90 is shown a very fine lead figure from Belcombe Brook, Bradford-on-Avon.

Several examples of lead vases are shown on Plates 109 and 110. No. 1, on the latter, is one of a pair at Iford Manor, Somersetshire, and although of quite a different shape, it has a bas-relief figure subject, similar to the example from Penshurst (No. 4) and that at Drayton House, Northants (where one of the finest collections in England is to be found), which is shown with three other examples from the same garden on Plate 30; and these, no doubt, share a common origin. Of the further examples on Plate 110, No. 2, without handles, has well modelled masks round the drum. No. 3 is one of a pair from Hampton Court Palace; they are 2 feet 3 inches high, and the little sitting figures are charmingly posed. No. 4, from Penshurst, came originally from old Leicester House, London. On Plate 109 are shown two examples of leaden vases from Wilton House, of rather an unusual type, and two from Chiswick House, Middlesex, of pleasing form.

The leaden cisterns, of which many good examples exist, show a particularly appropriate use of this metal. These cisterns were used to catch water for use in the garden, and were so ornamented as to form pleasant features, whether in large grounds or the smallest of gardens. The octagonal cistern from Charlton in Kent has nicely modelled shields, heads of angels, and other devices within ribbed borders. The examples from Enfield shown on Plate 112 are in very good preservation; one dated 1791 has ribbed patterns and small figures emblematical of the seasons; another is adorned with wreaths, and has ribbed panels formed of interlacing squares and semicircles; a third, dated 1769, with the initials F. S. has quaint floral decorations, with a fish and a crown, set within a ribbed panel.

Mr. Lethaby, in his interesting book on leadwork, speaking of these cisterns, says: "The ribs, with the stock enrichments in new combinations, the date and initials, were attached to a wood panel the size of the cistern front; this was moulded in the sand, and the casting made of good substance; stout strips were soldered across the inside as ties."

STONE VASES.

PLATES 113 AND 114.

I N almost every formal garden stone vases are to be found, and it would not be difficult to make a large collection of examples, differing in design, from all parts of the country. On Plates 113 and 114 several suggestive types are shown. The four handsome examples from Sion House, Isleworth, the seat of the Duke of Northumberland, are part of a series of ten vases arranged in front of the large conservatory, on a raised terrace overlooking the beautiful flower garden. They are of Portland stone, very richly undercut, and surmounted by bouquet of flowers. They are said to have been the work of Grinling Gibbons, and although direct evidence of this is not forthcoming, it is certain they must have been executed by a master possessing no less skill than that great carver.

The four subjects illustrated on Plate 114 show different types of pedestal vases. No. 1 is from Stoneleigh Abbey in Warwickshire, and stands amidst the stately gardens laid out in 1720, overlooking a classic terrace on the banks of the River Avon. It stands on a square pedestal about three feet in height. The second example is from the garden at Drummond Castle, more fully illustrated on Plates 88 and 89; the square form is very unusual and the top is supported by caryatid figures at either angle, between which are oval spaces; the square base is perhaps hardly satisfactory, and apparently does not form part of the original composition.

The vase from Wrest Park stands alone, in a grassy glade, among the French groves laid out about the middle of the eighteenth century. It is a well proportioned example about eight feet in height, including the pedestal, and is ornamented with swags of fruit and flowers and with two masks. The remaining example from Melbourne Hall dates from the middle of the eighteenth century. In this case the vase is somewhat simpler in form, and the circular pedestal which supports it has received more attention than the vase itself, being richly ornamented with amorini and garlands of flowers.

SUNDIALS.

EVER since the sixteenth century sundials have occupied a foremost place among the ornamental adjuncts of a garden. Although, of course, they were originally regarded entirely from the utilitarian standpoint, it was not long before it became the custom to devote considerable attention and skill to their design, and they have frequently survived in their position when all other trace of the garden has disappeared. In these days it cannot be claimed that a sundial is of much practical use, yet everybody has a tender regard for them, and no formal garden would be considered complete without one. Their mottoes often serve to suggest the constant flow of time, or to inculcate a spirit of quietude and meditation. From the point of view of the garden designer, a sundial is often a very valuable accessory, as it may mark some prominent point, perhaps as the centre of a rose garden, or, when placed on a terrace, to lead the eye along some pleasant vista. A sundial may be made to excite the spirit of curiosity, and like one that formerly existed at Whitehall, to plentifully sprinkle the onlooking stranger with water; a playful trick to which our ancestors were somewhat addicted.

"What a dead thing is a clock," wrote Charles Lamb, "compared with the simple altar-like structure and silent heart language of the old dial. It stood as the garden-god of Christian gardens. Why is it almost everywhere banished? If its business use be superseded by more elaborate inventions, its moral uses, its beauty, might have pleaded for its continuance." To-day its charm has been recognized, and it is reinstated amidst its most fitting setting, the garden.

The subject of sundials has already called forth much research and labour from such authorities as Mrs. Gatty, and Messrs. MacGibbon and Ross. In Mrs. Gatty's work[1] is to be found an extensive collection of mottoes, but the dials illustrated do not appear to have been selected with due regard to their artistic beauty. The Scottish examples illustrated by Messrs. MacGibbon and Ross,[2] although always quaint, are also frequently lacking in beauty.

On Plates 115 and 116 are illustrated some examples of English sundials. That from Northenden, Cheshire, which is in the churchyard, consists of a baluster-like shaft, with spiral flutings in the lower part. That from Chiswick House, which stands in a grass walk not far from the house, has its base ornamented with well modelled acanthus leaves. The leaden figure of a negro slave is well known both as a support for sundials and for vases. The example here illustrated is from Enfield Old Park, Middlesex, but similar figures exist at Arley Hall, Cheshire; the gardens of the Inner Temple, and elsewhere. One is also shown in the centre of the kitchen garden in Kip's view of Sandywell. Another dial from Enfield, shown on Plate 115, is of about the period of Grinling Gibbons, and consists of a fluted baluster raised on two circular steps, and ornamented with beautifully modelled Cupid heads, supporting the table. The remaining example is from the churchyard at Prestbury in Cheshire.

Two of the dials illustrated on Plate 116 are from the gardens at Wrest, in Bedfordshire, and both are of about the same date, namely, the middle of the eighteenth century. One contains an elaborate monogram both on the gnomon and on the base: the other has a gnomon of much simpler form, and the base is ornamented with acanthus leaves and delicate little swags of flowers and fruit. It is octagonal and supports a table of rather large dimensions. The example from Belton House in

[1] "The Book of Sundials," Fourth Edition, 1900.
[2] "The Castellated and Domestic Architecture of Scotland," 1887-1892.

Lincolnshire, is particularly good; the dial is supported by a figure of Father Time assisted by a cupid. It stands in the long walk on the north side of the house, and its date is about the middle of the eighteenth century. The one from Kew stands on a flight of square stone steps in front of the old red-brick Palace, and an exact replica of it exists on the south front of Hampton Court Palace. The remaining example on this plate now stands, forgotten and gnomonless, in the garden at Wilton House, a forlorn survivor of De Caux's famous gardens of the early seventeenth century.

On Plates 117 and 118 are some Scottish examples, mostly drawn from photographs kindly lent for the purpose by Mr. Thomas Ross. That from Pitmedden is believed to have been made about the year 1675. Its total height from the ground is 8 feet 9 inches, and the width at the base is 4 feet 11 inches. The elaborate dial from Woodhouselee consists of a broad spreading base from which rises a twisted shaft, ornamented with the rose and thistle. The example from Duthie Park, Aberdeen, is dated 1703, and, like most Scottish dials, has several gnomons; the pedestal supports a square block, above which is a globe with radiating incised lines. The other example on Plate 117 is from the little old world garden at Stobhall. It has a particularly charming and graceful pedestal, and is placed near the pillar dial, of which a measured drawing is given on Plate 72.

On Plate 118 are shown two monumental Scottish examples. The first is situated in the grounds of Holyrood Palace, and stands on a high wide-spreading base, consisting of three moulded steps divided into panels; the dial support is hexagonal, delicately carved and moulded. It belongs to a type known as "facet headed dials," and has about twenty different facets or sides, some ornamented with heart-shaped sinkings, others hollowed out and with gnomons, others again containing the royal arms, with the collar and badge of the thistle. There are also the initials of Charles I. and his queen, Henrietta Maria, for whom Charles is said to have had the dial made. It was made by one John Mylne in 1633 "for which he was paid the sum of £408 15s. 6d. Scots."

The sundial from Newbattle Abbey is one of a pair existing in the gardens there, and is probably the finest example in Scotland. Its total height is about sixteen feet from the level of the upper step. It was erected in 1635, and contains the arms and initials of the Earl and Countess of Lothian. The gnomon's figures, and the lines of the dials have all been gilt.

FOUNTAINS.

PLATE 119.

 FOUNTAIN is perhaps the most delightful of all the ornamental accessories that go to complete a garden, and one in which the sculptor may find the greatest scope and freedom for his fancy and skill. On the Continent, especially in the garden schemes of Italy and France, fountains and other waterworks held a much more important position than in this country, where immense schemes such as those inaugurated by Le Notre at Versailles were never attempted. Yet many interesting examples formerly existed in the gardens of this country, especially during the sixteenth and seventeenth centuries. Hentzner mentions several that existed at Hampton Court in 1598. In the pleasure and artificial gardens were many columns and pyramids of marble, "two fountains that spout water one round the other like a pyramid, upon which are perched small birds that stream water out of their bills: In the grove of Diana is a very agreeable fountain, with Acteon turned into a

stag as he is sprinkled by the goddess and her nymphs. There is besides another pyramid of marble, full of concealed pipes, which spurt upon all who come within their reach." Similar surprise fountains existed at Whitehall, Theobalds and Hatfield; they were held in some favour by our ancestors, ever fond of a practical joke, and even Bacon did not disapprove their use. The well-known copper tree at Chatsworth is probably a unique example of such fountains now remaining.

In the old gardens at Wilton designed by De Caux were several elaborate fountains, fragments of which may still be seen, though diverted from their original use. The example shown from a photograph on Plate 18 and drawn on Plate 119 stands in the centre of the Italian garden. It is surmounted by a graceful figure of a girl wringing the tresses of her hair. Of this figure a replica is to be seen on a fountain in the Villa Petraia near Florence. When the fountain is set in motion, the water trickles from the girl's hair into a small marble basin, from whence it falls into a larger one, and finally into the circular pool below. The total height above the water line is rather more than 12 feet, and the pool is 16 feet in diameter.

The other fountain illustrated on Plate 119 is from the Victoria and Albert Museum, South Kensington. It is of Italian origin, having been brought from the Palazzo Stufa at Florence. It is surmounted by a figure of Bacchus, and the water spurts from a small cup held in his hand into a white marble basin, from whence it issues through lions' mouths, and also from amorini supporting the quadrangular base. The total height of this fountain is 11 feet.

STONE BALUSTRADES.

PLATE 120.

IN the arrangement of a stone balustrade an important point to be noticed is the spacing of the balusters. These should never be too crowded, and the most satisfactory examples are those in which the distance from centre to centre almost equals the height from plinth to coping. The piers dividing the groups should not be set too far apart, from ten to fifteen feet being a good distance, but much will depend on the proportion of the balusters themselves. Some illustration of this point will be conveyed by the examples of balustrading given on Plate 120. That from Drayton House, Northamptonshire, is also shown in the view given on Plate 28. It encloses the garden on the east side of the house, extending a distance of 175 feet between the two garden houses. The total height is 4 feet 9 inches, the balusters being 2 feet 7 inches high, and spaced 2 feet from centre to centre; the distance between the piers is 14 feet.

In the balustrade from Brympton Manor House, the balusters are far more closely spaced, as they were intended to serve as a screen for the wall which divides the forecourt from the main road. The wall is 6 feet in height and the balusters are 12 inches from centre to centre, and 2 feet 6 inches high.

The other terraces on the plate are from the garden fronts of Berwick Hall in Westmorland and Cranborne Manor in Dorsetshire. The former has square balusters, set 2 feet 2 inches apart, and the intervening piers are formed of two half balusters, and are spaced at intervals of 11 feet 9 inches. The terrace now overlooks a meadow, for all trace of the old garden has disappeared. The terrace at Cranborne leads down to a delightful old garden, gay with flower-beds and grass walks. Like the one at Borwick Hall, it dates from the early part of the seventeenth century, and may have been designed by Inigo Jones, who superintended some alterations here about this time. It will be noticed that the flight of steps is slightly wider at the bottom than the top, and that the balls, instead of being quite circular, are flattened, two little variations worthy of notice. The terrace is raised some five feet above the garden level, and the balusters are 18 inches from centre to centre, and 2 feet 8 inches high, the piers being spaced 12 feet apart.

WALL GATEWAYS.

PLATE 121.

S the point at which a garden is entered, the frame, as it were, which is to disclose a view within, any architectural design devoted to a gateway will not be lost. Take for example the gateway shown on Plate 103, leading up to the old-fashioned Manor House at Sydenham; how inviting it looks, with its moss-grown piers and time-worn gates! Innumerable examples of old gateways are to be met with; but those shown on Plate 121 are gateways set in walls as distinct from those having gatepiers and forming independent structures in themselves.

The gateway from Penshurst Place is of Tudor date, and forms the entrance to the churchyard from the garden. It is flanked on either side by buttresses, and over the arch has the armorial bearings of the Sidneys. The example from the garden at Earlshall is of stone, and though having a somewhat ancient appearance, is of quite modern date. Its quaint motto is particularly fitting in such a position, and the one over the porch at Montacute[1] is also very appropriate.

The gateway leading to the forecourt of the interesting Elizabethan Manor House at Cold Ashton, near Bath, belonging to the early part of the seventeenth century, stands high from the road and has three semicircular steps, with a mounting block at the side. The iron gates have been removed and are replaced by wooden ones. The gateway is flanked by pilasters supporting an entablature, over which is the coat of arms of the Gunning family, consisting of a lion's head, and paws holding a shield with three guns. The height from the top step to the top of the cornice is 12 feet 6 inches.

The other example given forms the entrance to the Almshouses at Oundle in Northamptonshire. The three curious obelisks supported on little balls, a very favourite Italian device, lend a quaint aspect to the gateway. The opening is quite small, being only 2 feet 9 inches wide, and 6 feet 3 inches high.

MAZES.

PLATE 122.

AZES and labyrinths may be traced from very early days. In England they are mentioned in the thirteenth century, when we read how fair Rosamund met her fate, in the labyrinth which concealed her bower, at the hands of the jealous Queen Eleanor. In early days a maze consisted of low hedges of privet, box, or hyssop, and William Lawson, writing in 1618, says: "Mazes well framed, of a man's height, may perhaps make your friend wander in gathering of berries till he cannot recover himself without your helpe."

One of the earliest designs for a maze is that given in the quaint little work of Thomas Hill, "The

[1] See description of Plates 1-5.

Proffitable Arte of Gardening," published in 1568. He gives two designs, one of which is reproduced on this plate. He says that mazes are not "for any commoditie in a garden but rather that who so listeth, having such room in their garden, may place the one of them in that void place that may best be spared for the only purpose to sport in them at times."

During the seventeenth century, Mazes were frequently formed. One existed at Theobalds which had a mount known as the "Mount of Venus," placed in its midst. Another which existed in the gardens of Queen Henrietta Maria at Wimbledon is mentioned in a parliamentary survey of 1649. The celebrated maze at Hampton Court which still exists, covers an area of a quarter of an acre. It has hedges of hornbeam, and the walks aggregate a half a mile in length. The one at Hatfield (shown on Plate 25) is of more recent date; it is oblong in shape and has two entrances, north and south.

Two of the mazes shown on Plate 122 are from a small manuscript book among the Harleian Manuscripts at the British Museum. This book appears to have belonged to a journeyman gardener in the seventeenth century. The examples from Somerleyton Hall, Suffolk, and Arley Hall, Cheshire, have been constructed within the last fifty years, and both are good. The former has hedges of yew, and in the centre a quaint pagoda-like summer-house, while that at Arley has hedges of lime trees, and though quite small in extent is by no means easy to penetrate. The remaining example at Belton House is not a very difficult one and is very little used.

FINIS.

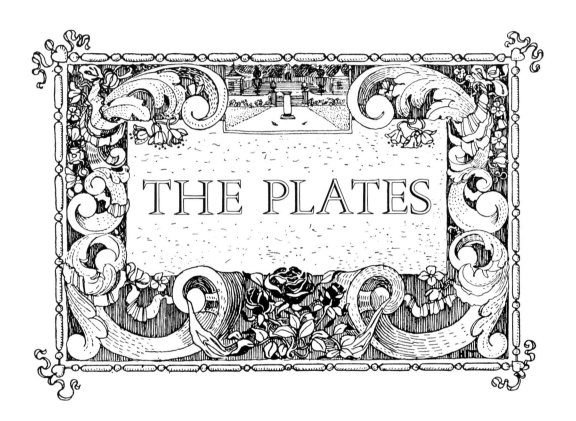

THE PLATES

Plate 1

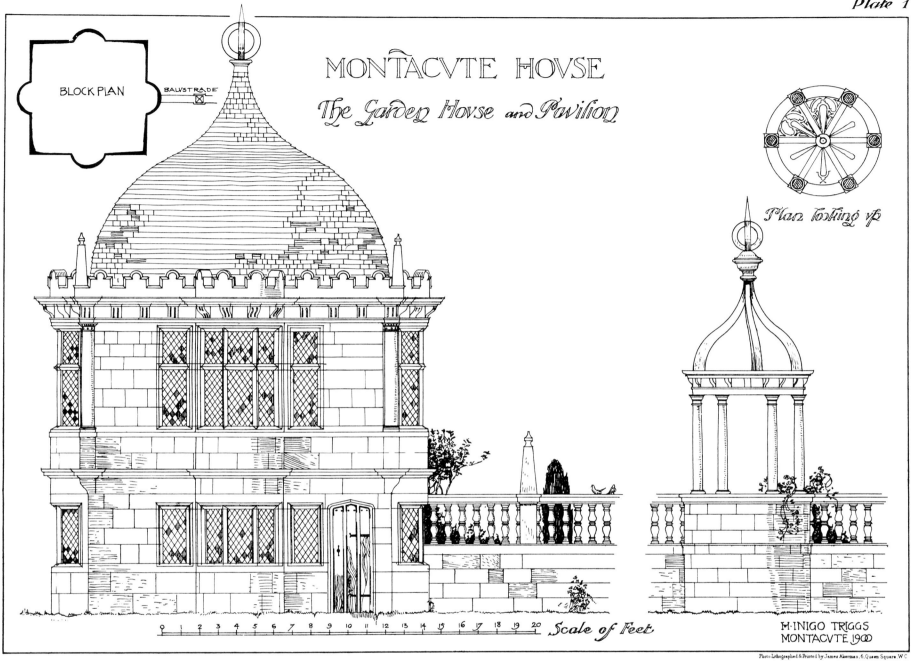

BLOCK PLAN

BALVSTRADE

MONTACVTE HOVSE
The Garden Hovse and Pavilion

Plan looking up

Scale of Feet

0 1 2 3 4 5 6 7 8 9 10 11 12 13 14 15 16 17 18 19 20

H·INIGO TRIGGS
MONTACVTE 1900

Photo-Lithographed & Printed by James Akerman, 6, Queen Square, W.C.

65

Plate 2

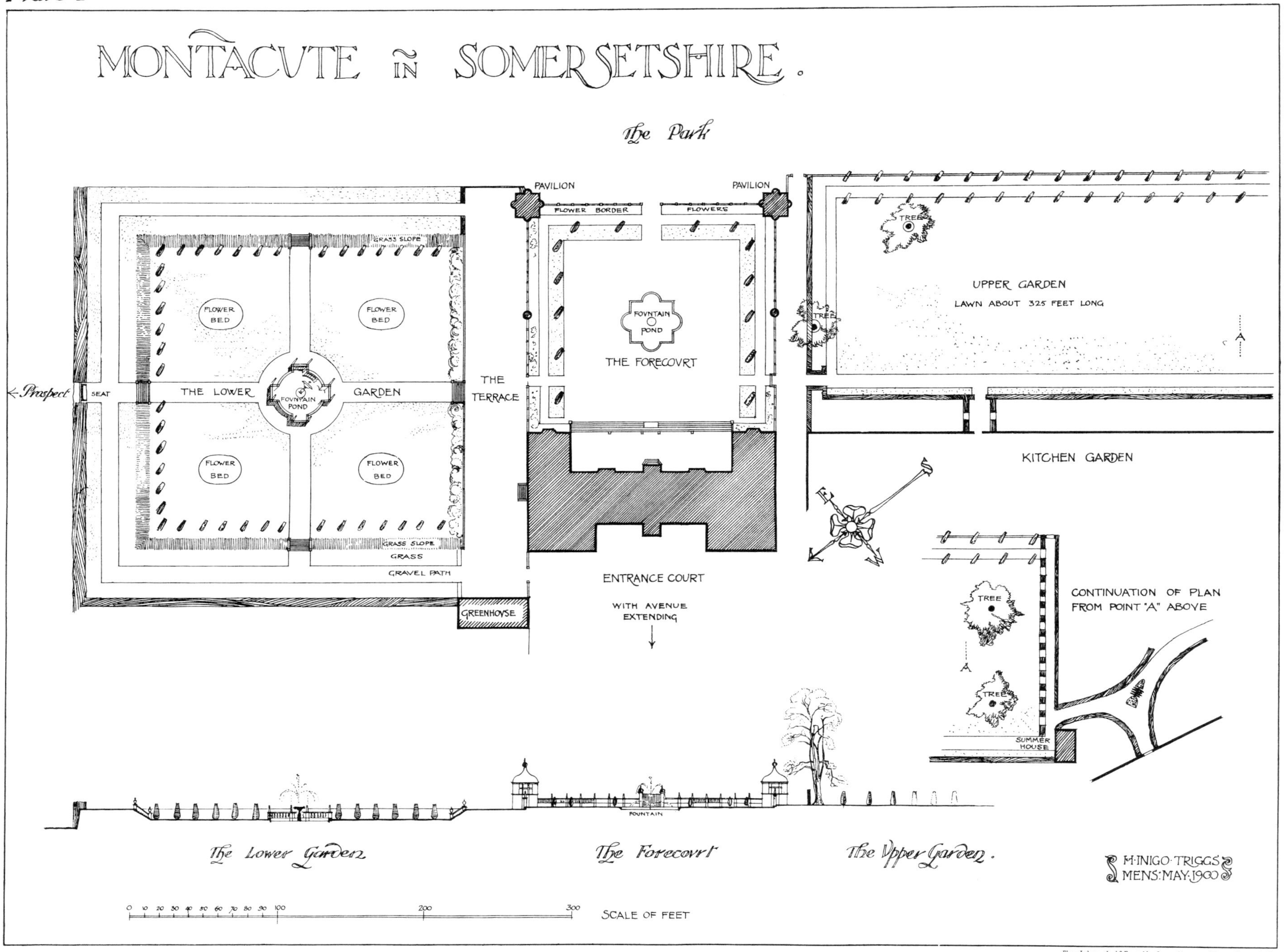

MONTACUTE in SOMERSETSHIRE.

The Park

FLOWER BED · FLOWER BED · FLOWER BED · FLOWER BED

THE LOWER GARDEN

FOUNTAIN POND

GRASS SLOPE
GRASS
GRAVEL PATH

Prospect · SEAT

THE TERRACE

GREENHOUSE

PAVILION · PAVILION

FLOWER BORDER · FLOWERS

THE FORECOURT

FOUNTAIN POND

ENTRANCE COURT

WITH AVENUE EXTENDING

UPPER GARDEN
LAWN ABOUT 325 FEET LONG

TREE · TREE

KITCHEN GARDEN

CONTINUATION OF PLAN FROM POINT "A" ABOVE

TREE · TREE

SUMMER HOUSE

The Lower Garden · FOUNTAIN · The Forecourt · The Upper Garden.

M. INIGO TRIGGS
MENS: MAY. 1900

0 10 20 30 40 50 60 70 80 90 100 · 200 · 300 · SCALE OF FEET

Photo-Lithographed & Printed by James Akerman, 6, Queen Square, W.C.

66

MONTACUTE HOUSE — AUGUST 1988.

PLATE 3.

MONTACUTE, SOMERSETSHIRE.

THE GARDEN HOUSE AND PAVILION.

PLATE 4.

MONTACUTE, SOMERSETSHIRE.

VIEW ACROSS THE POND.

MONTACUTE HOUSE — AUGUST 1988.

PLATE 5.

MONTACUTE, SOMERSETSHIRE.

THE TERRACE, LOWER GARDEN.

Plate 6

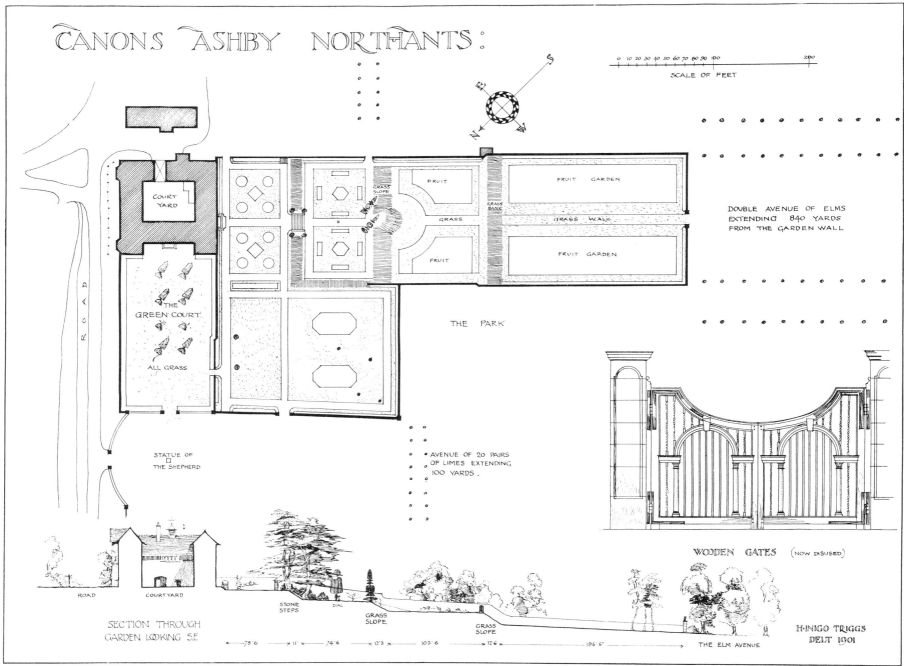

CANONS ASHBY NORTHANTS:

SCALE OF FEET
0 10 20 30 40 50 60 70 80 90 100   200

COURT YARD

THE GREEN COURT
ALL GRASS

FRUIT

FRUIT

FRUIT GARDEN

GRASS SLOPE

GRASS BANK

GRASS

GRASS WALK

FRUIT GARDEN

DOUBLE AVENUE OF ELMS EXTENDING 840 YARDS FROM THE GARDEN WALL

THE PARK

STATUE OF THE SHEPHERD

AVENUE OF 20 PAIRS OF LIMES EXTENDING 100 YARDS.

WODDEN GATES (NOW DISUSED)

ROAD   COURTYARD

SECTION THROUGH GARDEN LOOKING S.E.

STONE STEPS   DIAL   GRASS SLOPE   GRASS SLOPE   THE ELM AVENUE

H·INIGO TRIGGS DELT 1901

75'6   11"   74'6   12'3   102'6   12'6   196'6"

Photo·Lithographed & Printed by James Akerman, 6, Queen Square, W.C.

72

Plate 7

CANONS ASHBY.

Northamptonshire

Plan

The Green Court.   Piers at the Angles

The Height of all the Gatepiers
is about 11 feet to the Cap

Park Gates   Entrance to Flower Garden.

Photo-Lithographed & Printed by James Akerman, 6, Queen Square, W.C.

Plate 8

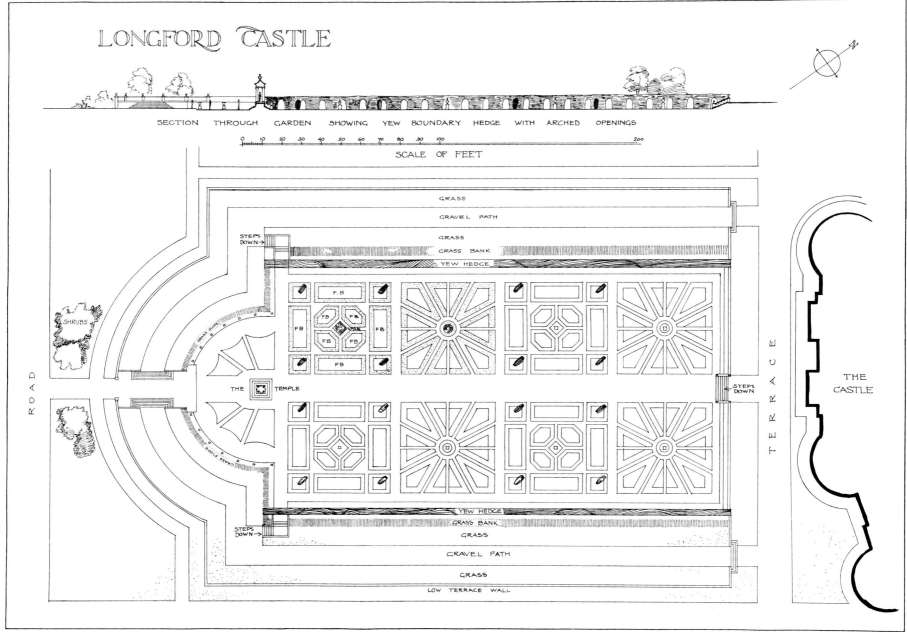

LONGFORD CASTLE

SECTION THROUGH GARDEN SHOWING YEW BOUNDARY HEDGE WITH ARCHED OPENINGS

SCALE OF FEET

0 10 20 30 40 50 60 70 80 90 100 200

PLATE 9.

LONGFORD CASTLE, WILTSHIRE.

GENERAL VIEW.

PLATE 10.

LONGFORD CASTLE, WILTSHIRE.

THE TEMPLE.

Plate 11

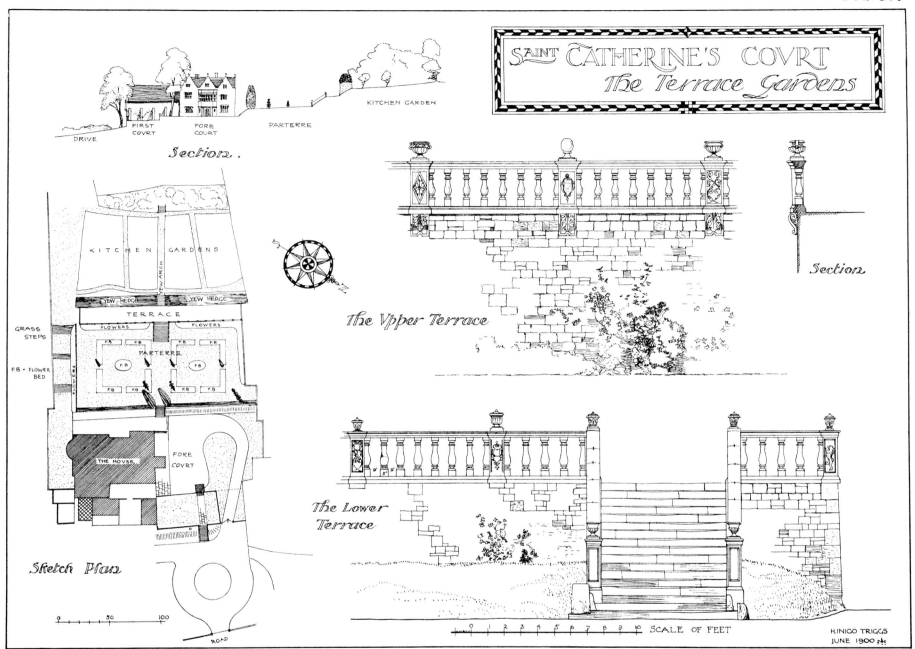

SAINT CATHERINE'S COVRT
The Terrace Gardens

Section.

DRIVE FIRST COVRT FORE COURT PARTERRE KITCHEN GARDEN

KITCHEN GARDENS

YEW ARCH

YEW HEDGE YEW HEDGE

TERRACE

FLOWERS FLOWERS

GRASS STEPS

PARTERRE

F.B F.B F.B F.B

F.B F.B F.B F.B

F.B = FLOWER BED

F.B

F.B F.B F.B F.B

FLOWERS

THE HOVSE.

FORE COVRT

Sketch Plan

0   50   100

ROAD

The Vpper Terrace

Section

The Lower Terrace

0 1 2 3 4 5 6 7 8 9 10 SCALE OF FEET

H.INIGO TRIGGS
JUNE 1900

Photo-Lithographed & Printed by James Akerman, 6, Queen Square W.C.

77

Plate 12.

ST. CATHERINE'S COURT, SOMERSETSHIRE.

VIEW FROM THE UPPER TERRACE.

ST. CATHERINE'S COURT, SOMERSETSHIRE.

THE UPPER TERRACE.

PLATE 13.

Plate 14

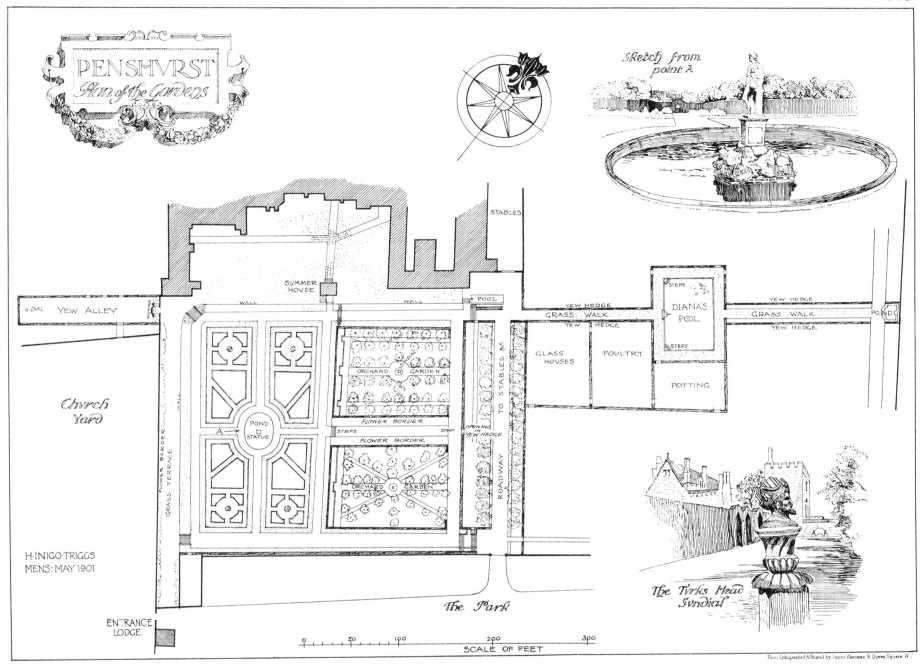

PENSHVRST
Plan of the Gardens

Sketch from point A

STABLES

o DIAL   YEW ALLEY

SUMMER HOUSE

WALL

POOL

WALL

YEW HEDGE

GRASS WALK

DIANA'S POOL

YEW HEDGE

GRASS WALK

POND

Church Yard

FLOWER BORDER   GRASS TERRACE   WALL

ORCHARD   GARDEN

FLOWER BORDER

STEPS

FLOWER BORDER

STEPS

ORCHARD   GARDEN

POND STATUE

A

TO STABLES &c

ROADWAY

OPENING IN YEW HEDGE

STEPS

STEPS

YEW HEDGE

GLASS HOVSES

POULTRY

POTTING

H·INIGO·TRIGGS
MENS: MAY 1901

The Park

The Tvrks Head Svndial

ENTRANCE LODGE

0   50   100   200   300
SCALE OF FEET

Photo-Lithographed & Printed by James Akerman, 6, Queen Square, W.C.

PLATE 15.

PENSHURST PLACE, KENT.

VIEW ACROSS THE POND GARDEN.

PENSHURST PLACE — 1987.

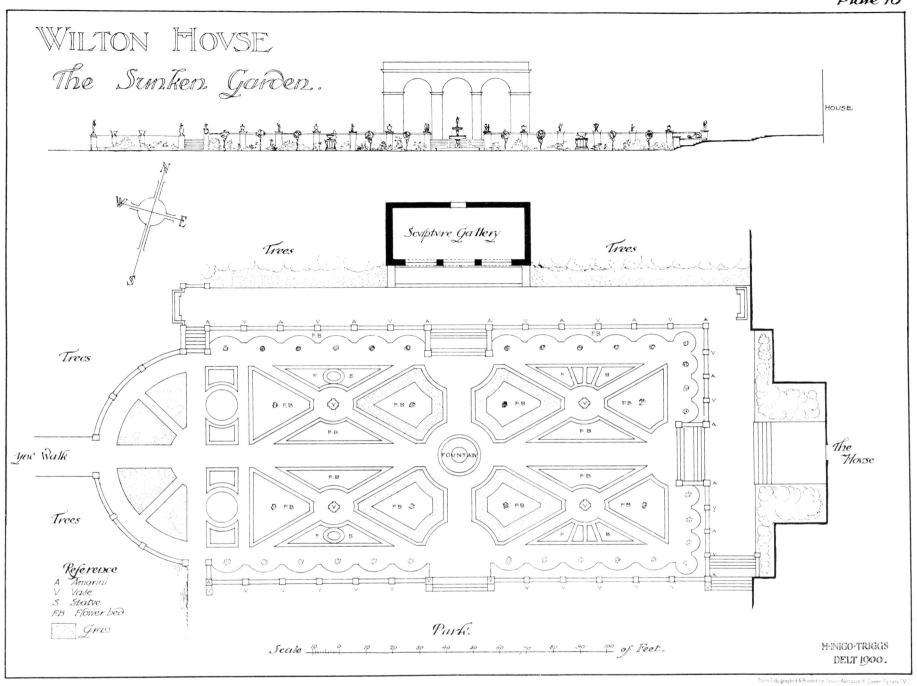

Plate 16

WILTON HOVSE
The Sunken Garden.

HOUSE

Scvlptvre Gallery

Trees

Trees

N
W E
S

Trees

Yew Walk

Trees

FOUNTAIN

The House

Reference
A   Amorini
V   Vase
S   Statve
F.B Flower bed
Grass

Park.

Scale 10 0   10   20   30   40   50   60   70   80   90   100   of Feet.

M INIGO TRIGGS
DELT 1900.

85

WILTON HOUSE — AUGUST 1988.

PLATE 17.

WILTON HOUSE, WILTSHIRE.

THE ITALIAN GARDEN.

Plate 18.

WILTON HOUSE. WILTSHIRE.

FOUNTAIN IN THE ITALIAN GARDEN.

WILTON HOUSE
1988.

PLATE 19.

LEADEN AMORINI FROM WILTON HOUSE.

PLATE 19.

LEADEN AMORINI FROM WILTON HOUSE.

BOWOOD HOUSE 1988.

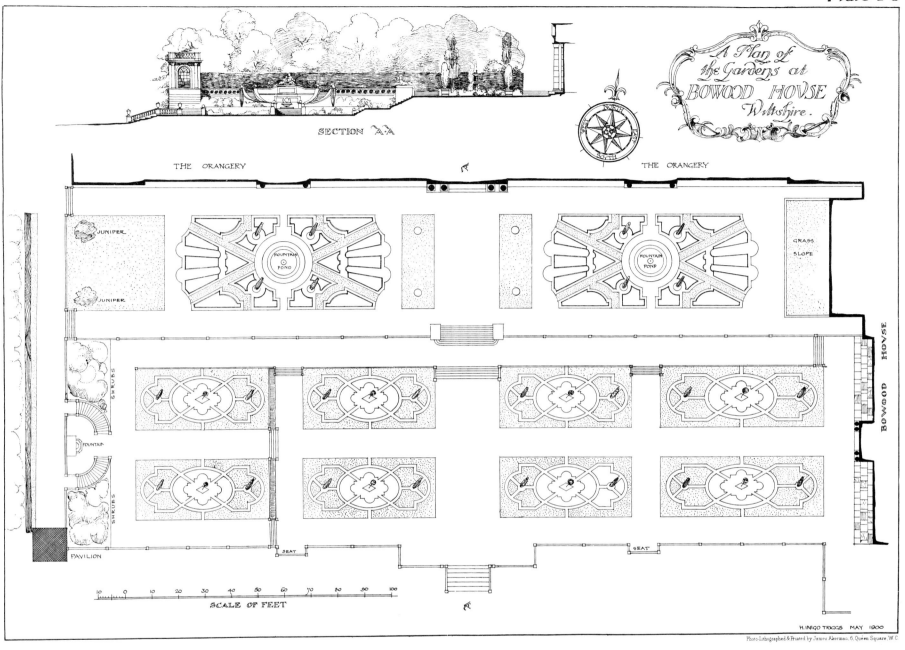

Plate 20

SECTION A·A

A Plan of
the Gardens at
BOWOOD HOVSE
Wiltshire.

NORTH
WEST · EAST
SOUTH

THE ORANGERY

THE ORANGERY

JUNIPER

JUNIPER

FOUNTAIN
POND

FOUNTAIN
POND

GRASS
SLOPE

SHRUBS

SHRUBS

FOUNTAIN

BOWOOD HOVSE

PAVILION

SEAT

SEAT

10 0   10   20   30   40   50   60   70   80   90   100
SCALE OF FEET

H. INIGO TRIGGS MAY 1900

Photo-Lithographed & Printed by James Akerman, 6, Queen Square, W.C.

Plate 21.

BOWOOD HOUSE, WILTSHIRE.

THE ITALIAN GARDEN.

Plate 22

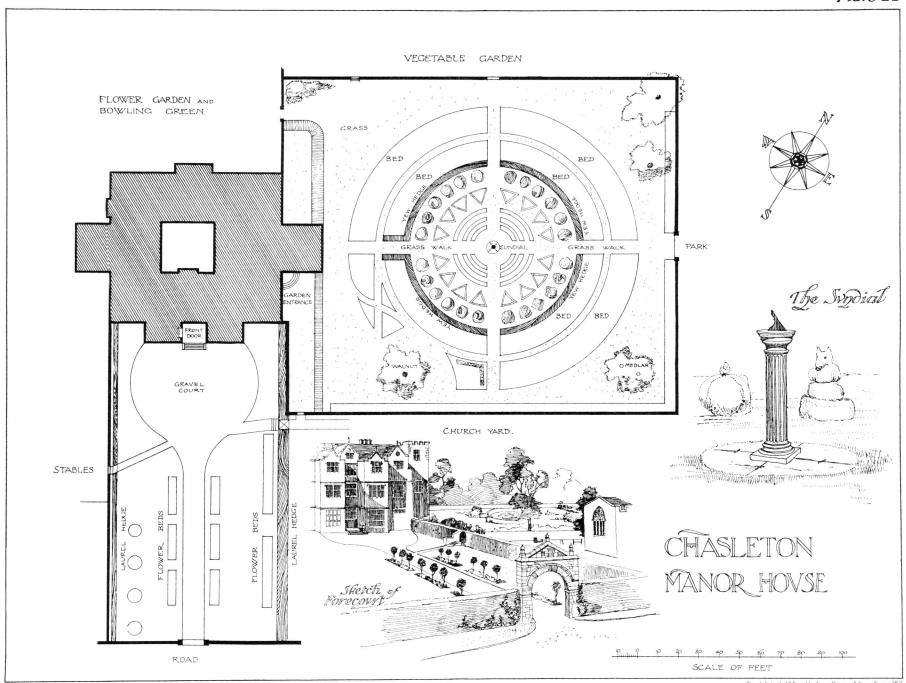

VEGETABLE GARDEN

FLOWER GARDEN AND
BOWLING GREEN.

GRASS

BED

BED

BED

BED

YEW HEDGE

YEW HEDGE

GRASS WALK · SUNDIAL · GRASS WALK

YEW HEDGE

YEW HEDGE

BED

BED

WALNUT

O·MEDLAR

GARDEN
ENTRANCE

FRONT
DOOR

GRAVEL
COURT

PARK

CHURCH YARD.

STABLES

LAUREL HEDGE

FLOWER BEDS

FLOWER BEDS

LAUREL HEDGE

The Sundial

*Sketch of
Forecourt*

ROAD

CHASLETON
MANOR HOVSE

SCALE OF FEET

Photo-Lithographed & Printed by James Akerman, 6, Queen Square W.C.

97

CHASTLETON MANOR HOUSE 1988.

PLATE 23

CHASTLETON MANOR HOUSE, OXFORDSHIRE.

VIEW OF THE CIRCULAR GARDEN.

Plate 24.

HATFIELD HOUSE, HERTS.

THE PRIVY GARDEN.

Plate 25

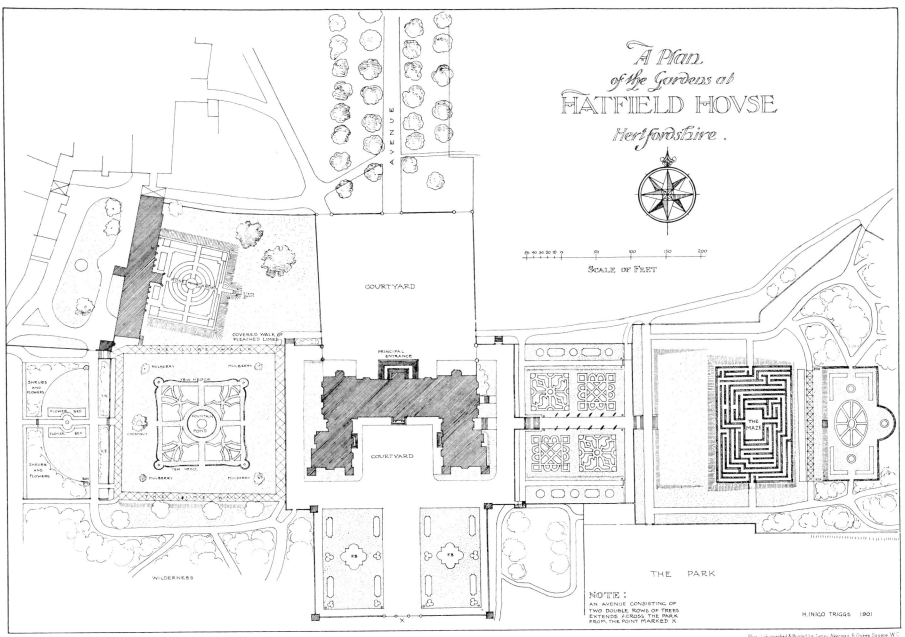

A Plan
of the Gardens at
HATFIELD HOVSE
Hertfordshire.

SCALE OF FEET

COURTYARD

COVERED WALK OF
PLEACHED LIMES

PRINCIPAL
ENTRANCE

COURTYARD

SHRUBS
AND
FLOWERS

FLOWER BED

FLOWER BED

SHRUBS
AND
FLOWERS

BAY

MULBERRY

MULBERRY

YEW HEDGE

CHESTNUT

FOUNTAIN
POND

YEW HEDGE

MULBERRY

MULBERRY

THE LIME WALK

WILDERNESS

THE MAZE

THE PARK

FB

FB

X

NOTE:
AN AVENUE CONSISTING OF
TWO DOUBLE ROWS OF TREES
EXTENDS ACROSS THE PARK
FROM THE POINT MARKED X

H. INIGO TRIGGS 1901

AVENUE

PLATE 26.

HATFIELD HOUSE, HERTS.

THE GARDEN AND MAZE.

CANONS ASHBY 1988.

LEADEN AMORINI AT MELBOURNE.

STONE FIGURE AT BELTON HOUSE.

Plate 27

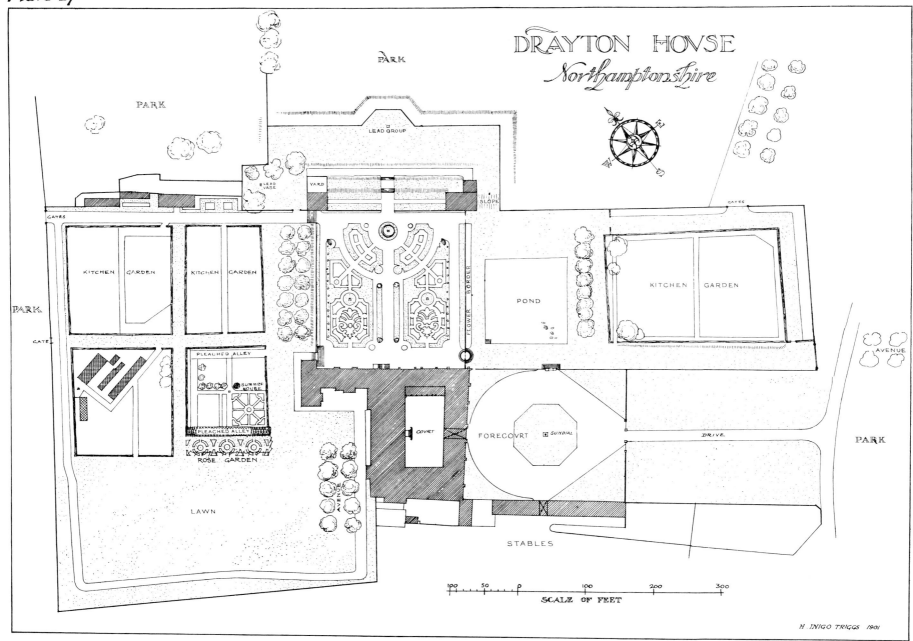

DRAYTON HOVSE
Northamptonshire

PARK

PARK

PARK

PARK

PARK

PARK

LEAD GROUP

LEAD VASE

YARD

SLOPE

GATES

GATE

GATES

KITCHEN GARDEN

KITCHEN GARDEN

KITCHEN GARDEN

FLOWER BORDER

POND

PLEACHED ALLEY

SUMMER HOUSE

PLEACHED ALLEY

ROSE GARDEN

COVRT

FORECOVRT

SUNDIAL

AVENUE

AVENUE

LAWN

DRIVE

STABLES

100   50   0   100   200   300

SCALE OF FEET

H. INIGO TRIGGS 1901

Photo-Lithographed & Printed by James Akerman, 6, Queen Square, W.C.

PLATE 28.

DRAYTON HOUSE, NORTHANTS.

GENERAL VIEW, LOOKING EAST.

PLATE 29.

DRAYTON HOUSE, NORTHANTS.

THE ENTRANCE GATES.

PLATE 30.

DRAYTON HOUSE, NORTHANTS.

FOUR LEADEN VASES.

PLATE 31.

A.

B.

ROSE GARDENS.

A. ROCKINGHAM CASTLE.   B. BROUGHTON CASTLE.

Plate 32

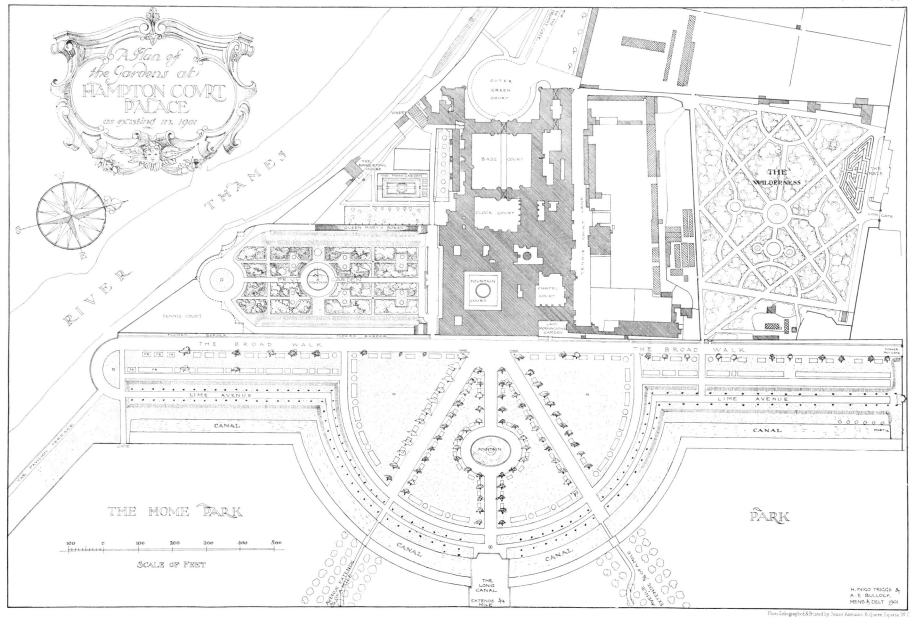

A Plan of the Gardens at HAMPTON COURT PALACE as existing in 1901

OVERLEAF

HAMPTON COURT

IN THE REIGN OF THE GEORGE I BY LEONARD KNYFF.

Plate 33

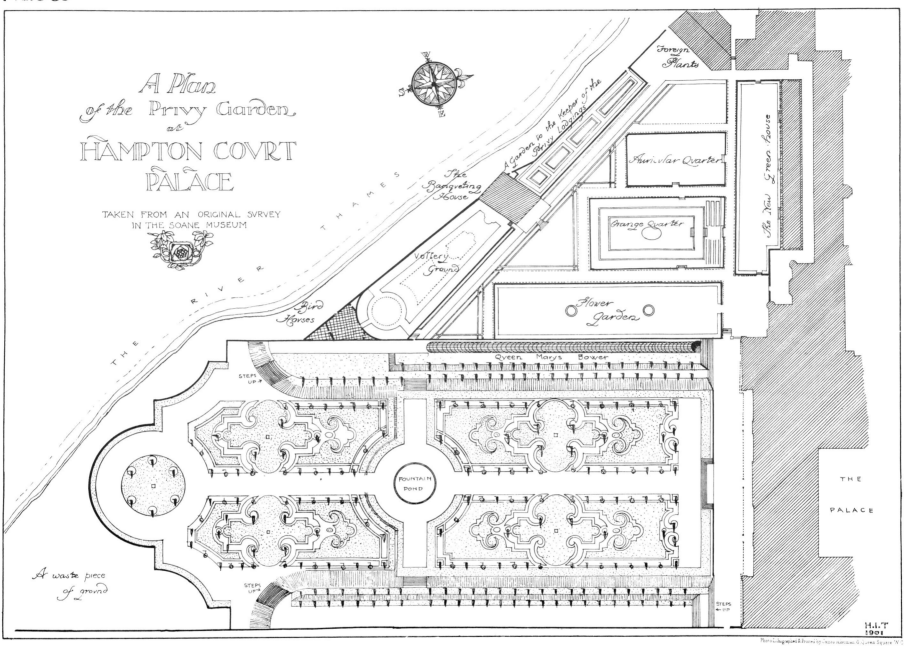

A Plan
of the Privy Garden
at
HAMPTON COVRT
PALACE

TAKEN FROM AN ORIGINAL SVRVEY
IN THE SOANE MUSEUM

Foreign Plants

A Garden to the Keeper of the Privy Lodgings

The Banqueting House

Vollery Ground

Bird Houses

Auricular Quarter

Orange Quarter

The New Green House

Flower Garden

Queen Marys Bower

STEPS UP

FOUNTAIN POND

THE PALACE

A waste piece of ground

STEPS UP

STEPS UP

THE RIVER THAMES

H.I.T
1901

PLATE 34.

HAMPTON COURT PALACE.

THE PRIVY GARDEN.

PLATE 35.

HAMPTON COURT PALACE.

THE POND GARDEN.

PLATE 36.

HAMPTON COURT PALACE.

THE "FLOWER-POT" GATES.

HAMPTON COURT PALACE 1988.

THE POND GARDEN.

Plate 37

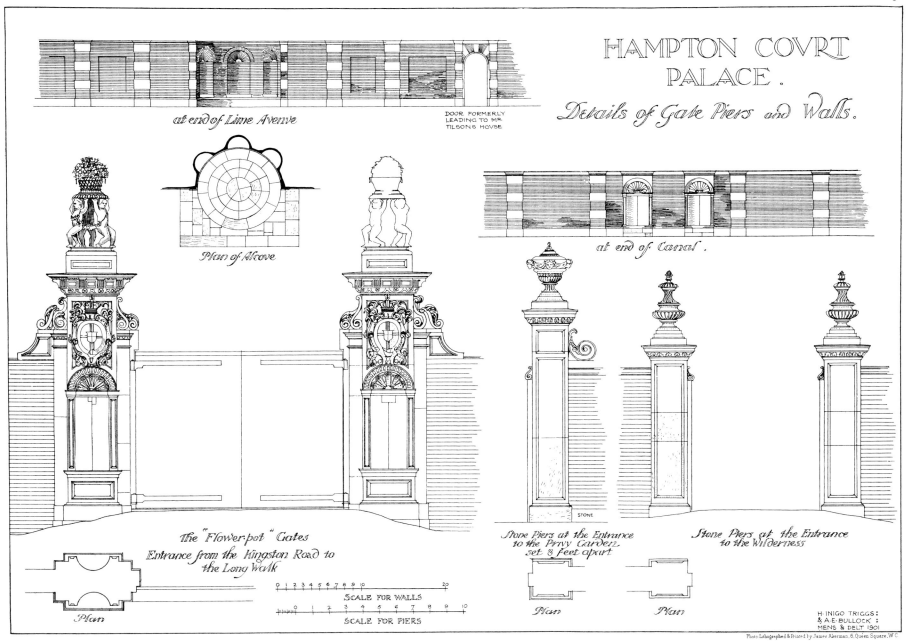

at end of Lime Avenue

DOOR. FORMERLY
LEADING TO MR.
TILSONS HOVSE

HAMPTON COVRT
PALACE.

Details of Gate Piers and Walls.

Plan of Alcove

at end of Canal.

The "Flower-pot" Gates
Entrance from the Kingston Road to
the Long Walk

Plan

Stone Piers at the Entrance
to the Privy Garden
set 8 feet apart

Stone Piers at the Entrance
to the Wilderness

STONE

0 1 2 3 4 5 6 7 8 9 10   20
SCALE FOR WALLS

0   1   2   3   4   5   6   7   8   9   10
SCALE FOR PIERS

Plan

Plan

H. INIGO TRIGGS:
& A.E. BULLOCK:
MENS & DELT 1901

Photo-Lithographed & Printed by James Akerman, 6, Queen Square, W.C.

117

PLATE 37*.

BRIDGE END GARDENS, SAFFRON WALDEN.

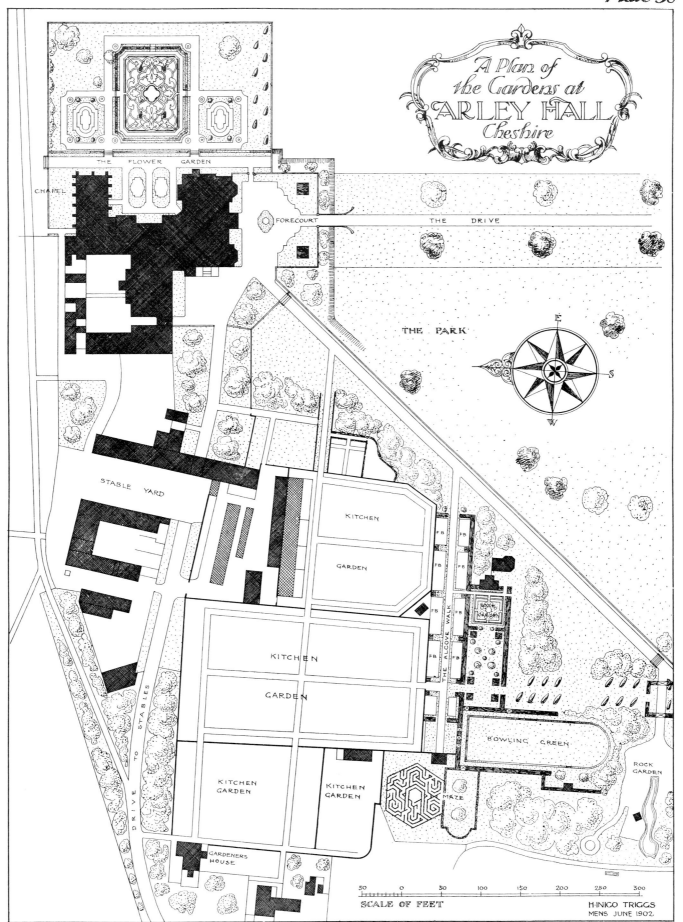

Plate 38

A Plan of
the Gardens at
ARLEY HALL
Cheshire

THE FLOWER GARDEN

CHAPEL

FORECOURT

THE DRIVE

THE PARK

E

S

W

STABLE YARD

KITCHEN

GARDEN

KITCHEN

GARDEN

THE ALCOVE WALK

FB
FB
FB
FB

FB

BOWLING GREEN

ROCK GARDEN

DRIVE TO STABLES

KITCHEN GARDEN

KITCHEN GARDEN

MAZE

GARDENERS HOUSE

50   0   50   100   150   200   250   300

SCALE OF FEET

H·INICO TRIGGS
MENS JUNE 1902.

119

Plate 39.

A.

B.

ARLEY HALL, CHESHIRE.

A. THE ALCOVE WALK.   B. THE YEW GARDEN.

ARLEY 1988.

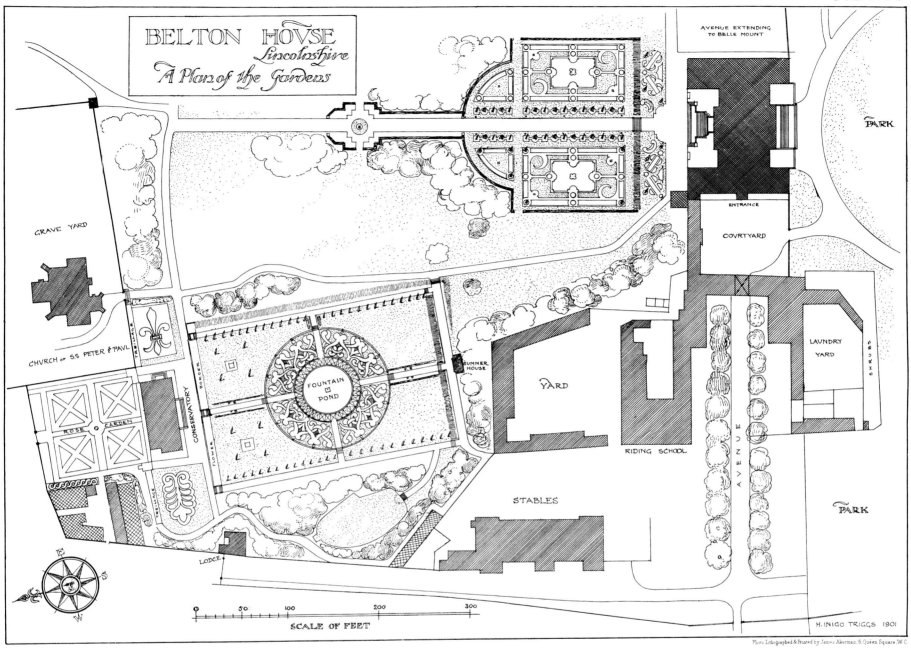

Plate 40

BELTON HOVSE
Lincolnshire
A Plan of the Gardens

AVENUE EXTENDING
TO BELLE MOUNT

PARK

GRAVE YARD

CHVRCH of SS PETER & PAVL

ENTRANCE

COVRTYARD

ROSE GARDEN

CONSERVATORY

FLOWER BORDER

TRELLIS

TRELLIS

FOUNTAIN & POND

SUMMER HOUSE

YARD

LAUNDRY YARD

SHRVBS

RIDING SCHOOL

AVENUE

LODGE

STABLES

PARK

E N S W

SCALE OF FEET
0   50   100   200   300

H. INIGO TRIGGS 1901

Photo Lithographed & Printed by James Akerman, 6, Queen Square, W C

Plate 41

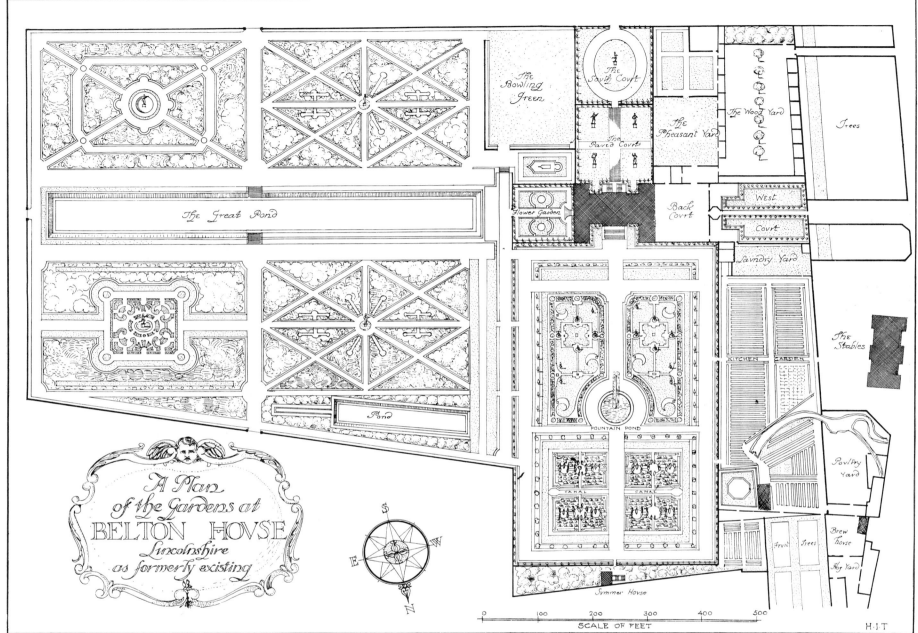

The Bowling Green

The South Court

The Wood Yard

Trees

The Pheasant Yard

The Paved Courts

The Great Pond

Flower Garden

Back Court

West Court

Laundry Yard

Pond

The Stables

KITCHEN GARDEN

FOUNTAIN POND

Poultry Yard

CANAL CANAL

Fruit Trees

Brew House

Hog Yard

Summer House

A Plan
of the Gardens at
BELTON HOVSE
Lincolnshire
as formerly existing

SCALE OF FEET

0   100   200   300   400   500

H·I·T

Photo-Lithographed & Printed by James Akerman, 6 Queen Square, W.C.

124

PLATE 42.

BELTON HOUSE, GRANTHAM.

THE LONG WALK.

PLATE 43.

BELTON HOUSE, GRANTHAM.

THE ROSERY.

BELTON HOUSE 1988.

PLATE 44.

TRENTHAM HALL, STAFFORDSHIRE.

GENERAL VIEW OF THE GARDENS.

TRENTHAM HALL 1988.

BELTON HOUSE 1988.

129

Plate 45

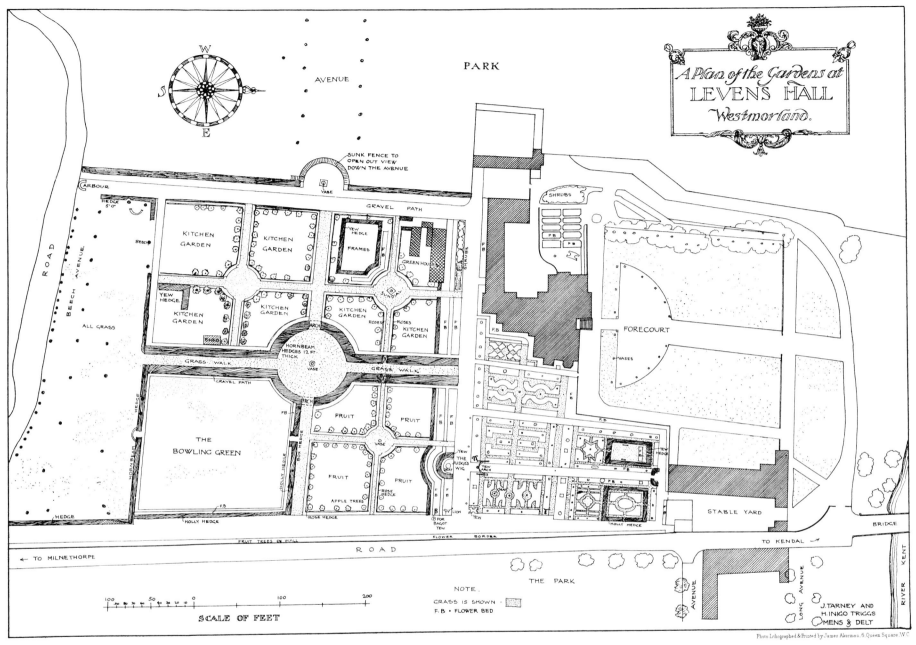

A Plan of the Gardens at
LEVENS HALL
Westmorland.

PARK

AVENUE

SUNK FENCE TO
OPEN OUT VIEW
DOWN THE AVENUE

GRAVEL PATH

ARBOUR

HEDGE
5'0"

BEECH

KITCHEN
GARDEN

KITCHEN
GARDEN

YEW
HEDGE

FRAMES

GREEN HOUSE

SHRUBS

SHRUBS

F.B

ROAD

BEECH AVENUE

ALL GRASS

YEW
HEDGE

KITCHEN
GARDEN

KITCHEN
GARDEN

KITCHEN
GARDEN

ROSES

ROSES

KITCHEN
GARDEN

SUNDIAL

F
B

F
B

F.B

FORECOURT

VASES

GRASS WALK

GRASS WALK

GRAVEL PATH

HORNBEAM
HEDGES 12 FT.
THICK

VASE

F.B

ARCH

FRUIT

FRUIT

F
B

F
B

F.B

HOLLY HEDGE

HORNBEAM HEDGE

THE
BOWLING GREEN

FRUIT

FRUIT

VASE

YEW
THE
JUDGES
WIG

YEW
ARCH

YEW
HEDGE

F.B

APPLE TREES

ROSE HEDGE

LION

YEW

STABLE YARD

F
B

F
B

F.B

HOLLY HEDGE

HEDGE

HOLLY HEDGE

B FOR
BAGOT
YEW

FRUIT TREES ON WALL

FLOWER BORDER

ROAD

BRIDGE

TO KENDAL

← TO MILNETHORPE

THE PARK

AVENUE

LONG AVENUE

RIVER KENT

100   50   10   0   100   200

SCALE OF FEET

NOTE.
GRASS IS SHOWN -
F.B - FLOWER BED

J. TARNEY AND
H. INIGO TRIGGS
MENS & DELT

Photo-Lithographed & Printed by James Akerman, 6, Queen Square, W.C.

LEVENS HALL 1988.

PLATE 46.

LEVENS HALL, WESTMORLAND.

LEVENS HALL 1988.

PLATE 47.

LEVENS HALL, WESTMORLAND.

THE HORNBEAM HEDGE.

PLATE 48.

HESLINGTON HALL, YORKSHIRE.

VIEW OF TOPIARY WORK.

PLATE 49.

ASHBRIDGE PARK, BERKHAMPSTEAD.

THE SKATING POND.

Plate 50

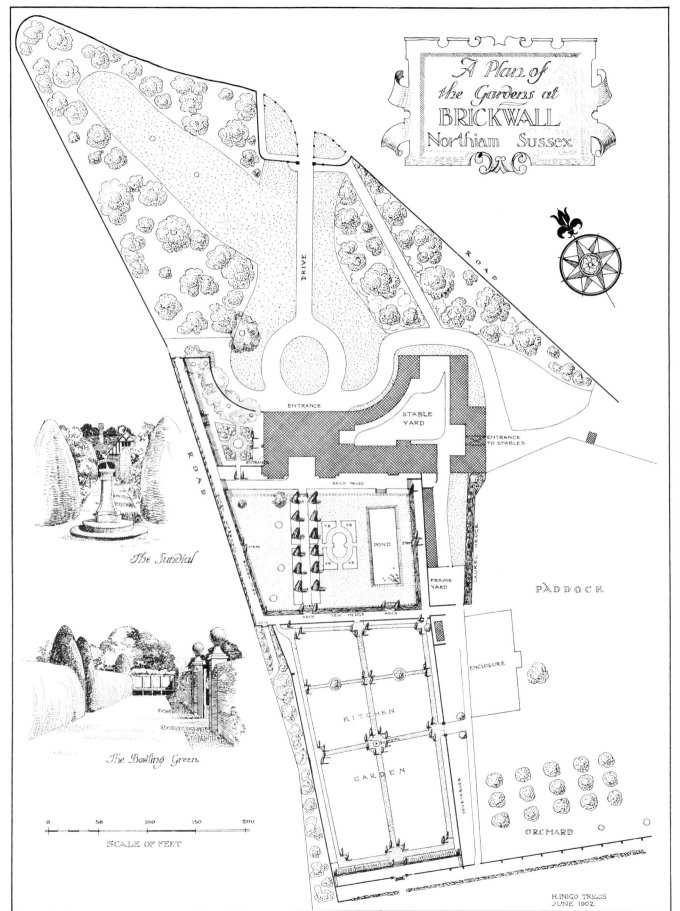

A Plan of
the Gardens at
BRICKWALL
Northiam Sussex

The Sundial

The Bowling Green

DRIVE

ROAD

ROAD

ENTRANCE

STABLE
YARD

ENTRANCE
TO STABLES

BRICK PAVED

ENTRAN

POND

FRAME
YARD

LAUREL HEDGE

PADDOCK

ENCLOSURE

ARCH   YEW HEDGE   ARCH

KITCHEN

GARDEN

VEGETABLES

ORCHARD

0   50   100   150   200
SCALE OF FEET

H INIGO TRIGGS
JUNE 1902

Photo-Lithographed & Printed by James Akerman, 6 Queen Square W C

139

BRICKWALL 1988.

PLATE 51.

BRICKWALL, NORTHIAM, SUSSEX.

VIEW FROM THE HOUSE.

MELBOURNE HALL 1988.

Plate 52

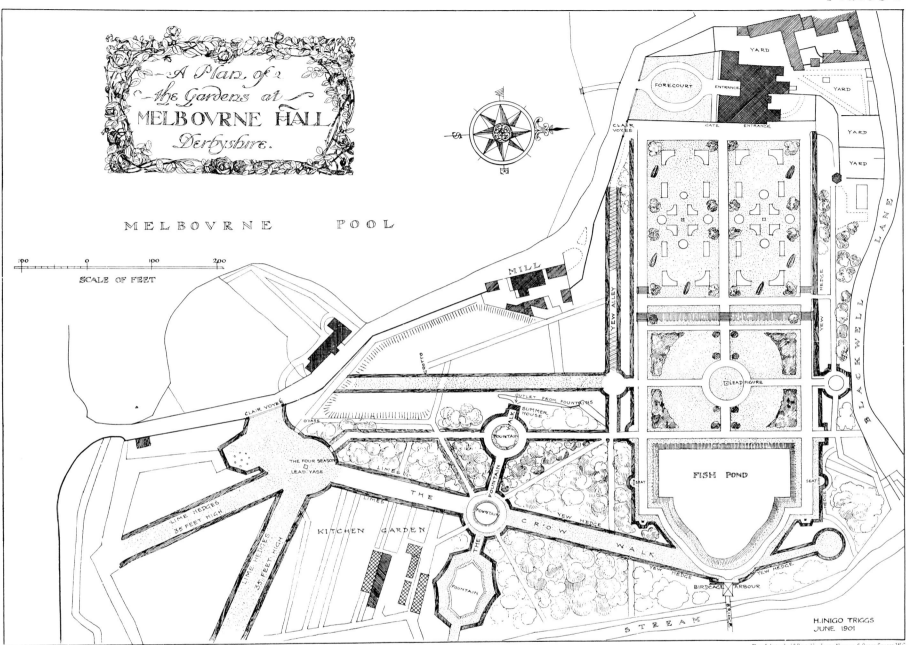

A Plan of the Gardens at
MELBOURNE HALL
Derbyshire.

MELBOURNE POOL

SCALE OF FEET

143

Plate 53

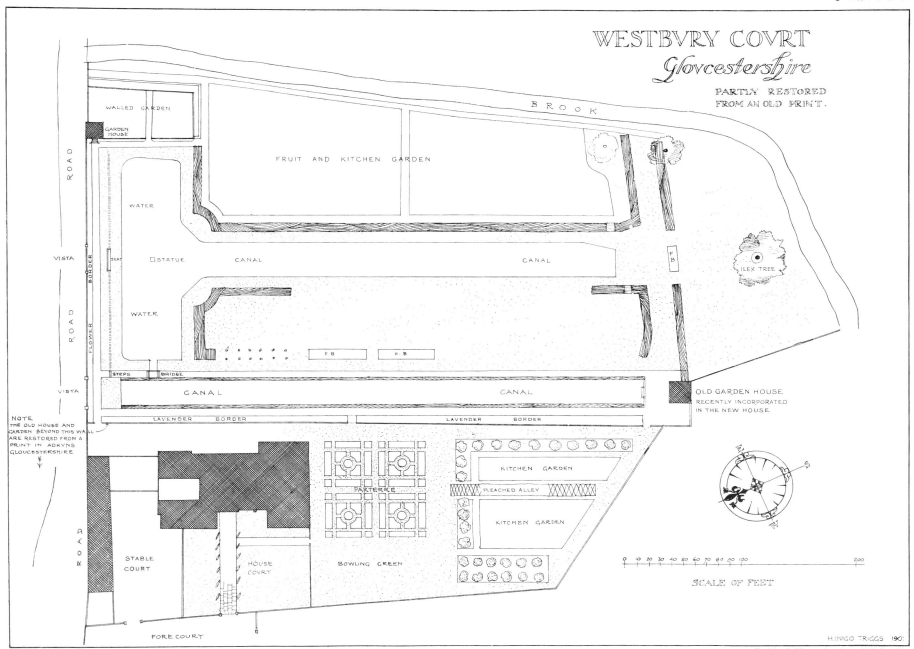

WESTBVRY COVRT
Gloucestershire
PARTLY RESTORED
FROM AN OLD PRINT.

BROOK

ROAD

WALLED GARDEN

GARDEN HOUSE

FRUIT AND KITCHEN GARDEN

WATER

VISTA

BORDER

SEAT

STATUE

CANAL

CANAL

F.B

WATER

ILEX TREE

FLOWER

F.B

F.B

STEPS

BRIDGE

VISTA

CANAL

CANAL

OLD GARDEN HOUSE
RECENTLY INCORPORATED
IN THE NEW HOUSE

NOTE.
THE OLD HOUSE AND
GARDEN BEYOND THIS WALL
ARE RESTORED FROM A
PRINT IN ADKYNS.
GLOUCESTERSHIRE

LAVENDER BORDER

LAVENDER BORDER

KITCHEN GARDEN

PARTERRE

PLEACHED ALLEY

KITCHEN GARDEN

ROAD

STABLE COURT

HOUSE COVRT

BOWLING GREEN

0 10 20 30 40 50 60 70 80 90 100   200
SCALE OF FEET

FORE COURT

H. INIGO TRIGGS 1901

Photo Lithographed & Printed by John Akerman 6 Queen Square E.C

PLATE 54.

WESTBURY COURT, GLOUCESTERSHIRE.

THE LONG CANAL.

WESTBURY COURT 1988.

PLATE 55.

WESTBURY COURT, GLOUCESTERSHIRE.

THE LOWER GARDEN.

Plate 56

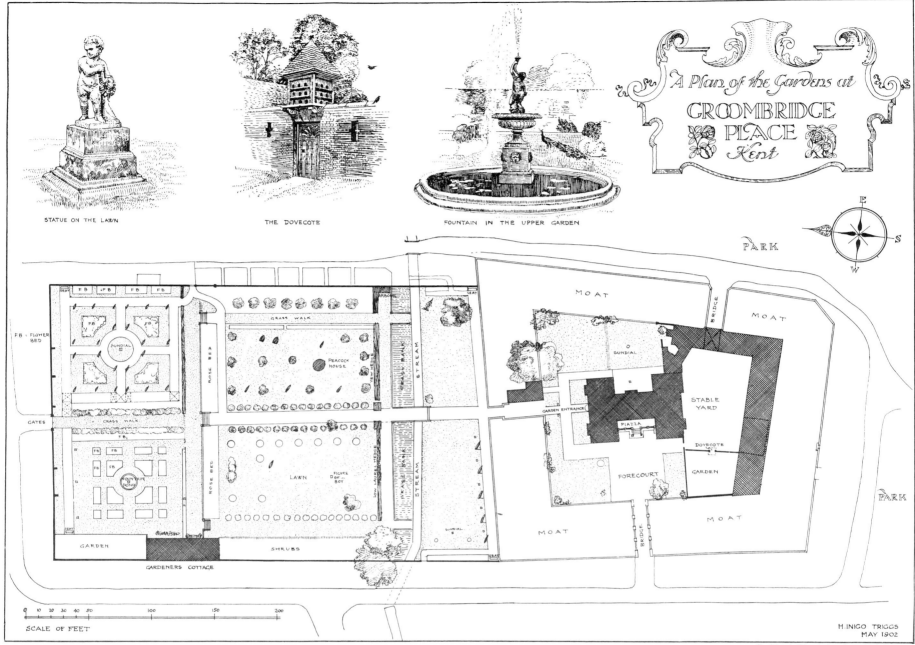

STATUE ON THE LAWN

THE DOVECOTE

FOUNTAIN IN THE UPPER GARDEN

A Plan of the Gardens at
GROOMBRIDGE
PLACE
Kent

PARK

PARK

MOAT

MOAT

MOAT

MOAT

STABLE
YARD

GARDEN ENTRANCE

PIAZZA

DOVECOTE

GARDEN

FORECOURT

BRIDGE

SUNDIAL

BRIDGE

SEAT

GRASS WALK

PEACOCK
HOUSE

STREAM

ARBOUR

SEAT

FB FLOWER
BED

SUNDIAL

ROSE BED

GATES

GRASS WALK

FB

LAWN

FIGURE
OF
BOY

ROSE BED

FOUNTAIN
& POND

GARDEN

GARDENERS COTTAGE

SHRUBS

SUNDIAL

SEAT

SCALE OF FEET

0 10 20 30 40 50   100   150   200

H. INIGO TRIGGS
MAY 1902

Photo Lithographed & Printed by James Akerman, 6 Queen Square W.C.

PLATE 57.

GROOMBRIDGE PLACE, KENT.

VIEW ACROSS LOWER GARDEN.

PLATE 58*.

HOLLAND HOUSE, KENSINGTON.

GATEWAY IN FORECOURT.

PLATE 58.

HOLLAND HOUSE, KENSINGTON.

THE DUTCH GARDEN.

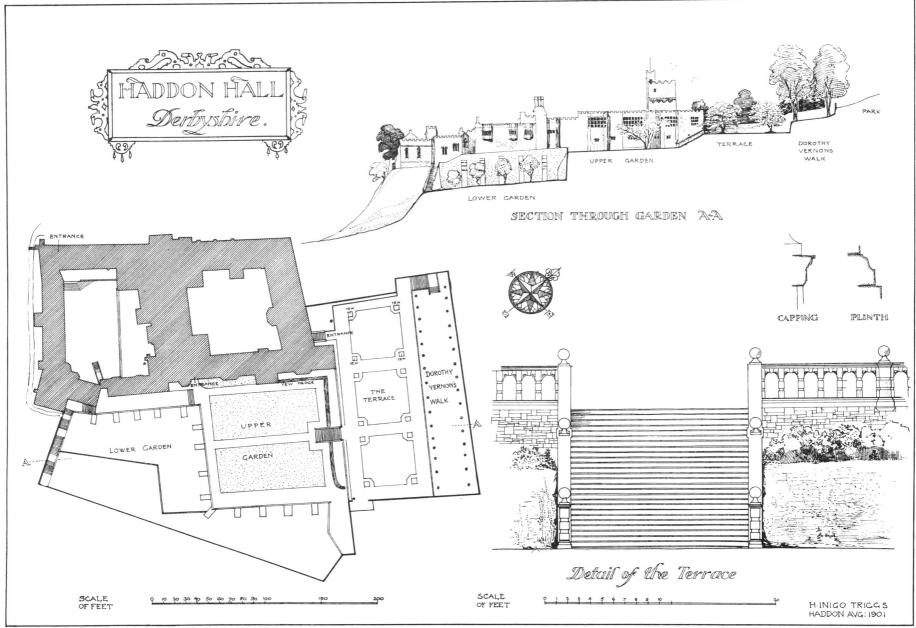

Plate 59

Detail of the Terrace

154

Plate 60

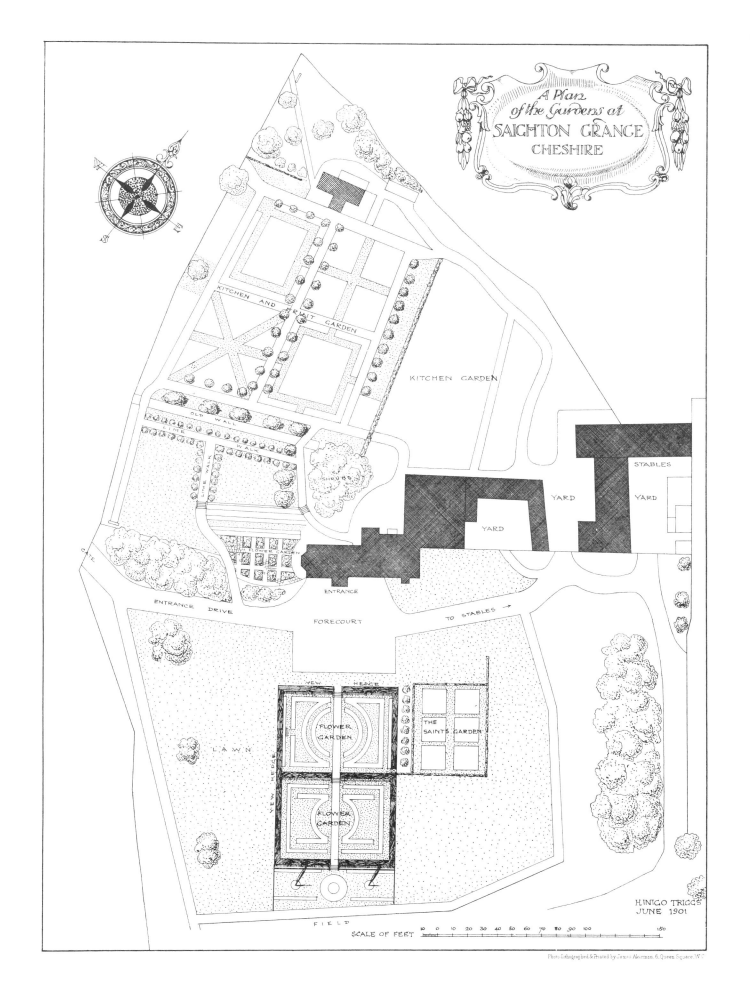

A Plan
of the Gardens at
SAIGHTON GRANGE
CHESHIRE

KITCHEN AND FRUIT GARDEN

KITCHEN GARDEN

OLD WALL

LIME WALK

LIME WALK

SHRUBS

FLOWER GARDEN

STABLES

YARD

YARD

YARD

ENTRANCE

ENTRANCE DRIVE

FORECOURT

TO STABLES →

GATE

NEW HEDGE

FLOWER GARDEN

FLOWER GARDEN

THE SAINTS GARDEN

LAWN

FIELD

H INIGO TRIGGS
JUNE 1901

SCALE OF FEET   10 0 10 20 30 40 50 60 70 80 90 100   150

Photo-Lithographed & Printed by James Akerman, 6, Queen Square, W C

Plate 61

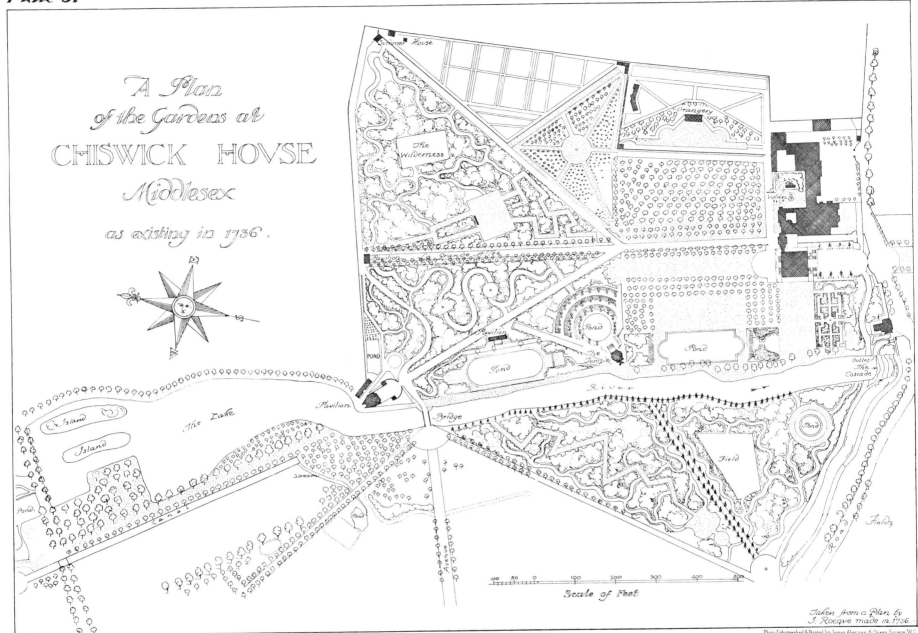

A Plan
of the Gardens at
CHISWICK HOVSE
Middlesex

as existing in 1736.

Summer House

The Wilderness

Orangery

Volier

Grande Alle

Bagnio

Pavilion

Pond

Pond

Pond

The Temple

Pond

Outlet
The
Cascade

Pavilion

River

Bridge

Field

Pond

Island

Island

The Lake

Stream

Pond

Pond

Avenue

Fields

Road

100 50   0   100   200   300   400   500

Scale of Feet

Taken from a Plan by
J. Rocqve made in 1736

Photo-Lithographed & Printed by James Akerman, 6, Queen Square, W.C.

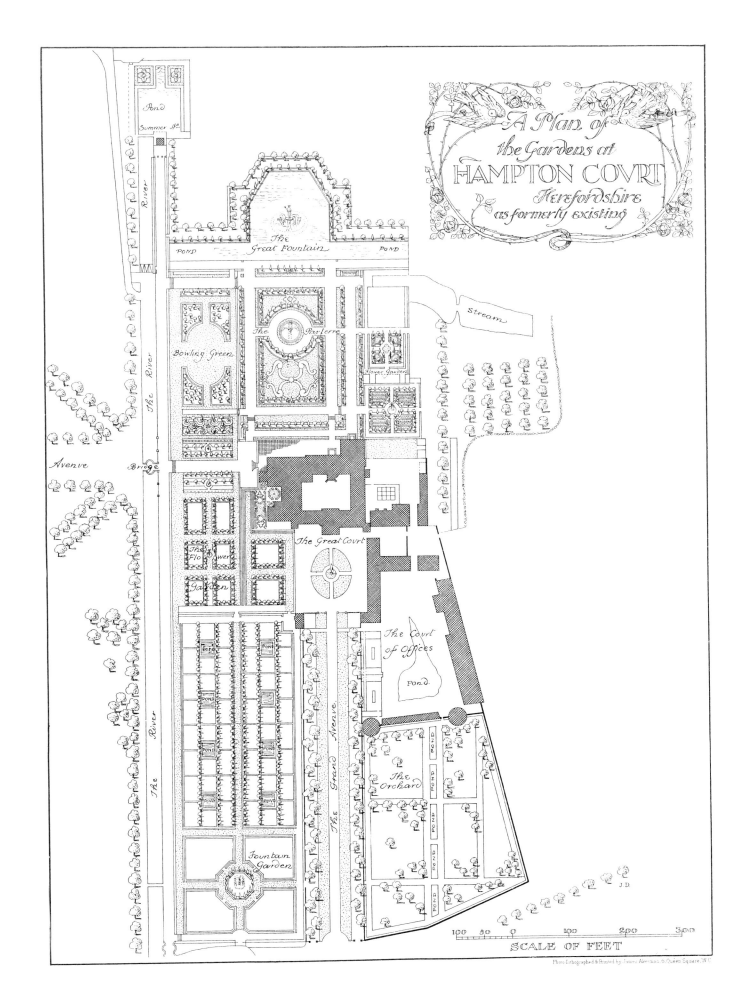

Plate 62

A Plan of
the Gardens at
HAMPTON COVRT
Herefordshire
as formerly existing

Pond
Summer H⁰
River
The Great Fountain
POND
POND
The Parterre
Bowling Green
Flower Garden
Stream
The River
Avenue
Bridge
The Flower Garden
The Great Court
The River
The Grand Avenue
POND
The Court of Offices
Pond.
The Orchard
POND
Fountain Garden
J.D.

Plate 63

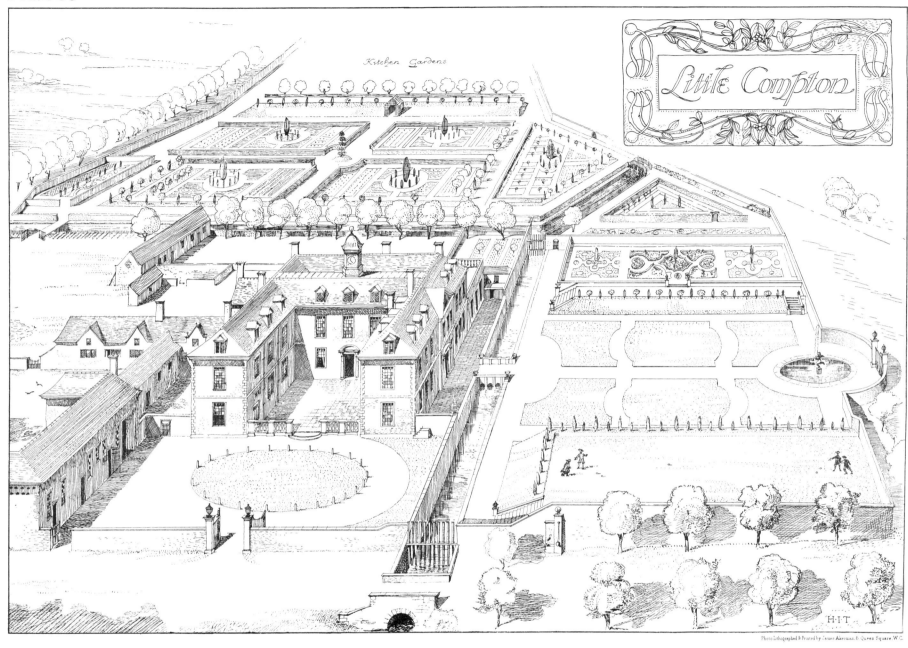

Kitchen Gardens

Little Compton

H·I·T

Photo Lithographed & Printed by James Akerman, 6 Queen Square. W.C.

Plate 64

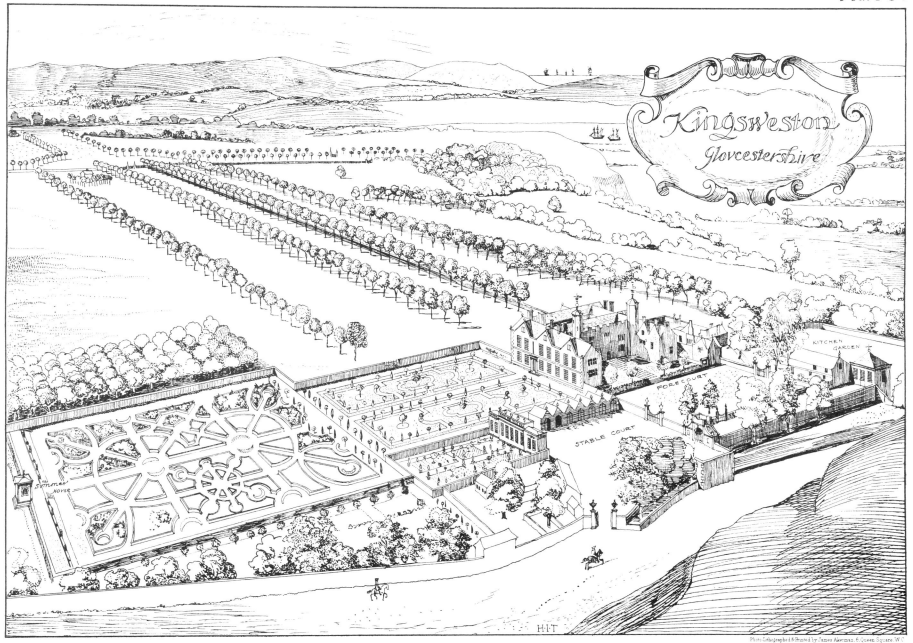

Kingsweston

Gloucestershire

KITCHEN GARDEN

FORECOURT

STABLE COURT

SUMMER HOUSE

H.I.T.

Photo Lithographed & Printed by James Akerman, 6, Queen Square, W.C.

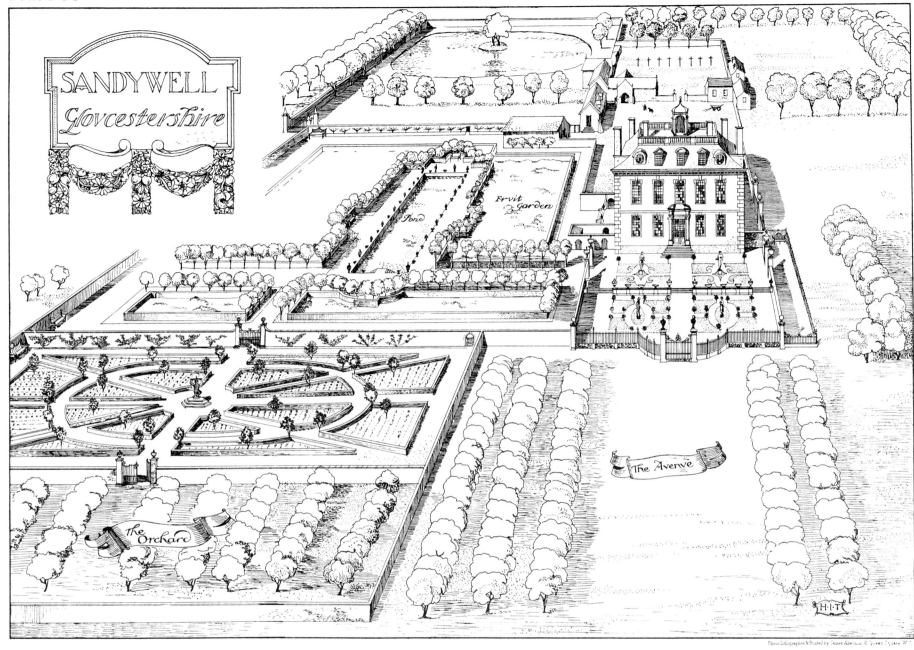

Plate 65

SANDYWELL
Gloucestershire

Pond

Fruit Garden

The Avenue

The Orchard

H·I·T

Photo Lithographed & Printed by James Akerman 6 Queen Square W.C.

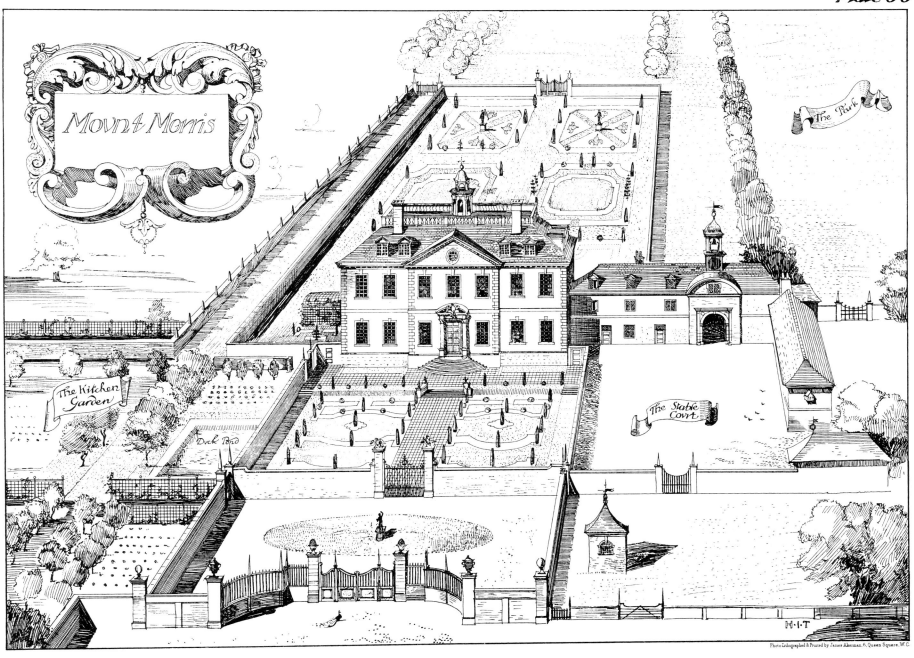

Plate 66

Movnt Morris

The Kitchen Garden

Dvck Pond

The Stable Covrt

The Park

H·I·T

Photo-Lithographed & Printed by James Akerman, 6, Queen Square, W.C.

Plate 67

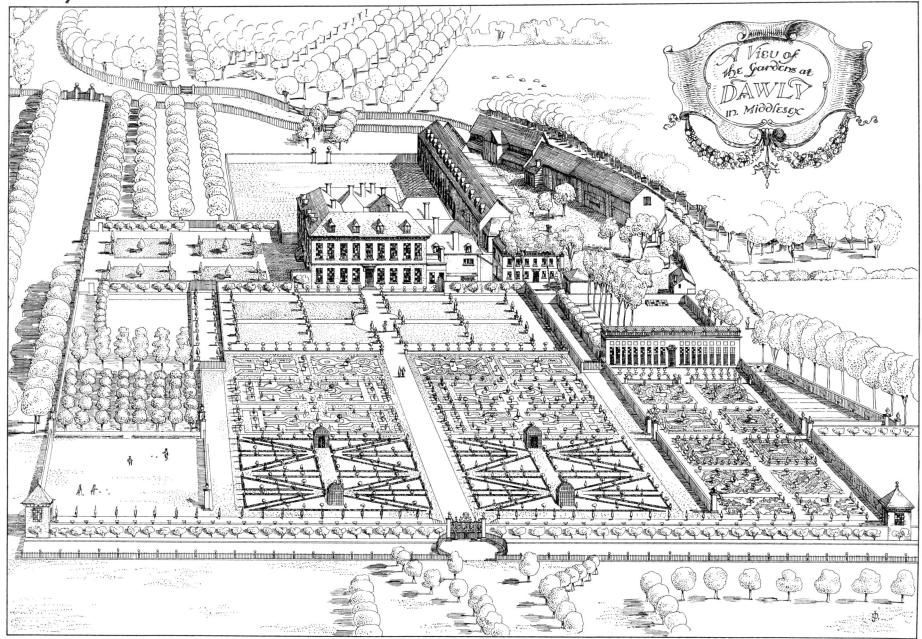

A View of the Gardens at DAWLY in Middlesex

Photo-Lithographed & Printed by James Akerman, 6, Queen Square W C

162

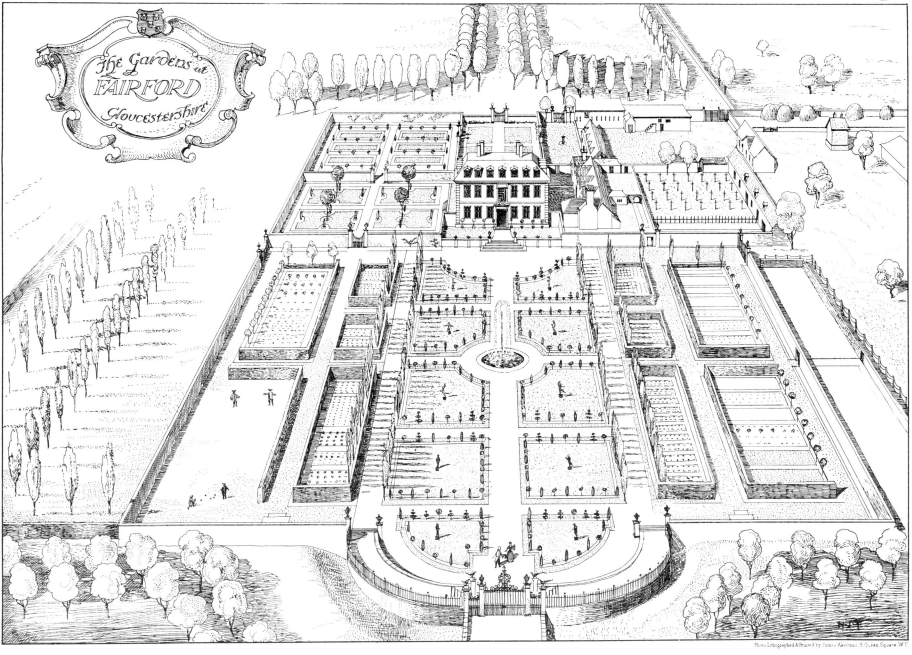

The Gardens at FAIRFORD Gloucestershire

Plate 68

Photo Lithographed & Printed by James Akerman, 5, Queen Square, W.C.

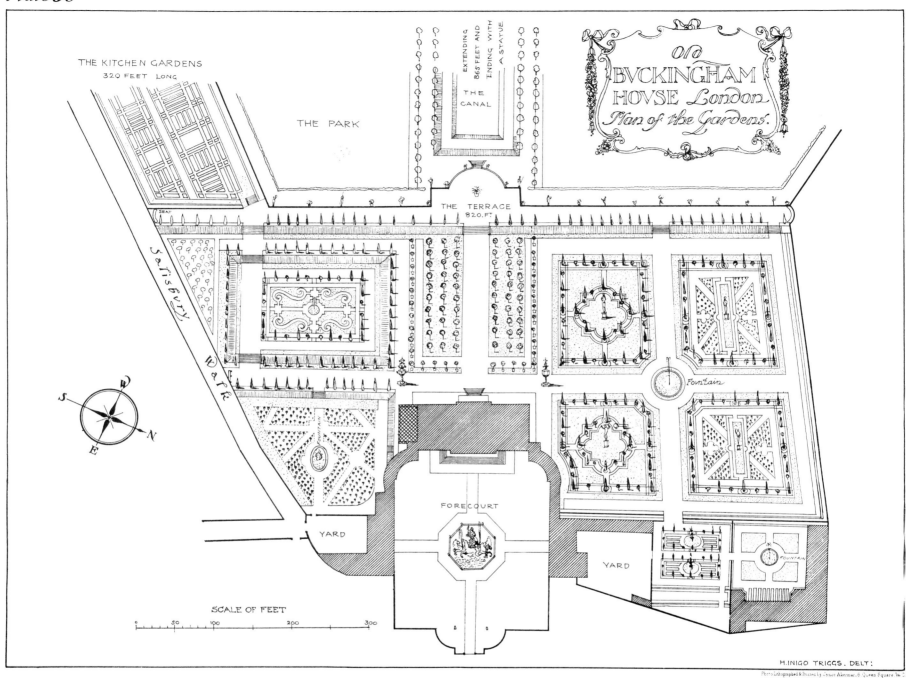

Plate 69

THE KITCHEN GARDENS
320 FEET LONG

THE PARK

EXTENDING 865 FEET AND ENDING WITH A STATUE

THE CANAL

Old
BVCKINGHAM
HOVSE London
Plan of the Gardens.

THE TERRACE
820. F.T

SEAT

Salisbury Walk

FOUNTAIN

Fountain

FORECOURT

YARD

YARD

Fountain

SCALE OF FEET

0   50   100   200   300

H. INIGO TRIGGS. DELT.

Photo Lithographed & Printed by James Akerman, 6 Queen Square, W.C.

164

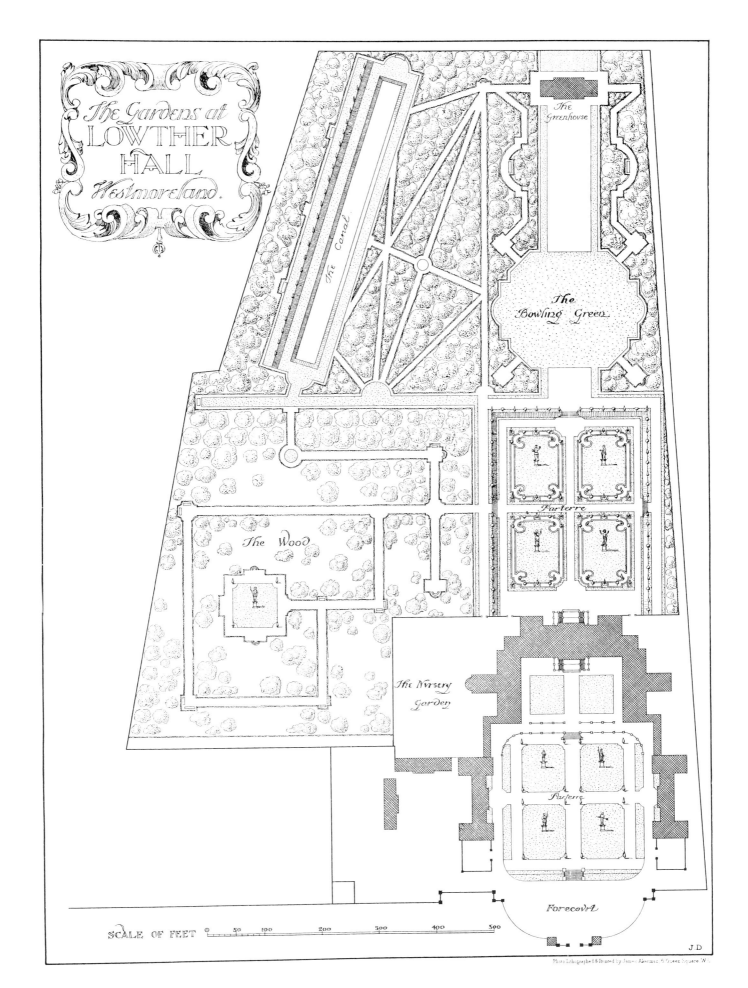

Plate 70

The Gardens at
LOWTHER
HALL
Westmoreland.

The Canal

The Greenhouse

The Bowling Green

Parterre

The Wood

The Nursery Garden

Parterre

Forecourt

SCALE OF FEET   0   50   100   200   300   400   500

J.D

Plate 71

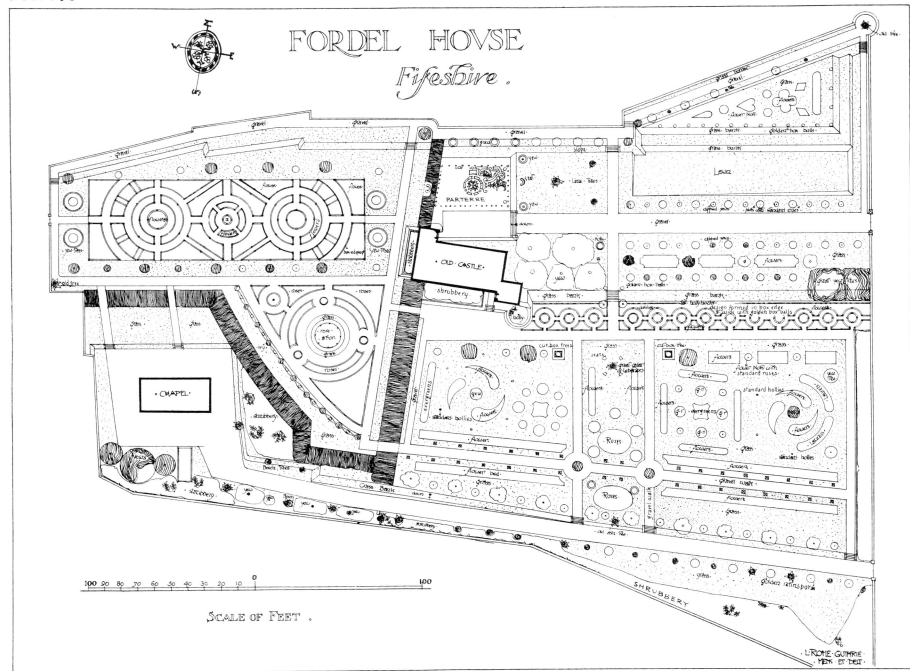

FORDEL HOVSE
Fifeshire.

SCALE OF FEET .

Plate 72

CIRCULAR ← ✳ SQUARE →

STOBHALL
PERTHSHIRE

The Sundial
HEIGHT 6 FEET 2 IN

FLOWERS

FLOWERS

GRASS WALKS

· L·ROME· GUTHRIE·

Phot: Lithographed & Printed by James Akerman 6 Queen Square W C

Plate 73

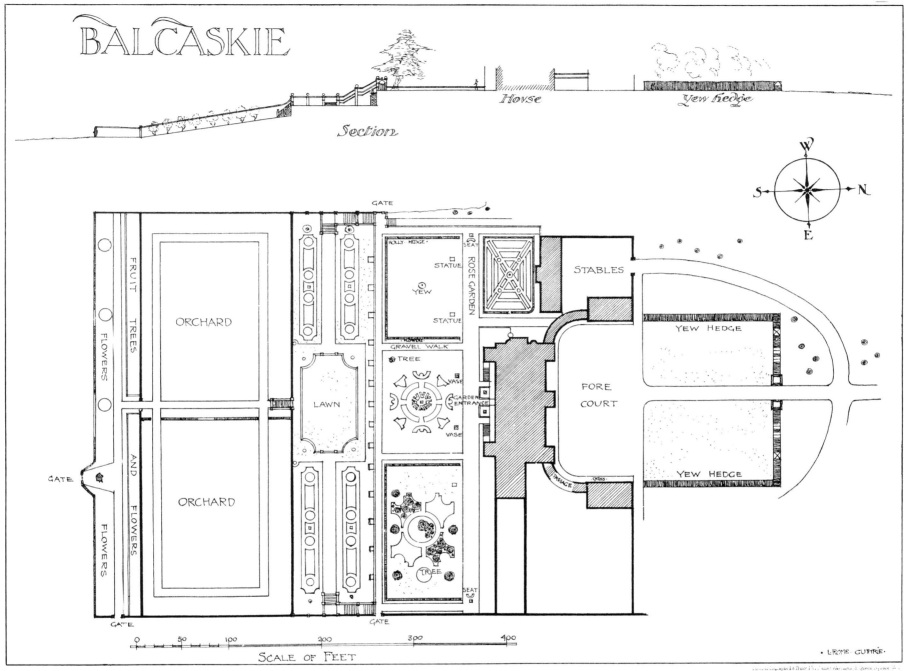

BALCASKIE

Section

House

Yew hedge

GATE

FRUIT TREES

FLOWERS

ORCHARD

ORCHARD

FLOWERS

GATE

AND FLOWERS

FLOWERS

GATE

LAWN

GATE

GRAVEL WALK

HOLLY HEDGE

YEW

STATUE

STATUE

TREE

VASE

GARDEN ENTRANCE

VASE

TREE

SEAT

GATE

ROSE GARDEN

SEAT

STABLES

FORE COURT

PASSAGE

CROSS

STABLES

YEW HEDGE

YEW HEDGE

W N S E

0   50   100   200   300   400

SCALE OF FEET

• JEROME GUTHRIE •

Plate 74

BALCASKIE
Birds-eye View

L·ROME·GUTHRIE·

Photo Lithographed & Printed by James Akerman, 6, Queen Square W.C.

PLATE 75.

BALCASKIE, FIFESHIRE.

THE TERRACE.

Plate 76.

BALCARRES, FIFESHIRE.

FROM THE TERRACE.

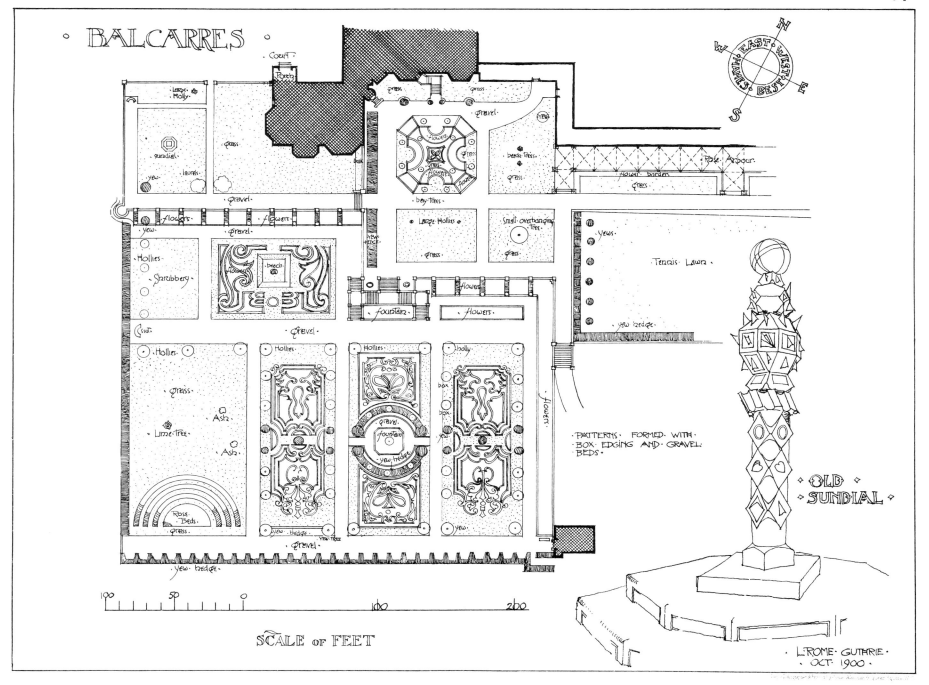

Plate 77

BALCARRES

PATTERNS · FORMED · WITH ·
BOX · EDGING · AND · GRAVEL ·
BEDS ·

SCALE OF FEET

OLD SUNDIAL

· L·ROME· GUTHRIE ·
· OCT · 1900 ·

173

Plate 78

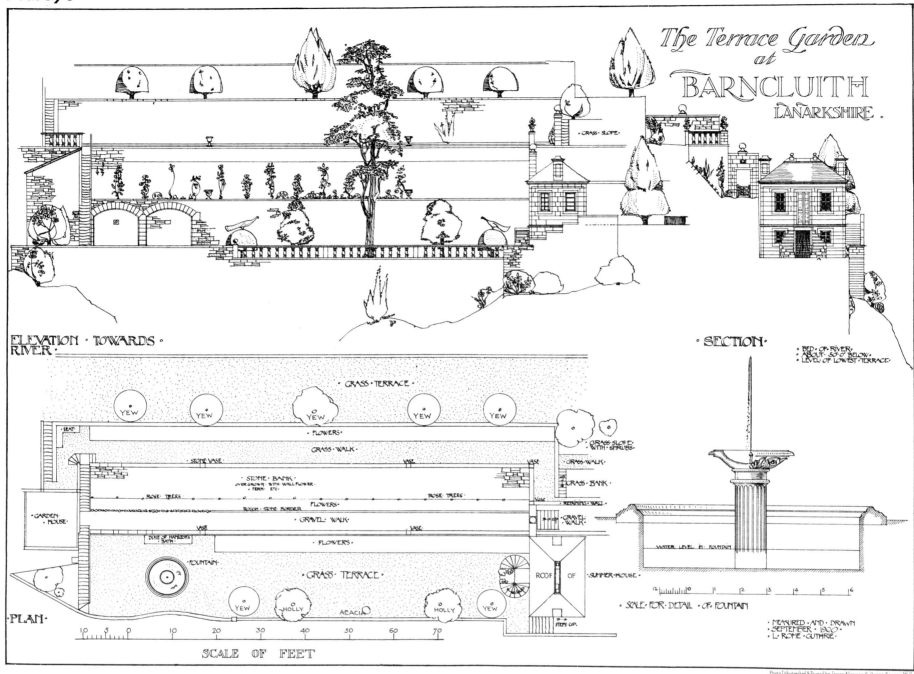

The Terrace Garden
at
BARNCLUITH
LANARKSHIRE.

ELEVATION · TOWARDS · RIVER ·

· SECTION ·

· BED · OF · RIVER ·
· ABOUT · 80'·0" · BELOW ·
· LEVEL · OF · LOWEST · TERRACE ·

· GRASS · TERRACE ·

YEW   YEW   YEW   YEW   YEW

· GRASS · SLOPE ·

· SEAT ·

· FLOWERS ·

· GRASS · WALK ·

· GRASS · SLOPE ·
· WITH · SHRUBS ·

· STONE · VASE ·   · VASE ·   · GRASS · WALK ·

· STONE · BANK ·
· OVERGROWTH · WITH · WALL FLOWER ·
· FERN · ETC ·   · GRASS · BANK ·

· ROSE · TREES ·   · ROSE · TREES ·

· ROUGH · STONE · BORDER ·   · FLOWERS ·   · VASE ·

· RETAINING · WALL ·

· GARDEN ·
· HOUSE ·

· GRAVEL · WALK ·   · GRAVEL ·
· WALK ·

· VASE ·   · VASE ·

· DUKE OF HAMILTON'S ·
· BATH ·

· FLOWERS ·

· FOUNTAIN ·

· GRASS · TERRACE ·   · ROOF · OF · SUMMER · HOUSE ·

YEW   HOLLY   ACACIA   HOLLY   YEW

· STEPS · UP ·

· PLAN ·

10 5 0   10   20   30   40   50   60   70

SCALE OF FEET

· WATER · LEVEL · IN · FOUNTAIN ·

12   0   1   2   3   4   5   6

· SCALE · FOR · DETAIL · OF · FOUNTAIN ·

· MEASURED · AND · DRAWN ·
· SEPTEMBER · 1900 ·
· L · ROME · GUTHRIE ·

Photo Lithographed & Printed by James Akerman, 6, Queen Square, W.C.

PLATE 79.

BARNCLUITH, LANARKSHIRE.

THE TERRACES.

PLATE 80.

NEWBATTLE ABBEY, EDINBURGH.

THE GATE-HOUSE.

Plate 81

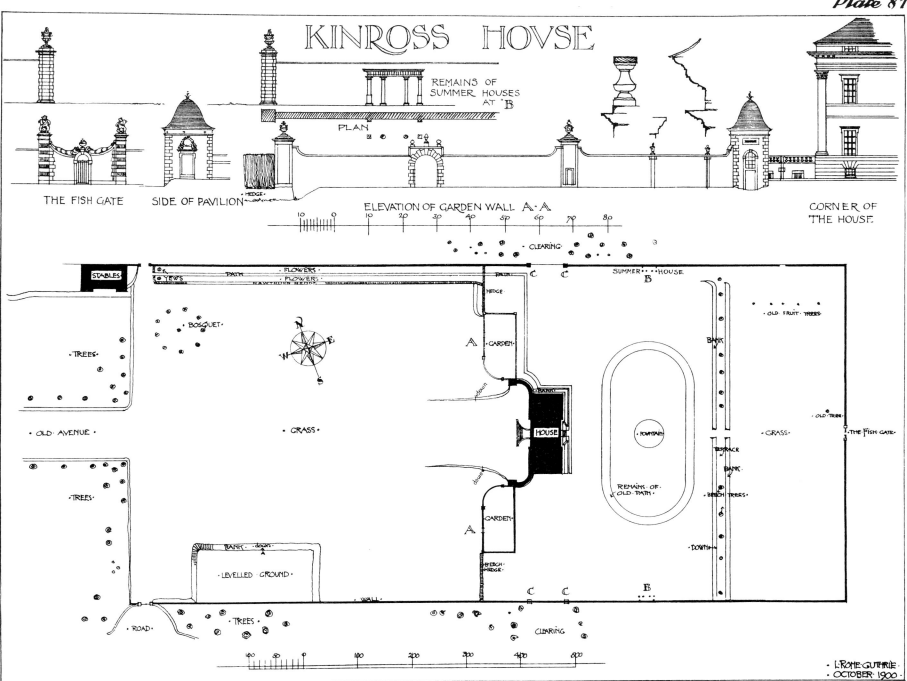

KINROSS HOVSE

REMAINS OF
SUMMER HOUSES
AT "B

PLAN

THE FISH GATE   SIDE OF PAVILION   ELEVATION OF GARDEN WALL A·A   CORNER OF THE HOUSE

L·ROME·GUTHRIE
OCTOBER·1900

Photo Lithographed & Printed by James Akerman, 6, Queen Square, W.C.

177

Plate 82.

KINROSS HOUSE.

THE GARDEN-HOUSE AND FISH GATES.

Plate 83

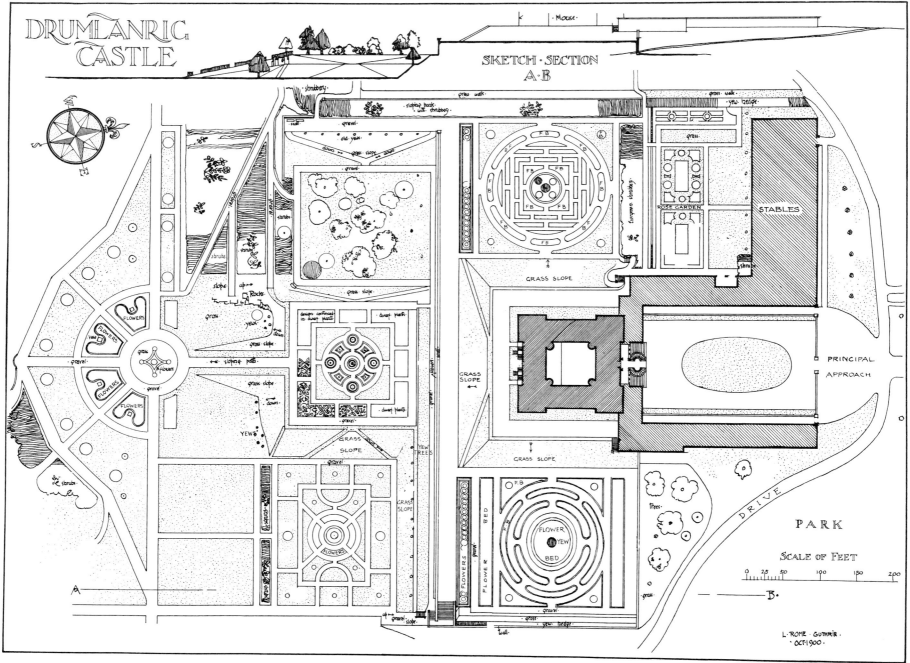

DRUMLANRIG CASTLE

SKETCH · SECTION
A · B

ROSE GARDEN

STABLES

PRINCIPAL
APPROACH

GRASS SLOPE

GRASS
SLOPE

GRASS SLOPE

FLOWERS

FLOWERS

FLOWERS

FLOWERS

FLOWERS

YEW
TREES

GRASS
SLOPE

GRASS
SLOPE

FLOWER
BED

FLOWER
YEW
BED

FLOWER BED

Trees

grass

DRIVE

PARK

SCALE OF FEET
0   25   50   100   150   200

A

B

L · ROME · GUTHRIE
· OCT · 1900 ·

PLATE 84.

DRUMLANRIG CASTLE, DUMFRIESSHIRE.

GENERAL VIEW.

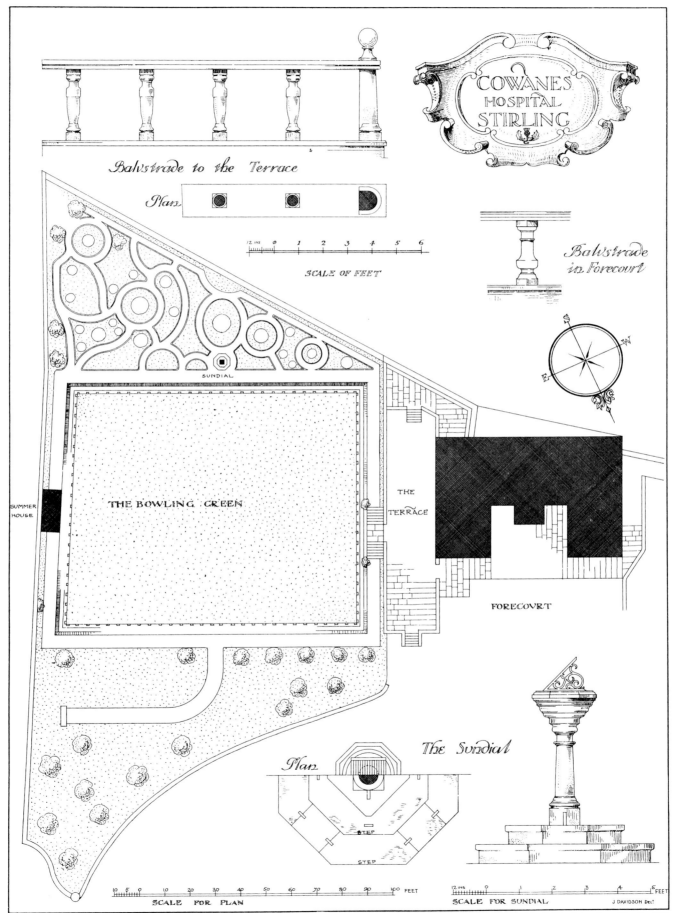

Plate 85

COWANES HOSPITAL STIRLING

Balustrade to the Terrace

Plan

SCALE OF FEET

Balustrade in Forecourt

THE BOWLING GREEN

SUNDIAL

SUMMER HOUSE

THE TERRACE

FORECOURT

Plan

The Sundial

STEP

STEP

SCALE FOR PLAN

FEET

SCALE FOR SUNDIAL

FEET

J DAVIDSON Delt

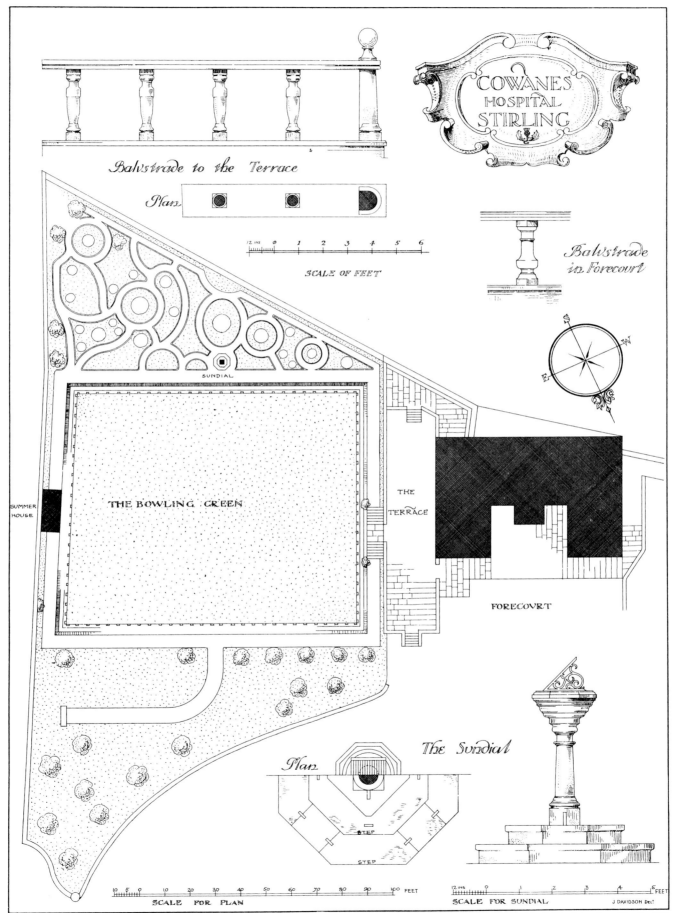

Photo-Lithographed & Printed by James Akerman, 6, Queen Square, W.C.

183

Plate 86

EARLSHALL Fifeshire.

Plan & Details of the Garden

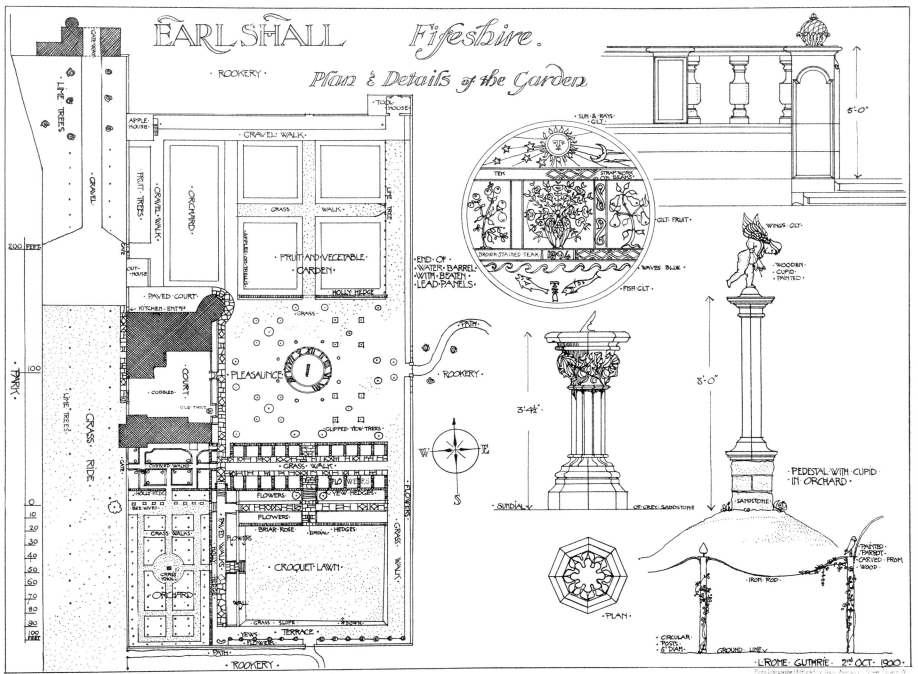

· ROOKERY ·

· LIME · TREES ·

· GRAVEL ·

200 FEET

· PARK ·

· LIME · TREES ·

· GRASS · RIDE ·

100

· GATE · WALK ·

· TOOL · HOUSE ·

· APPLE · HOUSE ·

· GRAVEL · WALK ·

· FRUIT · TREES ·

· GRAVEL · WALK ·

· ORCHARD ·

· GRASS · WALK ·

· FRUIT · AND · VEGETABLE · GARDEN ·

· APPLES · ON · TRELLIS ·

· HOLLY · HEDGE ·

· OUT- HOUSE ·

· GATE ·

· PAVED · COURT ·

· KITCHEN · ENT^CE ·

· COBBLED ·

· COURT ·

· OLD · TREE ·

· PLEASAUNCE ·

· GRASS ·

I

· CLIPPED · YEW · TREES ·

· GRASS · WALK ·

· COBBLED · WALKS ·

· FLOWERS ·

· FLOWERS ·

· YEW · HEDGES ·

· FLOWERS ·

· FLOWERS ·

· BRIAR · ROSE ·

· SUNDIAL ·

· HEDGES ·

· PAVED · WALKS ·

· HOLLY · HEDGE ·

· BEE · HIVES ·

· GRASS · WALKS ·

· GRASS · KNOLL ·

· ORCHARD ·

· WALL ·

· GRASS · SLOPE ·

· YEWS ·

· FLOWERS ·

· TERRACE ·

· PATH ·

· BOWN ·

· CROQUET · LAWN ·

· FLOWERS · GRASS · WALK ·

· END · OF · WATER · BARREL · WITH · BEATEN · LEAD · PANELS ·

· PATH ·

· ROOKERY ·

· ROOKERY ·

0
10
20
30
40
50
60
70
80
90
100 FEET

W · E · S (compass)

· SUN · & · RAYS · GILT ·

· TEK ·

· STRAP · WORK · ON · BEAMS ·

· GILT · FRUIT ·

· BROWN · STAINED · TEAK ·

1894

· WAVES · BLUE ·

· FISH · GILT ·

5'-0"

· WINGS · GILT ·

· WOODEN · CUPID · PAINTED ·

3'-4½"

8'-0"

· SUNDIAL ·

· OF · GREY · SANDSTONE ·

· PLAN ·

· PEDESTAL · WITH · CUPID · IN · ORCHARD ·

· SANDSTONE ·

· IRON · ROD ·

· PAINTED · PARROT · CARVED · FROM · WOOD ·

· CIRCULAR · POSTS · 8" DIAM ·

· GROUND · LINE ·

· L · ROME · GUTHRIE · 2ND · OCT · 1900 ·

Photo Lithographed & Printed by ...

185

EARLSHALL 1988.

KINROSS 1988.

Plate 87

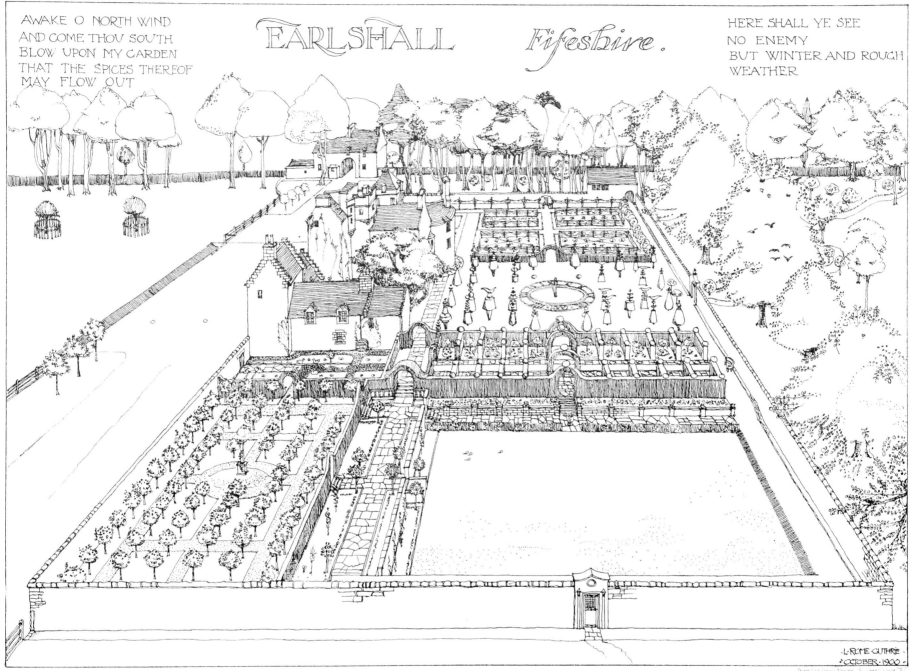

AWAKE O NORTH WIND
AND COME THOU SOUTH
BLOW UPON MY GARDEN
THAT THE SPICES THEREOF
MAY FLOW OUT

EARLSHALL   Fifeshire.

HERE SHALL YE SEE
NO ENEMY
BUT WINTER AND ROUGH
WEATHER

· L · ROME · GUTHRIE ·
· OCTOBER · 1900 ·

Plate 88

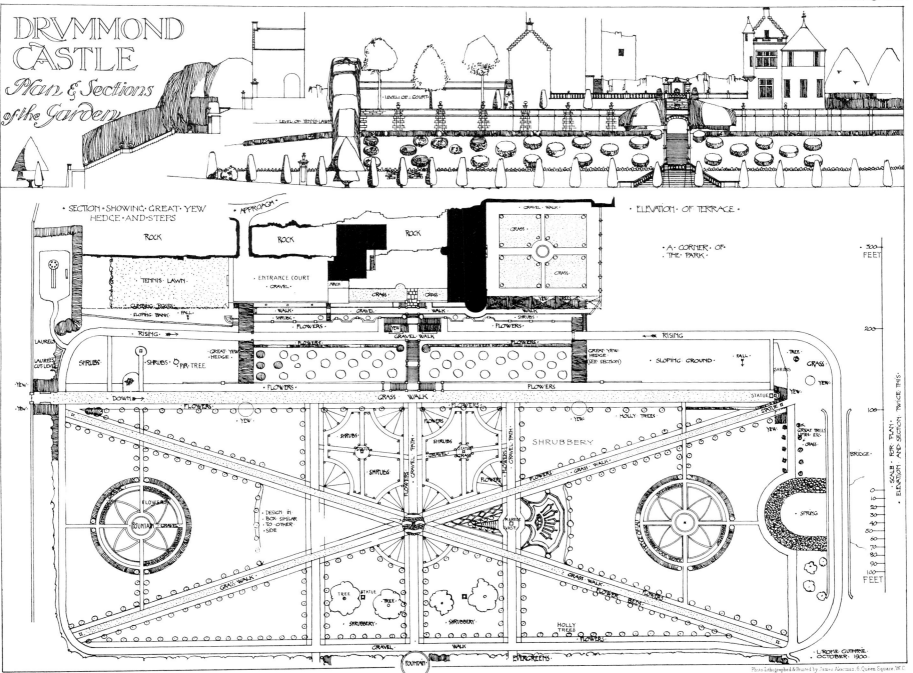

DRVMMOND CASTLE
Plan & Sections
of the Garden

· LEVEL · OF · COURT ·

· LEVEL · OF · TENNIS · LAWN ·

· SECTION · SHOWING · GREAT · YEW ·
HEDGE · AND · STEPS

· ELEVATION · OF · TERRACE ·

· A · CORNER · OF ·
· THE · PARK ·

ROCK   ROCK   ROCK

APPROACH

GRAVEL · WALK

GRASS

TENNIS · LAWN

ENTRANCE COURT
· GRAVEL ·

ARCH   GRASS   GRASS

WALK   GRAVEL   WALK

SHRUBS   · SHRUBS ·

· FLOWERS ·   · FLOWERS ·

CUTTING BOARD

SLOPING · BANK   FALL

RISING   YEW   RISING

· FLOWERS ·   · GRAVEL · WALK ·   · FLOWERS ·

LAURELS

LAURELS
CUT · LEVEL   SHRUBS   SHRUBS · FIR · TREE   GREAT · YEW ·
HEDGE ·   GREAT · YEW ·
HEDGE ·
(SEE SECTION)   · SLOPING · GROUND ·   FALL   TREE   GRASS   SHRUBS

· FLOWERS ·   · FLOWERS ·   SHRUBS   CRASS

YEW

YEW   DOWN   · FLOWERS ·   · GRASS · WALK ·   · FLOWERS ·   STATUE   YEW   YEW

· YEW ·   · YEW ·   · HOLLY · TREES ·   STATUE

· DESIGN · IN
· BOX · SIMILAR
· TO · OTHER
· SIDE ·   SHRUBS   SHRUBS   FLOWERS   · SHRUBBERY ·   YEW   OK
GREAT TREES
LIMES · ETC.
GRASS

FLOWERS
FOUNTAIN GRAVEL   SHRUBS   SHRUBS
STATUE
GRASS
GRAVEL   FLOWERS   GRAVEL PATH   FLOWERS   GRASS · WALK   FLOWERS   FOUNTAIN   SPRING

MARBLE
VASE   BRIDGE

TREE   STATUE
TREE   SHRUBBERY   SHRUBBERY   HOLLY
TREES   FLOWERS

· SHRUBBERY ·   · SHRUBBERY ·

GRAVEL   WALK   · EVERGREENS ·

FOUNTAIN

· SCALE · FOR · PLAN ·
· ELEVATION · AND · SECTION · TWICE · THIS ·

300
FEET

200

100

0
10
20
30
40
50
60
70
80
90
100
FEET

· L · ROME · GUTHRIE ·
· OCTOBER · 1900 ·

Photo Lithographed & Printed by James Akerman, 6, Queen Square, W.C.

189

PLATE 89.

DRUMMOND CASTLE, PERTHSHIRE.

VIEW FROM THE TERRACE.

DRUMMOND CASTLE 1988.

Plate 90

Plan

LEAD FIGURE

GILT

Garden Hovses

THATCHED ROOF

Plan

SCALE OF FEET
FOR PLANS

Belcombe Brook
Bradford on Avon

Lead figvre in Temple

Iford Manor.
near Bradford on Avon

M·I·TRIGGS 1900

Photo Lithographed & Printed by James Akerman, 6 Queen Square W

Plate 91

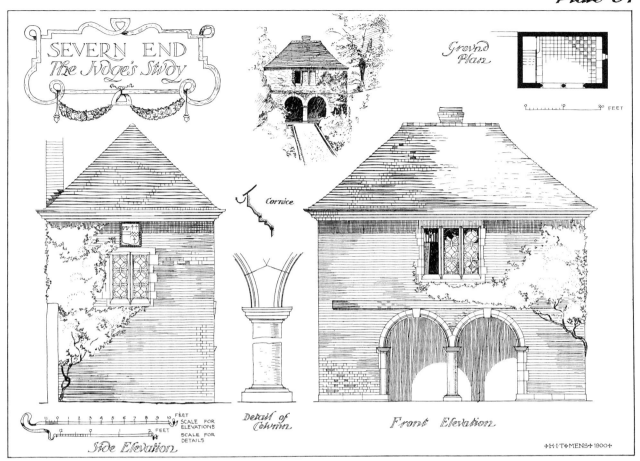

SEVERN END
The Judge's Study

Ground Plan

0   10   30 FEET

Cornice

Detail of Column

Side Elevation

FEET
SCALE FOR ELEVATIONS
SCALE FOR DETAILS

Front Elevation

+H·I·T+MENS+1900+

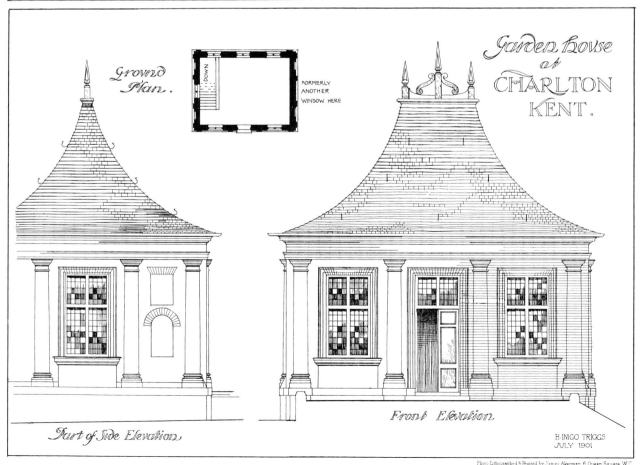

Garden House at CHARLTON KENT.

Ground Plan.

DOWN

FORMERLY ANOTHER WINDOW HERE

Part of Side Elevation

Front Elevation

H·INIGO TRIGGS
JULY 1901

Photo-Lithographed & Printed by James Akerman, 6 Queen Square W.C.

Plate 92

Plan

SVMMER HOVSES

Plan

Nvn Moncton near York

H.M.CAUTLEY MENS

The Cedars Beckington
Somersetshire

0   10   20   SCALE FOR PLANS
0 1 2 3 4 5 6 7 8 9 10 11 12 13 14 15   SCALE FOR ELEVATIONS

H.I.T 1901

Photo-Lithographed & Printed by James Akerman, 6, Queen Square, W.C

Plate 93

Shipton Court · Chasleton Manor

DOVECOTES

Dormstone · Oddingley

Photo-Lithographed & Printed by James Akerman, 6, Queen Square, W.C.

195

Plate 93*

Richard's Castle   Old Sufton

DOVECOTES

Much Marcle   Buttas

Herefordshire.

Photo-Lithographed & Printed by James Akerman, 6, Queen Square, W.C.

Plate 94

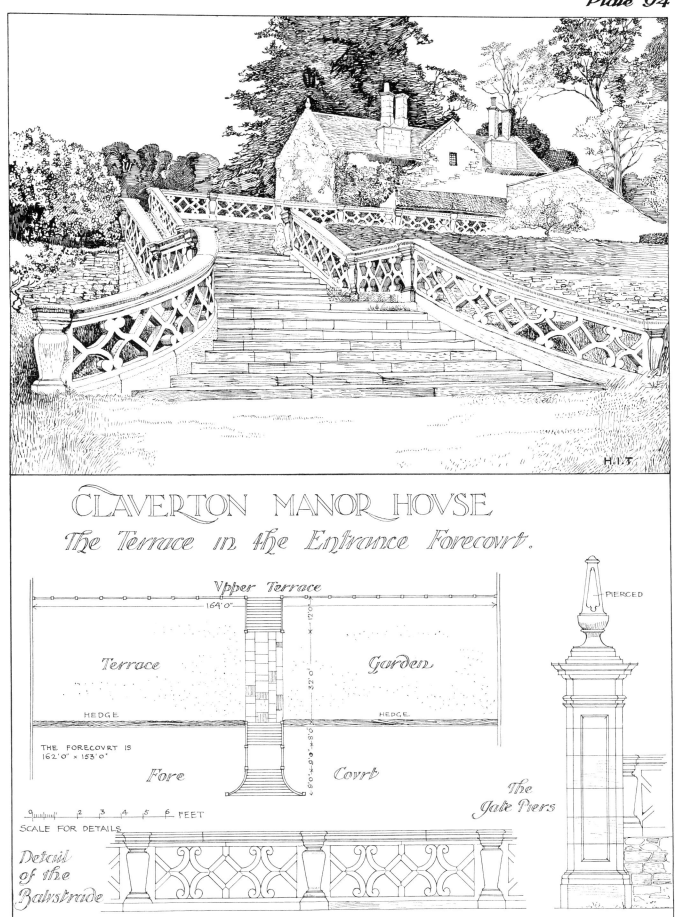

CLAVERTON MANOR HOVSE
The Terrace in the Entrance Forecovrt.

Vpper Terrace

164'0"

12'0"

Terrace

Garden

32'0"

HEDGE

HEDGE

THE FORECOVRT IS
162'0" × 153'0"

9'0"·9'0"·8'0"

Fore

Covrt

PIERCED

The
Gate Piers

0 1 2 3 4 5 6 FEET

SCALE FOR DETAILS

Detail
of the
Balvstrade

197

PLATE 95.

BRYMPTON MANOR HOUSE, SOMERSETSHIRE.

THE TERRACE.

PLATE 96.

KINGSTON HOUSE, BRADFORD-ON-AVON.

THE TERRACE.

PLATE 97.

A.

B.

BRAMSHILL, HANTS.

A.   GATEWAY IN GARDEN WALL   B.   THE TERRACE.

Plate 98

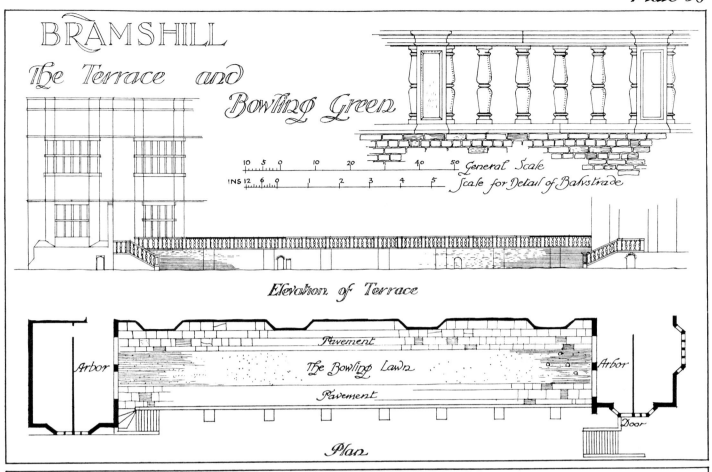

BRAMSHILL
The Terrace and Bowling Green

General Scale

Scale for Detail of Balustrade

Elevation of Terrace

Pavement

The Bowling Lawn

Pavement

Arbor

Arbor

Door

Plan

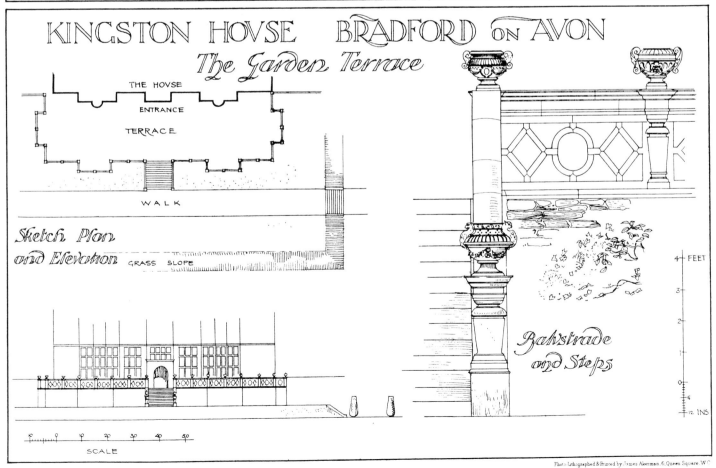

KINGSTON HOUSE BRADFORD ON AVON
The Garden Terrace

THE HOUSE

ENTRANCE

TERRACE

WALK

Sketch Plan and Elevation

GRASS SLOPE

Balustrade and Steps

SCALE

FEET

INS

Photo-Lithographed & Printed by James Akerman, 6, Queen Square, W.C.

PLATE 99.

CLIFTON HALL, NOTTINGHAM.

THE STEPS.

PLATE 100.

VEN HOUSE, SOMERSET.

THE TERRACE STEPS.

PLATE 101.

A.

B.

(A.) HADSOE.   (B.) BULWICK HALL, NORTHANTS.

     THE FOUNTAIN AND TERRACE.   GATE-ENTRANCE, THE LONG WALK.

Plate 102

ENTRANCE GATES AND PIERS

Penshurst Kent

Iford Manor Somersetshire

SQUARE ON PLAN

SQUARE ON PLAN

The Botanic Gardens Oxford

St John's College Cambridge.

Belton House Grantham

Scale of Feet

0 1 2 3 4 5 6 7 8 9 10 11 12 13 14 15

HADDON HALL 1988.

PLATE 103

STONELEIGH ABBEY, WARWICKSHIRE.

GARDEN GATES.

SYDENHAM HOUSE, DEVONSHIRE.

THE ENTRANCE GATEWAY.

Plate 104

KNOTS AND PARTERRES *from old Designs*

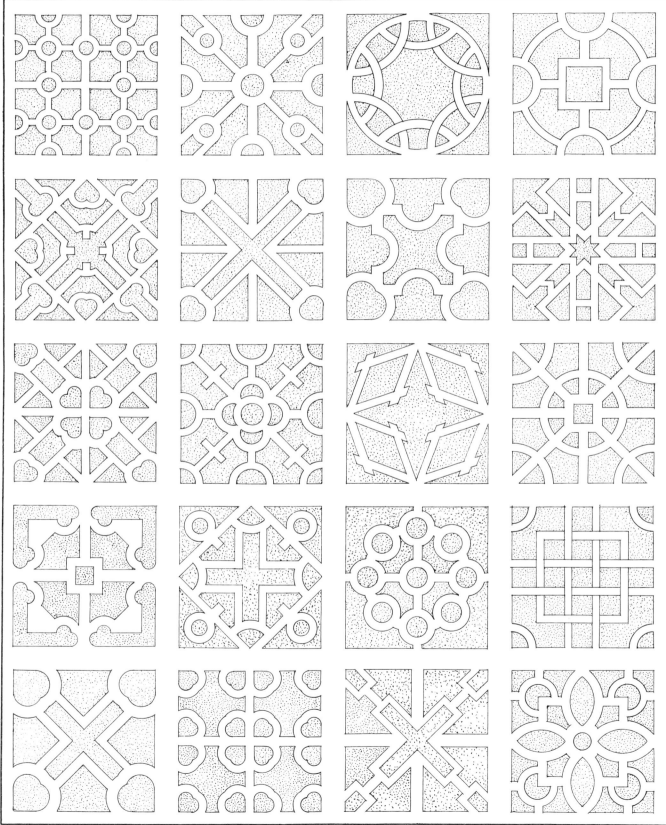

Photo-Lithographed & Printed by James Akerman, 6, Queen Square, W.C.

Plate 105

KNOTS AND PARTERRES *from old Designs.*

Phot. Lithographed & Printed by James Akerman 6 Queen Square W C

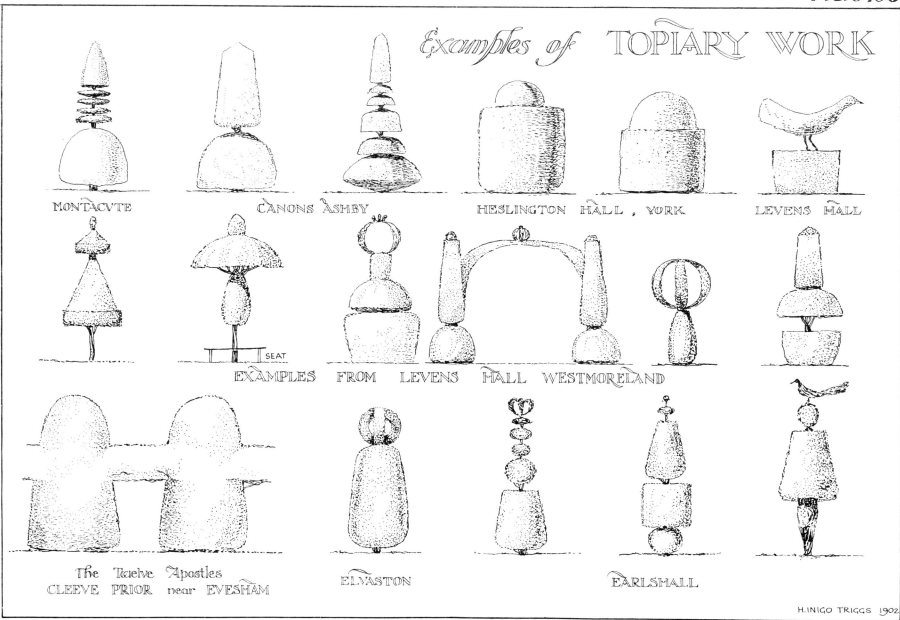

Plate 106

Examples of TOPIARY WORK

MONTACVTE

CANONS ASHBY

HESLINGTON HALL, YORK

LEVENS HALL

SEAT

EXAMPLES FROM LEVENS HALL WESTMORELAND

The Twelve Apostles
CLEEVE PRIOR near EVESHAM

ELVASTON

EARLSHALL

H.INIGO TRIGGS 1902

Plate 107

LEAD FIGVRES

4 FEET HIGH

A Pair of Figvres

at Enfield Old Park

Rovsham Oxon

at Rovsham Oxfordshire

The Shepherd at Canons Ashby

Photo-Lithographed & Printed by James Akerman, 6 Queen Square W.C.

NUN MONCTON, YORKSHIRE.

FOUR LEAD FIGURES.

Plate 109

I

II

III

IV

LEAD VASES

I & II *from Wilton House.*
III & IV *from Chiswick House.*

H·I·T

Photo Lithographed & Printed by James Akerman, 6, Queen Square, W.C.

Plate 110

1

Iford Manor,
Somersetshire.

LEAD

3

Hampton Court
Palace.

2

Enfield Old
Park.

VASES

4

Penshurst
Place.

Enfield Old
Park.

Photo-Lithographed & Printed by James Akerman, 6, Queen Square, W.C.

Plate 111

LEAD GARDEN CISTERNS

From the Victoria and Albert Mvsevm

Front

3 FEET 9½ INCHES LONG
2 „ 5 „ HIGH
1 FOOT 8½ „ BROAD

End

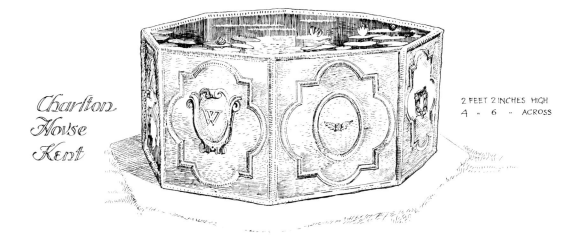

Charlton Hovse Kent

2 FEET 2 INCHES HIGH
4 „ 6 „ ACROSS

From the Victoria and Albert Mvsevm

Front

3 FEET 11½ INCHES LONG
2 „ 6¾ „ HIGH
1 FOOT 9 INCHES BROAD

End

Photo Lithographed & Printed by James Akerman, 6 Queen Square, W.C.

Plate 112

LEAD CISTERNS *From Enfield Old Park.*

2 FEET II INCHES

5 FEET 9 INCHES

THE FIGURES ARE EMBLEMATICAL OF THE FOUR SEASONS

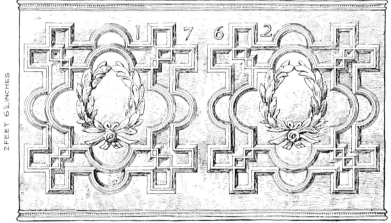

2 FEET 6½ INCHES

4 FEET 2 INCHES

1 FOOT 8½ INCHES

2 FEET 3 INCHES

3 FEET 8 INCHES

1 FOOT 10 INCHES

J. DAVIDSON. MENS

Plate Lithographed & Printed by James Akerman, 6 Queen Square, W.C.

PLATE 113.

SION HOUSE, ISLEWORTH.

FOUR STONE VASES.

Plate 114

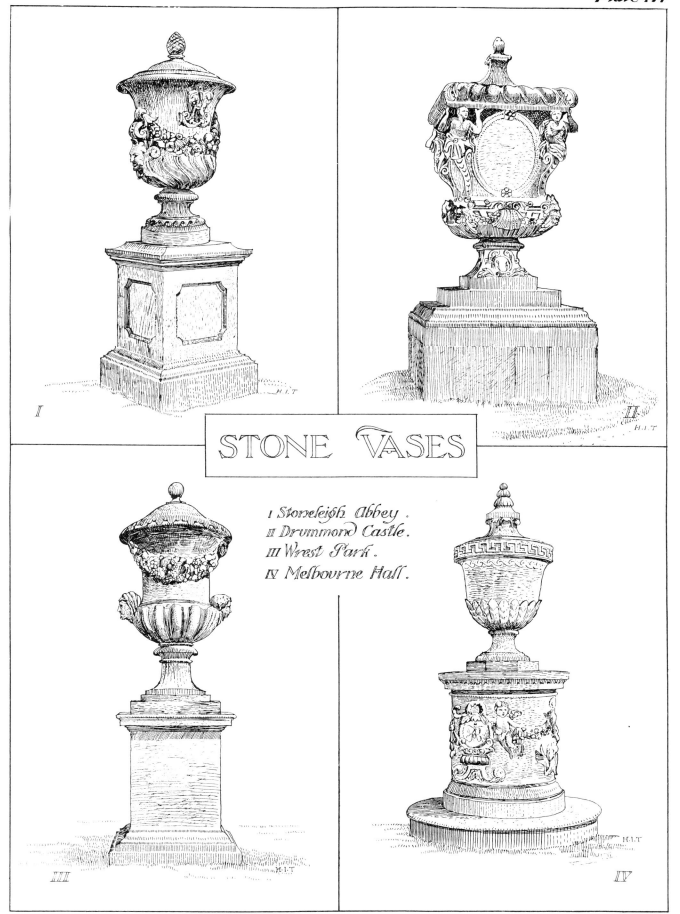

STONE VASES

I Stoneleigh Abbey.
II Drummond Castle.
III Wrest Park.
IV Melbourne Hall.

Plate 115

Northenden
Cheshire

Chiswick House
Middlesex

Enfield

Old Park

The Figvre
is of lead:

Enfield Old Park
Middlesex

Presthvry
Cheshire

H·I·T

Photo-Lithographed & Printed by James Akerman 6 Queen Square W.C.

Plate 116

SVNDIALS

4' 1" HIGH

3' 10" HIGH

Wrest
Bedfordshire

Wrest
Bedfordshire

Kew Palace
Svrrey

Wilton Hovse
Wiltshire.

5' 1" HIGH

Belton Hovse
Lincolnshire

BRONZE

GNOMON GONE

OCTAGONAL

OCTAGONAL

SQVARE STEPS

Photo Lithographed & Printed by James Akerman, 6 Queen Square, W C

221

PITMEDDEN 1988.

DRUMMOND CASTLE 1988.

Plate 117

Pitmedden
Aberdeen
Dvthie Park

SVNDIALS

Woodhovselee

Stobhall
Perthshire

H·I·T

H·I·T

Photo-Lithographed & Printed by James Akerman, 6 Queen Square W.C.

Plate 118

QVEEN MARYS DIAL
HOLYROOD PALACE

M R

Plan

Section thro' Pedestal

Scale of Feet

FEET

Scale for Plan

SVNDIAL AT NEWBATTLE ABBEY.

H·I·T

Photo-Lithographed & Printed by James Akerman, 6, Queen Square, W.C.

Plate 119

FOVNTAINS
I Wilton Hovse
III Victoria & Albert
Mvsevm

I

II

BRONZE

MARBLE

BRONZE

BLACK MARBLE

WHITE
MARBLE
BASIN

BRONZE
SVPPORTS

ROUND

SQUARE

KERB

GROUND
LINE

WATER LEVEL

SCALE OF FEET

12 INS   0   1   2   3

H. INIGO TRIGGS
DELT MAY 1902

Photo Lithographed & Printed by James Akerman, 6, Queen Square, W.C.

225

Plate 120

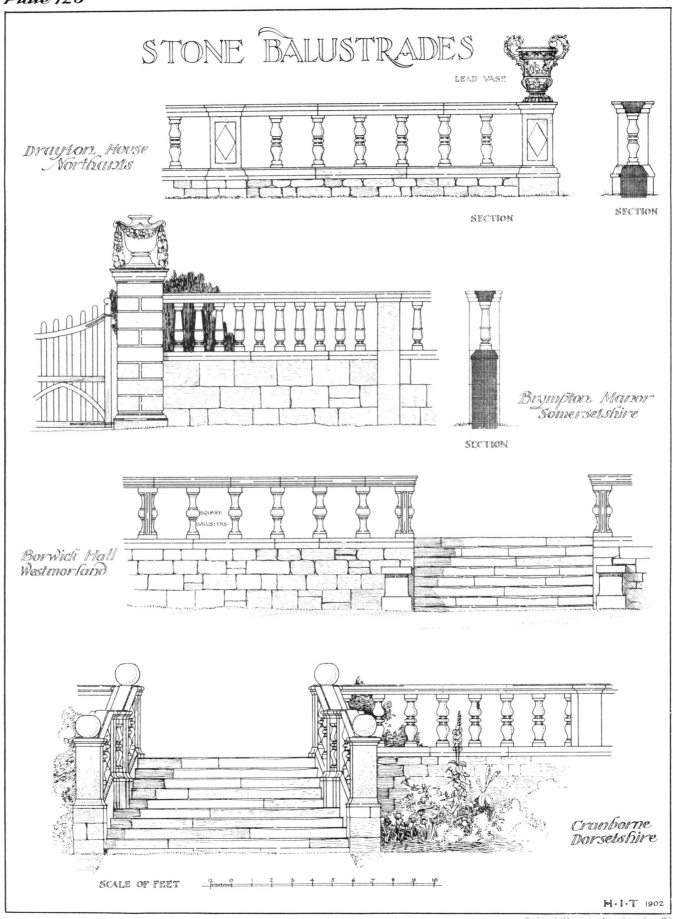

STONE BALUSTRADES

LEAD VASE

Drayton House Northants

SECTION

SECTION

Brympton Manor Somersetshire

SECTION

SQUARE BALUSTERS

Borwick Hall Westmorland

Cranborne Dorsetshire

SCALE OF FEET

H·I·T 1902

CRANBOURNE 1988.

Plate 121

Penshurst

Earlshall

WALL GATEWAYS

Cold Ashton.

Oundle

228

Plate 122

MAZES

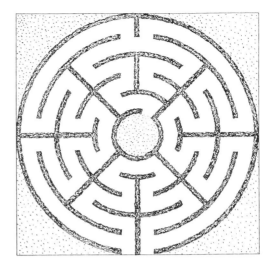

From the British Museum. Harl: MSS:

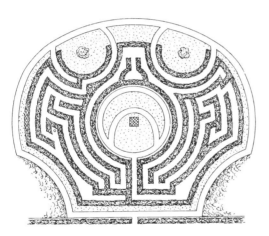

Somerleyton Hall Suffolk

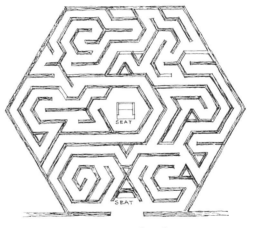

Arley Hall Cheshire

Belton House Lincolnshire

From Thomas Hills "Arte of Gardening" 1568